PRAISE FOR *DRINKING FI*

D1649093

"The world seems to have moved away from the written .... made to endure time, imprinted on paper. Dr. Carlson's gatherings are worthy of the paper and press. I found myself relating to moment after moment as she used her perspective to lure me into imagining. There were times I was not sure what would happen next, and times I anticipated and found myself amazed at her cleverness. Read this and you will find, like me, that you wished there was just more of it."

—Bo A. Brock, DVM, DABVP (equine),
author of *Crowded in the Middle of Nowhere*,
and 2007 Texas Equine Practitioner of the Year

"*Drinking from the Trough* has the wit of a modern day James Herriot. These stories will have the reader equally laughing and grieving over the personal struggles and triumphs in the life of veterinarian Dr. Mary Carlson."

—Kris Abbey, DVM,
Certified Veterinary Acupuncturist

"Student, teacher, veterinarian, friend—now Dr. Mary Carlson can add "gifted storyteller" to her long list of achievements. *Drinking From the Trough* is a delightful meander through a life filled with colorful people and memorable animals, from Keli, a husky with a gift for singing, and Marcie, a horse with the kind of heart that comes along only once in a lifetime of owning horses, to any of the many other animal companions Mary has known. Through her tales, Mary reminds us of the value of the friendship of people and animals alike, the grief we know at their loss, and the enrichment they bring us as they travel through our lives."

—Anna Dee Fails, DVM, PhD, professor of
anatomy and neurobiology, Colorado State University

Drinking From the Trough

Drinking From the Trough

A Veterinarian's Memoir

Mary Carlson, DVM

SHE WRITES PRESS

Published 2018
Printed in the United States of America
ISBN: 978-1-63152-431-8 pbk
ISBN: 978-1-63152-432-5 ebk
Library of Congress Control Number: 2018936738

For information, address:
She Writes Press
1563 Solano Ave #546
Berkeley, CA 94707

She Writes Press is a division of SparkPoint Studio, LLC.

Dedicated to my mother, Carol Lederer Elson, and my husband, Earl Dwight Carlson, two amazing people gone too soon. You, more than anyone else, influenced the course of my life.

Table of Contents

Preface

As I settle into my office upstairs, fingers ready to tap out my personal stories about animals, people, and myself, Matthew, my orange tabby cat, pads silently into the office. He leaps gracefully onto the small guest bed beside my computer and table, strolls across the plastic drop cloth that protects the quilt from cat hair, and stretches out in quiet companionship.

I smile and get back to work. I have no doubt that Matthew is my muse; if he isn't here next to me, he's around the corner in the hall, lying beside the door, the tip of his tail twitching in thought. It's comforting to write with him close by.

Pages later, I stop and stretch, convincing blood to circulate in my chair-swollen calves, and Matthew is there, purring loudly and giving me the "slow blink." That slow blink is a gesture of love and respect unique to cats; it means I'm his trusted friend—as he is mine.

I pet him, kiss his forehead, and thank him for staying with me all these years—years that included a shattered hip, my husband's death, four moves in four years, a brief foray into law school, and my return to Colorado with occasional winter migrations as a "snowbird" to Arizona.

Matthew was diagnosed with chronic renal failure when he was fifteen years old, making our remaining time together even more precious. I cherish every moment with him, even when he beats up on the other cats, goes on his nightly tear around the house, smashes antique Staffordshire china to smithereens, or takes the finish off my dresser with retched-up hairballs.

A writer needs a muse, and Matthew is mine, for better or worse. He's kept an eye on me as I've written pieces that have been published in newspapers, professional journals, and lay publications over the years. He's been there through rough drafts and revisions. And he's been there while I've created this, my first book. It's a work of love and remembrance; I hope you enjoy it.

1

Cupcake

Out of vet school for barely two months, newly licensed, and wet behind the ears, I accepted a job offered by my friend Rachel to be a part-time veterinary practitioner at her private clinic. She couldn't pay much, but she promised to train me in the nuances of private practice. And with me on hand, she'd finally be able to take longed-for time off. I'd have to handle some night calls, but that was okay; I was just relieved that I would have a mentor so soon after graduation.

As soon as I walked in the door of her clinic, Rachel bombed out to go elsewhere—not just my first day but every day I worked. No training in nuances or anything else! Being the only vet on duty was bad enough, but Rachel let her one and only vet tech—the assistant who helps the veterinarian with patients in many different ways—go home at the same time too. I felt utterly abandoned.

I was technically qualified to treat sick and injured animals, but being totally on my own, without even a tech to help restrain patients, I was only comfortable with healthy patients coming to the clinic for wellness exams.

My first night call was for a house call to a bitch that had just delivered puppies. By the time I got there, the pups were dead. I talked to the client, who turned out to be a friend of my husband, Earl, and then

I left. I didn't charge him anything for the house call, because I really didn't do anything.

Rachel was furious when she found out I hadn't charged him—so furious I thought she would punch me out. She ranted at me: all calls get at least a night call charge.

How was I supposed know that?

This was definitely not the kind of "teachable moment" I'd expected from a mentor. Maybe taking this job hadn't been such a good idea. Low pay and no doctor present weren't helping me learn what was not taught in vet school. I began wondering if vet school itself had been a bad idea, if it had been a bad decision to leave my tenured teaching job four years ago.

But I was here, and I had a job to do, at least for the time being. And at least the next time I got a nighttime request for a house call, I'd know what to do.

But no two calls are ever the same.

Jamie had gone to school with my husband and was the daughter of one of my mother-in-law's best friends. A few days after the dead-puppies incident, Jenny, Jamie's six-year-old middle daughter, came into the clinic carrying a tiny kitten.

"Dr. Carlson, Cupcake is mine, all mine! My very own kitten!" she said with pure delight. As a middle daughter myself, I understood that having her own kitty made Jenny feel extra special.

Cupcake was an adorable buff-colored female tabby with an enormous purr. I took her through her first physical examination and first round of vaccinations and deworming, then pronounced her in excellent health. Jenny asked me many questions, and we had a serious discussion about proper care for Cupcake. Teaching clients how to properly care for their cats is still my favorite part of practice; I guess that's the teacher in me coming out. Jenny paid close attention, and I was sure she and Cupcake would be just fine.

It seemed to me that Cupcake was a wonderful kitten for Jenny. I imagined her telling her closest secrets to Cupcake, just as I had told mine to my gray tabby, Smokey, when I was young. Cupcake would be there for her when she felt ignored and stuck in the middle, neither the bossy big sister nor the baby of the family. As I sent Jenny and Cupcake on their way that day, I remember thinking that childhood kittens and their owners are meant to have long, happy relationships filled with love, joy, and delicious secrets.

One evening, not too long after Jenny and Cupcake's clinic visit, Earl and I were sitting outside our house chatting, playing with the horses, and just enjoying being together after a hectic day. My pager beeped, disturbing the peaceful twilight.

When I called the number, Jamie answered, her voice frantic. Her husband, Steve, had run over Cupcake with his car and would not come out of their room. Jenny was in hysterics. Could I please come to their home right away?

With rookie inexperience and confusion blowing around in my brain, I asked Jamie what I could possibly do for her if the kitten was already dead.

I could hear the shaking in her voice as she said she would pay a house call fee if I would come and officially pronounce Cupcake dead, just for Jenny's sake. A terrible thing had just happened, and this was beyond her experience as a mother. She needed my help.

I agreed to come right away.

I hung up the phone, feeling slightly panicked. Oh my gosh! What was I supposed to do? Perform an exam on an already-dead patient? How does one do that? Was this to be a theatrical performance? My acting skills were nonexistent. Those skills are not taught in vet school.

I thought back to when I was Jenny's age. We'd had a small Pekinese dog named Tang. Tang had been on the sidewalk with our family when the neighbor's Airedale, Kip, raced across the street and bit through Tang's chest, killing him instantly. It happened without warning, right in front of me.

I remembered my dad having to use a cane for the next few days because he had sprained his ankle when he'd kicked the stuffing out of Kip.

I remembered my mom picking me up and holding me in her arms for days afterward while I sobbed uncontrollably.

No matter how anxious I felt, I knew I had to look like the professional Jenny needed me to be. I pulled on a crisp white lab coat and looped my stethoscope around my neck, which I never do. I think wearing stethoscopes as necklaces is stupid unless you have no pocket to put them in, and white coats are impractical. Veterinary medicine can trash a white coat pretty quickly with nasty, smelly fluids.

I walked up the driveway, carrying the vet bag I knew I wouldn't need, looking like an experienced doctor of veterinary medicine.

As I approached the pretty little stone-and-wood house, I saw curly-haired Jenny backlit by light spilling from the open garage. She ran to me, sobbing and gasping, her face red from crying. She stared up at me and whimpered, "Dr. Carlson, my k-k-kitten is dead."

I knelt down and gave her a long, silent hug.

She took me by the hand and, still sniffling, led me to Cupcake.

Cupcake's body was lying on its side in the garage, slightly flattened and clearly dead.

Jenny held her breath as I grabbed my stethoscope and listened for a sound I knew I would not hear. I adjusted the stethoscope, moving it gently over the little kitten's soft chest with great care.

Even now, sometimes I listen to a patient's chest for a long time. It looks as though I am doing a really thorough cardiac exam, but I am actually thinking, *What in the world should I do next?*

This time, I had some help knowing what to do; rigor mortis was setting in. What I needed to do wasn't easy, but it was clear.

I turned to Jenny and said, "Yes, sweetheart, Cupcake is gone."

Jenny let out a long sigh, then burst into tears and fled into the house.

I carefully wrapped Cupcake's body in an old towel and glanced around, unsure of what to do next.

Jamie answered that question by leading me to the front porch and putting a glass of iced tea in my hand. We settled into chairs and chatted for a while in the quiet night.

When I asked about Steve, Jamie said that he was so mortified by what he'd done that he wouldn't come out of their bedroom.

"It really wasn't his fault," I said, knowing this grisly accident was perfectly understandable to a veterinarian but unthinkable to Cupcake's family. I explained what had most likely happened.

Cats will seek out warm, cozy places, places no one imagines a pet will hide in. Steve had no way of knowing that Cupcake was napping on top of a comfortable tire. When he'd put the car into reverse and backed up, the tire had crushed the sleeping Cupcake.

Jamie and I talked about grief, how people process grief in their own way, and how Jamie might help her husband work through his feelings, as well as how to help Jenny and her sisters cope.

That evening was a powerful "teachable moment" for me too. I learned that I should talk to clients about possible accidents and how to prevent them when discussing how to care for a pet. I learned that house calls aren't only about caring for a beloved pet but also about being there for the humans who loved the pet.

Losing Cupcake would leave a void in Jenny's life. That's a tough thing to experience, especially when you're a little girl who had finally had her very own kitten. I couldn't bring Cupcake back, but I could be there for Jenny and her family.

On the way home, I thought about whispering secrets to Smokey all those years ago, about Tang's awful death, and about why I had become a veterinarian.

And I knew that becoming a vet had been the right decision. It didn't matter if I stayed at this particular clinic or found work as a veterinarian elsewhere; I was where I belonged.

Tom

How does a slight girl from suburban Chicago grow up to love horses and the wild landscapes of the Rocky Mountain West?

In my case, it was thanks to my mother's brother, Thomas Lederer.

My mom and Tom were born and raised in Chicago, where their parents, Margery and Carl Lederer (known as Nana and Bapa to my sisters and me), owned a wallpaper business.

Tom was a sickly child and suffered from asthma all his life. Treatment options were limited in the 1920s; Mom told stories of how Nana and Bapa walked the floor with Tom at night to try to relieve his asthma attacks. One winter, his attacks were so bad that they pulled up stakes and moved to Phoenix in hopes that Arizona's dry, warm climate would help. It didn't, so they returned to Chicago.

Despite his health challenges and slight frame, Tom grew up to be fun loving and adventurous. After attending college and earning his certification at aviation mechanic school, he decided to move "out West" for two important reasons: he didn't want to work in my grandfather's wallpaper business, and Colorado's climate was better for his health.

He found work as a dude wrangler on a guest ranch that straddled the Colorado–Wyoming border. He wasn't a big man, but he had a knack for working with horses, even with his asthma. His personal ranch horse was a palomino quarter horse named Shane.

Eventually, Tom settled in Fort Collins, Colorado, which back then was a sleepy college town of about fifteen thousand people. He purchased a garage on a large plot of land that had been part of an estate sale. He converted the garage into his home and a new business repairing all kinds of appliances—radios, stereos, record players, even reed (pump) organs. He could fix anything.

Growing up, my sisters and I got to know him primarily through his annual Christmas visits to our grandparents and the recorded "letters" we sent back and forth. It was fun talking into the microphone of the reel-to-reel tape recorder and telling him what was going on in my junior high world.

Tom came home every Christmas, and he spent a lot of time playing with us kids. In many ways, he was just a big kid too; he loved toys and bought plenty for himself. I especially loved racing his HO model slot cars on the track he kept at Nana and Bapa's house.

Tom's visits were a treasure. He had an infectious giggle; I have never known anyone who could laugh so hard at his own jokes. He regaled us with stories about the adventures of Mitts, the long-haired tuxedo barn cat he'd adopted and brought home from the dude ranch.

Tom's stories of life in Colorado and Wyoming made the world west of the Mississippi River seem mysterious, exotic, and exciting. I longed to see it for myself, but we'd never taken family vacations or gone to sleepover camp, as our friends had. My parents had divorced when I was young, and Mom never had the money for travel. Dad wasn't interested in vacationing with his daughters.

One cold February day in 1968, my mother woke me in the early morning with the news that Nana had just died. Her death was completely unexpected, and I burst into tears. Nana and Bapa were madly in love with each other. "What will Bapa do now?" I sobbed.

Tom flew in to be with Bapa and say goodbye to Nana. I remember him waiting in the sanctuary of the funeral chapel when we arrived for the service. He stood beside Mom and said quietly, "They're closing it up now." I knew he meant the casket. They ushered us into the adjoining family waiting room; even though we weren't children any more—Margo was nineteen years old, I was fifteen, and Natalie, fourteen—they didn't want us to see Nana's body.

That April, Bapa arranged a trip for us to visit Margo, who was a sophomore at the University of Arizona in Tucson, as well as Tom in Colorado.

Arizona was an amazing and alien world to Nat and me. We'd never been beyond the lush, tree-filled green of Chicago's North Shore. Home was beautiful, we never doubted that, but Tucson was a hot world of sand, brilliant blue sky, and vivid green cacti. It had roadrunners, whose odd-looking antics made us laugh. It had skittering lizards, rattlesnakes, and dust storms. It had exotic dishes—we'd never heard of Mexican food, let alone lollipops with scorpions embedded in them.

We drove to Phoenix, where Mom and Bapa tried to find the house they had lived in when Tom was so ill. We didn't find it, but we did find a riding stable, and Natalie and I got to ride horses with a guide.

We both loved horses, but Natalie was the one who'd taken lessons. Mom had been willing to shell out eight hundred dollars every summer for several years for Nat's English riding lessons, in the hope that riding would keep her off the streets and out of trouble. I longed for lessons too, but I knew the financial strain of Nat's lessons; I didn't think it was right to demand that Mom spend more money on lessons for me, so I never even asked.

Natalie was clearly an experienced rider—even though she had learned on an English saddle, not the western saddles we were using—but I got up to speed quickly, and I loved it.

After Tucson, we flew to Denver in a new Boeing 737. Tom picked us up from the airport, and we headed north to Fort Collins.

Tom had long since established his Precision Radio shop, offering both repairs and parts sales in the converted garage. He'd also built half a house—a bedroom, bathroom, and living room—set well back from Mountain Avenue. No kitchen as yet; he still used the one he'd built in the garage.

Tom was a great tour guide. He knew the best scenic spots to visit, showing us the grand landscapes of northern Colorado and southern Wyoming. He drove us up to the guest ranch where he had worked and, while Mom and Bapa relaxed in chairs on a broad wooden porch, Tom saddled up horses for Natalie, himself, and me and led us on our first-ever mountain trail ride. The wondrous mountain beauty (and the seven-thousand-foot altitude) took my breath away. I was fascinated with all of it: the scenery, the wildlife—we even found old bones and a cattle skull! Quite an adventure for a fifteen-year-old suburban girl.

I loved the wide-open spaces of the West, and I was intrigued by Fort Collins and Colorado State University. Until this trip, I hadn't known CSU existed. College was still three years away, and I was just beginning to think about where I wanted to go. All I knew for certain was that I didn't want to stay in Illinois. CSU was now high on my list of possibilities.

The next summer, Natalie and I visited Tom together—by then, he'd finished building the other half of his house—and the summers after that, we took turns, first one visiting, then the other. It was our first time traveling solo. For a week or two, I had Tom all to myself.

During my visit, we went sightseeing, horseback riding, and swimming. We flew in his little two-seater 1959 Cessna 150. We did plenty of eating too—Tom was a great cook and loved to barbecue.

Most nights, I slept on his wonderfully comfortable couch. It wasn't a sleeper sofa, but with a set of sheets on it, it was as comfortable as any bed. I still have that couch; it's been reupholstered twice in fifty years. It may not be the most fashionable piece of furniture, but its comfort still makes up for its lack of style.

The nights I wasn't at Tom's house, I was at the ranch. That was amazing.

Tom loved to ride, and he fostered our love of horses. Every time we visited him, he took us up to the ranch for a day or more of riding. The first summer, when Natalie and I were there together, he let us stay overnight at the ranch, the closest we'd ever been to sleepover camp. The summer before I began college at CSU, I stayed with him during the freshman preview event. As a special treat afterward, he let me spend the night by myself at the ranch. I had my own cabin room. It was my first time being on my own; I didn't know anyone there other than Tom's friends. For supper, I shared a divine meal of roast bison and mashed potatoes, served family style, with the other guests. I felt quite grown up.

As an undergraduate at CSU, I lived in the dorms, but it was nice to have a relative nearby, and Tom and I visited often. I'd walk the mile and a half to his house, cutting through City Park, and borrow his AMC Javelin each week to run errands and enjoy a little more freedom than my bicycle allowed. When I returned, he'd either cook dinner or take me out to a local restaurant.

Tom would call me on the occasional Sunday morning to see if I wanted to go flying with him. He was an excellent pilot and a Civil Air Patrol (CAP) officer, flying missions to find planes lost in the Rocky Mountains.

Sometimes, the Sunday flight meant flitting over to Boulder and back to practice touch-and-go landings. Sometimes, if it was Christmas break and the weather was nice, it meant flying me to the Denver airport, where I'd board my commercial flight home for winter break. Sometimes it meant a two-hour jaunt to visit his friends, Cliff and Dorothy, in Glendo, Wyoming, often after a brief detour to circle over Fort Laramie.

Fort Laramie is a National Historic Site. What I remember most from our flyovers is how isolated it was. The barracks and other buildings enclosed by the fort were stark white, surrounded by a seemingly endless expanse of empty rangeland.

Glendo, a tiny town roughly a hundred miles north of Cheyenne and about forty miles from Fort Laramie, was a bustling metropolis by comparison. Technically speaking, it did have an airport, but it was only for daytime use by small private aircraft. Pronghorn occasionally wandered onto the unpaved runway. There weren't any regular on-site employees or nearby ground transportation, so we'd circle Glendo from the air. Someone would spot us and figure the circling plane was going to land, and one of the townspeople would drive their pickup truck to collect the passengers, whether or not they knew who they were. We'd get a lift into town and have lunch with Cliff and Dorothy at a greasy spoon that had outstanding grub. I'd never heard of chicken-fried steak before coming out West; every bite at that little hole-in-the-wall diner was delicious.

Tom had a '63 Rambler Classic in addition to his Javelin. One day, he announced that it was time I learned how to drive a stick shift; after all, the Javelin might not always be available.

He drove us half a block to one of the little-used streets in City Park. I sat in the driver's seat; he sat in the passenger's seat, holding a paper bag of peanuts. In between instructions on how the shift stick, clutch, and accelerator worked, he shelled and munched on the peanuts.

I eased up on the clutch and down on the accelerator. The Rambler jerked and bumped erratically. It stalled. I started over. It stalled again. It lurched. Peanut shells flew everywhere. I tried again. The gears ground together with a frightening *scrunch*, and the engine died again.

After more tries than I could count, I'd managed to move us forward by maybe ten inches.

I looked at Tom with a hangdog expression. I felt like a complete and utter failure.

Tom looked down at the bag of peanuts he'd been clutching tightly to his chest. He set the sack carefully on the dashboard and wiped his sweaty palms on his jeans.

"You know, Mary," he said, carefully avoiding eye contact, "I can make sure the Javelin is always available, whenever you need it."

After graduating from CSU with a physical education degree, I returned home to Highland Park and, with my brand-new Illinois teaching certificate in hand, began looking for work. Teaching jobs were hard to find; it felt as if every baby boomer had graduated on the same day, and we were all vying for the same handful of jobs.

I finally lucked out and landed a half-time job teaching physical education at the end of October. The salary was pretty small, so I taught gymnastics in three park districts and occasionally worked at Art and Evelyn Wienecke's hardware store, where my mother worked and where I'd worked in the summers during my college days.

The following spring, Tom was diagnosed with cancer of the larynx.

He wasn't a smoker, but asthma alone does slightly increase the risk of lung cancer. I have always wondered if his asthma inhalers contributed to his developing laryngeal cancer.

Tom had surgery to remove part of his larynx. I flew to Colorado to visit him as soon as school was out and before I started summer quarter at Northwestern University, where I was enrolled to begin my master's degree. The surgeons had managed to save his voice, although its timbre sounded a little different. I think he was relieved that he didn't have to use an electrolarynx, one of those battery-powered wands you hold against the throat to buzz out words.

He seemed fine; he was back to living his life, cooking large meals for himself to regain the weight he'd lost. He even took me flying again—this time, rolling the plane so we were sideways, one wing up and the other down, sky on one side, ground on the other. Then he'd roll to the other side. Terrifying, but definitely cool.

But the cancer wasn't gone. I got the news spring quarter while at grad school: it had metastasized to both lungs. Surgery wouldn't help; the only treatment options were chemotherapy and radiation.

Fort Collins was too small back then to have its own oncology center. Tom's friends drove him the 130-mile round trip to Denver for those treatments. Mom traveled back and forth to Colorado several times to help care for him. At the same time, she tried to shield Bapa, who was in his eighties, from the worst of the details about Tom's illness. Bapa knew more than Mom wanted him to know, I'm sure; after every phone call with Tom, Bapa wept.

Somehow, when Mom left our Illinois home for that final visit, she knew it would be the last one. Before she left, she showed me the dress she wanted me to bring to Fort Collins, the dress she wanted to wear at the funeral. In retrospect, I wonder if she deliberately left the dress behind, hoping in some strange way that if she didn't take it with her, Tom would survive a little longer after all.

Tom was admitted to Poudre Valley Hospital in Fort Collins on October 5. When visiting hours ended that evening, Mom went back to his house, where she was staying. The next morning, when she returned to the hospital, a nurse met her at the door to Tom's room; Tom had died moments before.

It had been nineteen months since his initial diagnosis.

I flew to Colorado the next day to help Mom with final arrangements. She didn't want to stay at Tom's house when I arrived—it was clear that she needed a break from the place where Tom had suffered so much—so we checked into a local hotel for the week.

Tom's wishes included clear instructions regarding Mitts, the black-and-white cat he'd adopted as a kitten and brought home from the ranch so many years ago.

Mitts was fifteen and in failing health. She had been Tom's constant companion and was as much a member of our family as Tom was. Tom had asked that after he died, Mitts be put to sleep and placed in his casket, so that the two of them would be cremated together. He'd had a friend photograph the two of them to show exactly how he wanted Mitts to be laid to rest; they would be in a perpetual hug. One of Tom's friends, who was a pilot and Tom's ownership partner in a newer airplane, had agreed to scatter their ashes over the Rockies.

Mom and I waited at the house for the funeral director, who took Mitts to the veterinarian for euthanasia. Knowing that it was the right thing to do didn't make it any easier, and we both cried for a long time after they left.

Mom scheduled the funeral for the Sunday following Tom's death to allow enough travel time for his out-of-town friends to attend. That Sunday happened to be my birthday. She apologized to me about the timing, but we both knew that Sunday was the only day Tom's far-flung friends could gather together.

Tom's friends filled the funeral home chapel. As Mom entered, they all stood up, in complete silence. During the service, the pastor read the poem I'd requested, "High Flight."

High Flight

Oh! I have slipped the surly bonds of Earth,
And danced the skies on laughter-silvered wings;
Sunward I've climbed, and joined the tumbling mirth
Of sun-split clouds—and done a hundred things
You have not dreamed of—wheeled and soared and swung
High in the sunlit silence. Hov'ring there
I've chased the shouting wind along, and flung
My eager craft through footless halls of air.
Up, up the long, delirious, burning blue
I've topped the wind-swept heights with easy grace
Where never lark or even eagle flew—
And, while with silent lifting mind I've trod

The high untrespassed sanctity of space,
Put out my hand, and touched the face of God.

John Gillespie Magee, Jr.

After the service, we went to Tom's house to visit and remember. Thelma, one of Tom's best friends, knew that it was my birthday and understood how hard it was to say goodbye to my uncle, so she had baked a double-chocolate birthday cake for me and hidden it from the guests.

Long after everyone had left, I settled into a quiet corner with a piece of birthday cake. I thought about the profound impact Tom had had on my life and the lives of my sisters, how he had encouraged our love of all things that involved adventure, horses, and playfulness. I imagined him giggling up in Heaven with all the other angels, probably telling silly jokes. I was sure Mitts would be curled up in his lap too.

I hope he knows that all of his nieces became horse owners. I hope he knows that by opening my eyes—and my life—to the wonders of Wyoming and Colorado, he set me on the path that would lead me to Earl, veterinary medicine, and this remarkable life I've had.

No Chrome

Earl was so excited that I could barely understand what he was saying. Finally, he calmed down enough to make sense: he had been up to Larry Greene's ranch near Sheep Mountain in the windy, high-altitude short-grass prairie west of Laramie, Wyoming, to visit family friends and get some good grub. He'd been enthralled by the horses he'd seen at the Greenes' ranch, especially a little three-year-old filly—a young female horse. All he could talk about was the gorgeous little sorrel quarter horse, who, he said, had "no chrome."

Earl and I had been good friends for five years, and he had taught me a lot about horses, but I honestly had no idea what "no chrome" meant. It happens that no chrome indicates that the horse is totally solid in color with no white markings anywhere. White coloring is the chrome. Sorrel is one of the red colors of quarter horses, so the filly was red—sorrel—with no white markings—no chrome.

Now that Earl was back from his year away after veterinary school graduation and living in the family farmhouse across the street from his grandparents, he was busy setting up his new practice in Fort Collins.

He already had two horses in the corral: his childhood nag, Chico—a cranky eighteen-year-old bay gelding—and an elderly retired barrel racing horse named Pappy, which he kept for Larry Greene. That tall horse, Pappy (registered name Little Levis but called Pappy because he was the color of paprika), had won the National Little Britches barrel race when he was eighteen years old. He was a huge horse, but he had a lot of kindness in his immense body. I adored him, and I rode him quite a bit.

The year before, we had taken both horses up to the Albany County Fairgrounds in Laramie so we could ride during graduation weekend. Earl was graduating from vet school at Colorado State University in Fort Collins on the same weekend his sister was graduating in nursing at the University of Wyoming in Laramie, where their father was president.

After the Wyoming graduation ceremony, we saddled up the horses and rode to the quarter horse track, part of the regular oval racetrack that had an extension at the start. Quarter horses are called *quarter* horses because of the track—they run at top speed on a straight track for a quarter of a mile.

Earl started out on Chico to get a lead, leaving me on twenty-three-year-old Pappy, who was prancing to go. He was disciplined, thanks to all his training and experience, and didn't run away with me. All I did was let up on the reins, and off we went at warp speed.

Whew! What a ride! I have never ridden so fast in my whole life! Pappy ran straight as an arrow, never wavering side to side at all. I am small enough to be a jockey, but this was my introduction to the adrenaline rush of racing, and I was hooked.

Dr. Larry Greene was a Laramie surgeon and team doctor for the University of Wyoming Cowboys, as well as a long-time rancher. The little sorrel's registered name was Tee Barwood, but Larry called her Franny after his wife Fran, who had died not long after Franny's arrival. He offered to sell Franny to Earl for nine hundred dollars. As an added bonus, or because he was trying to reduce his stock, he'd include another horse, Marcie (Liberty Sunshine), for only one hundred dollars more. Marcie was a beautiful palomino paint filly with white mane and tail and one blue eye and one brown eye. Earl said yes to both, and from that moment on, we always referred to Marcie as our hundred-dollar horse. I didn't know it then, but Marcie would turn out to be the horse of my life.

It had been two years since Uncle Tom had died of cancer. My mom was his heir and had inherited his house and other property he owned, including a Craftsman-style bungalow formerly owned by United States Supreme Court Justice Byron "Whizzer" White, both in Fort Collins.

I was comfortably residing in Tom's house, and I'd finally found a job teaching physical education in a Fort Collins elementary school. The teaching job was only one day a week at first, but I earned enough to pay nominal rent to my mother, plus I worked as her agent for the bungalow property and to help finish up settling Tom's estate.

Thanks to her brother, Mom had a little more money for herself and could come out to Colorado to visit me. We decided to drive up to the ranch so Earl could show off Franny.

We headed north on US 287 in Uncle Tom's AMC Javelin (technically Mom's car but left in my care; it was the last of the pony cars, and I drove it when I wasn't driving my VW Super Beetle). This two-lane highway is one of the most gorgeous roads anywhere. It runs from Texas to Montana, and the Fort Collins to Laramie section is spectacular.

This stretch of Highway 287 is a hazardous, undivided highway with curves, straightaways, and a two-thousand-foot increase in altitude in the last forty miles before the state border, but it is amazing, with pronghorn, mule deer, cattle, and eagles dotting the mountainous countryside. When we crossed the state line into Wyoming, the clouds seemed low enough to touch.

It was sixty-five miles to Laramie from Fort Collins, then a turn west to the ranch, about another twenty-five miles or so. It was clean and beautiful, all brilliant blue skies, bright sunshine, and vivid green grass.

There, in a field on the ranch, was a small red horse with no white on her. She was tiny, only fourteen hands tall, the smallest height to still be a horse and not a pony.

The way horses are measured for height is in hands. You put your hand with fingers sideways, and one full width of the four fingers (not the thumb) pointing east to west is a hand. If the horse measures 14.2 hands, or "fourteen two," it means fourteen hands plus two fingers going up the horse's side from the ground to her withers (the highest part of her back, just above her shoulders at the base of her neck). It's not very scientific, of course. My fingers do not equal the width of a ranch hand's fingers. But generally, a hand is considered four inches, which means that at the top of her withers, Franny was fifty-six inches tall—fourteen hands.

Mom enjoyed the ranch, the monumental steak lunch from one of the Greenes' cattle, and all the horses, especially the two fillies. She laughed when Marcie put her teeth on the car, biting it. Mom thought Marcie was trying to eat the Javelin. We had a great day and went home with the two fillies on hold for Earl.

After Mom went back to Highland Park, it was time to bring the fillies home. Earl had made arrangements to have them trained to be ridden and worked with at Steve and Mike Bowers' ranch. We were so excited to finally get them to Fort Collins.

It would be wonderful to say that on the ranch we haltered the youngsters, took the lead ropes, and asked them to go into Earl's trailer and that they went in calmly—but no such luck. What Franny and Marcie saw was a big maroon monster on wheels attached to a three-quarter-ton pickup truck. No way were they going into the Chamber of Doom.

We literally pulled them off the ranch. Marcie went into the horse trailer after much equine arguing. That's fair: she was a three-year-old baby, and she didn't know how to get in. She would have to learn later. After a struggle and a bloody bang to her forehead, she finally bolted in.

One down, one to go—halfway there!

Lawrence Atkinson, a gigantic ranch hand, looked sideways at little Franny, who was starting to get upset watching what was happening. Lawrence stepped forward, wrapped his arms around Franny as if she were an oversized dog, picked her up, and deposited her in the trailer. That massive man actually picked up a horse!

Fortunately, the ninety-mile ride downhill toward home was without any mishaps. We drove from the Greenes' ranch back into Colorado and directly to the Bowers' ranch in Fort Collins. Steve and Mike Bowers, identical twin brothers who had done just about every horse-related job from jockeying to training, spent the month of August teaching Franny and Marcie to have manners, to be ridden, and to be loaded into a horse trailer. They even trained us how to ride "the girls."

It seemed like forever, but we got the horses back to Earl's place after their month of training. After riding them in the corral for a few days, we decided to go for a trail ride in the mountains. Earl was riding Franny, and I was up on Marcie using an old saddle. I was hesitant to ride Franny. She was so quick she scared me a little.

Our judgment had been questionable in choosing where to take them for our first ride. We hauled them in the trailer to the Arthur's Rock trailhead at Lory State Park, a beautiful area of grasslands, foothills, and mountains only ten miles from home.

We saddled up the girls and rode on a tenuous trail to the top of a ridge. That was a fine ride. The fillies did well, even though the trail was really for more experienced horses. We had no blowups in behavior, no spooking at birds or the wind. It was lovely. Nothing smells as good as pine trees on a trail, especially when mixed with the odor of horses.

After we crested the trail, we wanted to ride the full loop back down to the trailhead, not just go back down the way we came. Going down the other side, the trail was steep and narrow, with a harrowing drop-off close by. Pebbles from the trail skittered down the mountainside, never to be seen again.

I didn't have a back cinch on my saddle, and because it was so steep, the back of the saddle tipped straight up in the air, depositing me on Marcie's neck, with my feet in the stirrups and my arms around her neck. I hung on for dear life—if I slid off her neck or if Marcie got off-balance or upset, we would disappear down the side of that precipitous mountain—but Marcie was very mellow about it. We eventually made it back to the trailer in good shape.

A year later, when the girls turned four, we took jumping lessons every Friday night and participated in local equitation competitions. Our jumping instructor told us to switch horses to better match the sizes of the riders and the horses, so I began riding Franny, and Earl rode Marcie.

Every time Franny and I came around the corner in the ring to where Marcie and Earl waited outside, Franny whinnied loudly at Marcie from the riding ring. She wanted to be with Marcie, not all these strangers. Definitely not cool in competition to have a screaming horse trotting around in a circle.

Natalie had sent me her old English riding clothes and ancient knee boots. When I rode Franny in a competition, I wore Nat's hand-me-downs.

When Earl rode Marcie in these jumping competitions, my Wyoming man (actually a fifth-generation Coloradan, but he wouldn't admit it, so much did he love Wyoming) absolutely refused to wear the froufrou English attire.

He wore his grubby old cowboy boots, chaps, and a helmet designed for cross-country riding. Snooty mothers complained that a man dressed that ridiculously should not be allowed to participate.

But Marcie blew the other horses out of the ring with her enthusiastic and excellent jumping form. Clothes do not make the champion!

We rode the girls everywhere, at Rocky Mountain National Park, at Lory State Park, in the city's natural areas, and through the streets of Fort Collins to get to fields.

The only thing wrong with our relationship with the girls was that they couldn't be separated from each other. We had to ride them together. They had gotten to the Greenes' ranch at the same time and were best friends as well as blood cousins, even though tiny Franny had been the boss mare of all the horses on the ranch.

One afternoon, I tried to ride alone. I got Marcie all tacked up with English equipment and rode through the streets to a field. Everything was copacetic. We rode around the field a little. Then we stopped for a moment before turning back.

All of a sudden, while standing still, Marcie bucked just once, and I flew off into outer space. I landed straight up and down on the top of my head. The rest of me flopped to the ground. I was going to get up but decided to just wait a minute and find my senses. I looked up at Marcie, who was wondering why I had turned into a crumpled body; then she bolted and ran off through the streets of Fort Collins.

As I stumbled out of the field, a kind man stopped his car. He had seen a running saddled horse without a rider and figured there must be a human around somewhere. Not caring that he might be a serial killer, I accepted his offer of a ride to Earl's house.

I called Earl at his clinic and wailed about what had happened and that I couldn't find Marcie. He came speeding home in his maroon Chevy pickup, the one that pulled the matching horse trailer we used to haul the girls.

He found Marcie at the side of the barn door, placidly eating hay. Long before I got there, she had run back to Franny.

Earl called my physician father to ask what to watch for in a head injury. My father said, with his typical dry wit, "Death." I went home to lie down.

I did wake up the next morning, I am happy to report, and went to teach school. Teaching physical education to elementary students was difficult that day. Staff members asked why I looked so out of touch. In an incidental conversation with my neurologist years later, he told me it is extremely rare in a fall to land exactly vertically on the top of the head. Well, this fall left a hole in the dirt, but by some miracle, I didn't break my neck or anything else. (I did start wearing a helmet after that ride, though.)

That was the end of riding the girls separately for the rest of their lives together.

Earl and I spent a lot of time with Franny and Marcie. We even took them to an elementary school that was putting on special programs, where the girls helped one group of little kids learn about horses. We spent most of our free time riding, growing closer as a couple.

We were married four years after we brought the girls home from the ranch in Wyoming. As we were honeymooning in Hawaii, lying on a beautiful Maui beach, Earl turned to me and said, "Next time, let's bring the children." I smiled. I knew he meant Franny and Marcie. How lovely it would have been to ride our girls on those pristine beaches.

Franny was such a sweet mare. She loved to be stroked and to have her soft coat brushed. She was truly gorgeous. I loved to kiss her right on the nose. Nothing is softer than a horse's nose.

At around five years of age, Franny developed asthma due to an allergy to molds. The major clinical sign is a deep, dry hacking cough, called heaves. She responded well to treatment and had no restrictions as long as we bought premium grass hay with as little dust and mold as possible.

Over time, heaves leads to chronic obstructive pulmonary disease, COPD. Usually, a horse has this for five years or so. Franny lived with COPD for sixteen years.

Periodically, we would call the ambulatory equine medicine crew to come out and take care of her, usually with a slug of dexamethasone, a powerful steroid. Franny always bounced back to health. We continued to enjoy her and Marcie in all types of horseback riding.

My classmate Anna and I rode the girls to the CSU Veterinary College anatomy building when we were teaching assistants in anatomy our senior year, on our trimester off. At the time, the senior vet students were on a trimester system, with the student in school two of the three trimesters. One trimester was scheduled with large animal rotations plus elective clinic work, and the other was small animal rotations and electives. The third trimester was not spent in school. Some students went away to work in practices, some went to ranches, some studied dairy herd management, and some got jobs unrelated to school to pay tuition.

Anna and I won the grand prize: being teaching assistants for the anatomy teachers. Anna got the job because she was a genius on the subject—she later became the vet school's anatomy professor. I got the job because I was an experienced teacher who loved anatomy. We would set up the lab stations, for learning things such as horse teeth and how to tell the age of the horse, and generally be there to help the students.

How neat is it to ride a horse to vet school?

It was fun to ride bareback across the busy street to CSU with Anna, getting quite the looks from those walking or riding bikes. We rode the girls to the anatomy building to let students enter the stalls when they had time, to palpate live equine anatomical structures, such as bony protrusions; locate the jugular veins; and find the "frogs" on the hooves and other structures pictured in their textbooks.

Some students had never touched a horse before and were frightened. That was fair—I had only touched a beef critter when it was in my Crock-Pot.

Our horses enjoyed being with people, and their calm and friendly demeanors went a long way toward helping vet students become comfortable with horses. Some days, instead of riding to campus, Anna and I let students, from both our own class and the class we later helped teach, come over to the Carlson corral to palpate living anatomical structures.

Our little red horse was also really fast for a backyard lawn ornament. She wasn't a pro rodeo horse, of course, as Pappy had been; she was a pet. But I rode Franny in the barrel racing competition at three of our annual vet school rodeos. (The fourth year, senior students are working on clinics at the hospital and can't really get a team together.)

I love to barrel race. The race has a cloverleaf pattern with rules about distances between the barrels. Three barrels are set up in a triangle formation. The rider has to circle each barrel while crossing the line she made. For example, the first barrel is usually the lower right barrel and is taken on the right lead (right front limb is last). Then, you cross over to the other lower barrel using the left lead, crossing that line. Finally, you take the top barrel, using the left lead again, and race for the finish line. Some racers like to take the barrels in the opposite direction, which is acceptable.

When given the go signal, Franny and I would fly through the air, trying to circle the barrels with as little space between us and the barrels as possible. It was fun to have everyone cheer for us, even though we didn't come close to winning. But my bright red mare sure looked good. Our class won the rodeo three years in a row, not because of Franny and me but more likely thanks to a classmate who was the New Mexico state roping champion.

At age twenty-one, Franny began coughing almost constantly, a dry, gut-wrenching cough that made me feel edgy. We stopped riding her. She ate her food and felt fairly well, but when that cough started up, it made me contemplate what would be in Franny's best interest in the near future.

As a doctor of veterinary medicine, I treat horrible illnesses of other people's pets, but I cannot stand to see one of my own unwell. I get a terrible feeling of doom that makes me wonder if I really should be a veterinarian. So I become the client when one of our own horses needs medical attention, bringing in another trusted veterinarian to provide treatment.

On Sunday of Presidents' Day weekend, Franny was suffering through an especially rough time. She coughed constantly. She wouldn't eat. Earl and I could hear her dry hacking cough way up in our bedroom overlooking the barn and corral.

I burst into tears at Franny's side. I couldn't stand seeing our little red mare suffer anymore. Franny was failing. She was no longer happy being a horse.

Any time one of our pets was clinically ready for euthanasia, I always waited until Earl agreed, unless it was an emergency situation.

On this Sunday, I was so upset about Franny that I went into our bedroom. Sleeping until noon on Sunday was Earl's weekend luxury, so he was still in bed. I cried even harder in our room and said that Franny really should be put down. He agreed.

I have learned over many years of clinical practice that the hardest part of euthanasia is deciding that the time is right, and next, having the actual procedure performed. Since Earl had agreed, I called Dr. Traub, a professor at the hospital who happened to be the clinician on call. She had treated Franny before and knew us and our horses well. We took Franny in to the CSU Veterinary Teaching Hospital, where she was admitted as an emergency, because it was a Sunday.

It was tough to wait while the students examined the patient and had us sign the permission papers, then watch as the students practiced placing a jugular catheter for the administration of euthanasia solution.

Dr. Traub had the students use sterile technique. I asked, "Why?" Jeez, my mare was going to die, but it was standard procedure. It took more time and put more stress on us, but the students had to learn proper technique.

During and after the catheter placement, Earl and I hugged Franny, cried, and held each other. As I always do when one of our animal friends is euthanized, I whispered into her ear, mostly instructions about whom to greet for me on the other side, some prayers for her safe journey, and a thank you for being my friend, all with tears flooding down my face.

The students put Franny into a padded induction stall used for horses being anesthetized before surgery. The horse is gently guided into a well-padded stock-like enclosure so that when the medicine goes in, the horse will lie down without injuring anyone. No one wants a hoof in the face or an eight-hundred-pound horse falling on them.

Once everything was set up, I asked Dr. Traub to let me euthanize Franny. She deviated from standard procedure and allowed me to administer the solution. Earl couldn't watch but waited outside the padded room. All was silent as Franny went down quietly and quickly when I pushed the solution into her catheter.

Franny's body went to the necropsy lab, but we donated Franny's legs to the anatomy department for first year students to learn about equine limb structures. Her head, I learned later, was used for students to practice dental procedures. I don't really like to think of that too much. It reminds me of the scene in *The Godfather* when the racehorse's head is found under the sheets of a movie producer's bed.

We didn't watch the necropsy because the usual room was being remodeled that winter, and necropsies were temporarily being done in the barn. I didn't want to see Franny's body spread all over the floor of the barn where I had spent so many happy hours as a student. I did, however, want to see her lungs and the slides of their microscopic structures, so I went to pathology rounds Friday afternoon.

The pathology resident knew little about the case and fumbled through it, so the pathology professors asked me to present the case.

I became the pathologist. Grossly (meaning visibly to the naked eye without a microscope), Franny's lungs looked normal. The only organ abnormality was that Franny had a smaller than average liver. It was an incidental finding. The results from the microscope slides of her lungs gave no further insight into the course of her disease. There was nothing to show why she had become so ill.

No one who makes the decision to say goodbye to an animal friend should be made to feel that the decision was wrong. Franny probably could have gone on, but we felt that she had had enough. Grieving for a pet is often just as difficult as grieving for a human. Earl and I grieved for a long time, even though we knew we'd done the right thing.

Franny's death was of value to the students and faculty who learned from her unusual course of illness, its treatment, the preparation for her death, her euthanasia, the necropsy, and the use of her body for learning structures and procedures. We felt fortunate to have had so much fun with her in all the things we did together. Most importantly, there was a peaceful end of life for the beautiful little mare who had no chrome.

Calproonio

I never thought I would have a pet who lived for half my life.

Pruney was born in my sister Natalie's bedroom in the spring of my senior year in high school. She wasn't my first cat, and she wasn't my cat at all in the beginning.

Natalie was the first of us to have a kitten. She was home from third grade, recovering from an asthma attack, when she and Mom discovered that a stray had delivered her litter in the window well. The kittens were old enough to be weaned, but the grate over the well had prevented the stray from carrying them out.

I arrived home from school—I was in fifth grade—and was confronted with Natalie's prize.

Natalie, the youngest (who always got what she wanted), had a kitten. Margo, the oldest, already had a guinea pig; she wasn't interested in kittens (though I must mention that Margo grew up to found Friends of Alley Cats of Tucson, known as FACT).

Why didn't I have a kitten? I wanted to know. I had seen the kittens, and I'd fallen in love with the white one that had gray spots. How could Mom not know that?

Mom didn't have an answer, but she didn't have a kitten either; the people from the animal shelter had already retrieved the others.

But persistence (and a certain amount of moping) works, even for a middle child, and not long before sixth grade began, I got my first kitten. Unfortunately, shortly after that, Natalie had a series of asthma attacks, and Mom gave both our cats away to Orphans of the Storm Animal Shelter.

We weren't cat-less for long: despite Nat's asthma (which didn't seem that much worse when cats were around), by the end of summer, I had Smokey and Natalie had Dusty, gray tabby littermates. Dusty eventually died of a urinary blockage, and Lynny became Natalie's new cat. Mom never considered spaying Lynny—not many people thought about fixing their dogs and cats in those days—and by the time we reached high school, Lynny had had several litters. The kittens stayed until they were weaned, then went to other homes or to the shelter.

The summer before my senior year, Smokey developed a urinary blockage and had surgery, but the surgery was unsuccessful. We had to send him to the Rainbow Bridge, that mysterious multicolored bridge connecting Heaven and Earth, where our precious pets wait for us after they die. I knew I'd be leaving home for college in a year, so it didn't make sense to adopt another cat. That didn't mean I wasn't tempted!

On April 8, when I got home from a student–faculty basketball game, Natalie was stretched out on her bed, watching Lynny deliver her latest litter. Periodically, Natalie would lift her head, peer blearily at Lynny, and say, "Look! There's another one!"

I thought Nat was just sleepy; later, I realized that my little sister, ever the wild child, was thoroughly stoned.

Natalie wanted an all-black cat, and that night, Lynny delivered one. That's the kitten Natalie kept. As she grew, we discovered she wasn't solid black; she turned out to be a black tabby.

Natalie was studying *Julius Caesar* in her sophomore literature class, so she named the new kitten Calpurnia, after Caesar's last wife.

When Jody, the little girl who lived across the street from us, tried to pronounce "Calpurnia," it came out "Calproonio," and from then on, the little cat was called Calproonio, Pruney for short.

Pruney was an amazingly mellow cat. I've always suspected that Natalie puffed a little marijuana smoke into young Pruney's mouth and wondered if that was why Pruney was so docile.

Natalie took Pruney everywhere, cradling her in her arms, and Pruney never objected. She purred constantly. And unlike any other cat I've ever had, she would walk with us around the neighborhood, off leash, like a well-behaved dog. Natalie even taught her to come into the house from outside when she whistled for her.

I went off to college, and not long after, Natalie decided she'd had enough of high school. She dropped out during the final semester and moved in with her boyfriend. Pruney stayed behind with Mom.

Mom was not happy with this arrangement. Pruney was a sweet, well-trained cat, but for reasons that have never been clear, she became the bane of Mom's existence.

Some of it, I'm certain, was due to Pruney's fertility. She had several litters before Mom had her spayed. I'm sure another big reason was Pruney's hunting prowess. She was a ferocious hunter and left a daily "gift," usually a dead chipmunk or bird, by the back door. Once, when I was home on break, she managed to take down an adult squirrel—astonishing for a petite eight-pound cat.

When cats eat their prey, they begin at the head and work downward. Pruney didn't get far with the squirrel; she left most of it in the garage. I shoveled the remains into the trash can before Mom saw it.

Mom completely lost it when Pruney left a half-eaten adult rabbit in the driveway. Bunnies are like candy to cats. Mom stormed into the house, shrieking, "That goddamn cat caught a rabbit! Half of it is in the driveway. Its intestines are hanging out, and there is *shit* coming out of them! *You are going to clean up that mess!*"

I started to snicker halfway through her tirade, and the angrier she got, the harder I laughed. And the harder I laughed, the angrier she got. I finally managed to promise to take care of poor Mr. Bunny, and I disposed of the unfortunate rabbit.

When I graduated from college, Natalie still hadn't started college, though she had passed her GED. She was broke and had no graduation gift for me. She asked me what I wanted. I pointed to Pruney.

"Fine, you can have her," Natalie said.

"A proper present should be gift-wrapped," I teased, not believing she'd really give up her precious Pruney.

She reappeared a few minutes later with Pruney, who now had a big bow wrapped around her neck. A card proclaiming "Congratulations!" was attached to the bow.

And so Pruney became my cat.

I'd moved back home after graduating from college. I spent my first year teaching, then earned my master's degree at Northwestern the next year.

Then Mom's brother, Tom, died. Tom was the reason I'd moved to Colorado for college, the reason my sisters and I had fallen in love with horses and the beautiful and wild western states. He'd left his house and most of his belongings to Mom, and she needed someone to take care of his house.

I was ready to move west again, so I happily returned to Colorado, leaving Pruney alone with Mom. Mom wasn't thrilled, but it seemed like a reasonable tradeoff at the time.

A year later, when I visited during the winter holidays, Mom declared that she wanted Pruney gone. "You are going to take that goddamn cat to Colorado with you!" No excuses, no discussion, no delays.

Pruney had always felt like my confidante and best buddy, and I really had missed her. I coaxed her into her cat carrier, loaded cat and carrier into my VW, and headed west.

Pruney hated being confined in the carrier. She yowled, screeched, and clawed nonstop. Twenty miles later, I detoured into the O'Hare Oasis Travel Plaza so I could pop a tranquilizer into her mouth.

It did nothing for her.

I covered the carrier with my good wool coat, partly to muffle the noise but mostly hoping that the darkness would help her relax and maybe she'd fall asleep.

She shredded the lining of my beautiful coat.

We weren't even halfway to the Mississippi River; we still had eight hundred miles to go.

I'd had enough. I turned around and took her back to Mom's.

I walked into Mom's house exhausted and flaming mad. Natalie heard what had happened and laughed herself into an asthma attack. But Mom agreed to keep Pruney for the time being. I left her behind, along with my ruined coat, and chugged west again.

A year later, knowing that I needed to bring Pruney back with me, I flew to Illinois for my winter break visit. I again loaded Pruney into her cat carrier, but this time, she flew with me, safely ensconced under the airplane seat in front of me. My ruined coat was in a suitcase in the plane's cargo hold.

Pruney was fine. I took the tranquilizer.

My longtime friend Nancy flew with me; she'd changed her return flight to Denver so she could accompany Pruney and me. I suspect a little cash changed hands between Mom and Nancy so I wouldn't have to travel alone with the cat. Or to make sure that the cat actually made it to Colorado this time.

We settled into Uncle Tom's old house on Mountain Avenue as if we'd lived there our whole lives. Pruney loved to sit in my lap and cuddle, and she purred all the time. She was the perfect cat, and we both knew it.

Earl agreed; he was in love with Pruney from day one.

Earl and I had met when I was a student teacher in my senior year of college and he was a first year student at the CSU vet school. We'd remained friends during my sojourn in Illinois, and when I'd moved back to Fort Collins permanently, we'd begun dating. We were serious about each other, but when Earl proposed that year, I turned him down. I loved him, but I knew we weren't ready.

Two years later, Mom died unexpectedly. After doing all the things necessary after a death in the family, I returned to my Colorado home and wept for days. Pruney never left my side.

Life began to settle back into place. I finished out the school year, still mourning Mom but comforted by Pruney. She kept watch as I sorted through boxes of Precision Radio electronics and other paraphernalia that Tom had amassed during his life, things that Mom and I had always planned to sort through together but never did.

On July 30, 1979, just four months after Mom's death, heavy storm clouds crowded the afternoon sky. Pruney had wandered off on her own. Fat raindrops began to fall. Within seconds, the rain turned to leaf-ripping, roof-smashing hail. I called for Pruney, but there was no response. I whistled our special "emergency" whistle, which usually brought her running. Still no response.

There wasn't anything else I could do; staying outside was dangerous. I retreated into the house and hoped for the best.

After almost an hour, the storm finally eased. I stepped outside to assess the damage. Hailstones the size of softballs covered my yard. One had punctured the metal roof of my carport. Later, I would learn that my neighborhood had been the epicenter of the storm. Over two thousand houses were damaged; twenty-five people were injured, and one, a babe in arms carried by a frantic mother trying to reach shelter, had been killed.

Where was Pruney?

Finally, she limped to the door. I crouched down and carefully pulled her into my lap, heaving a sigh of relief. She was bruised and battered, but nothing was broken. We were okay.

Life once again settled into place—a very busy place. Earl had opened up the fascinating world of veterinary medicine to me, and I'd decided to apply to vet school. In addition to teaching elementary school physical education, I was taking classes required for vet school admission. We still made time for horseback riding—some couples go to dinner and a movie on their dates; Earl and I rode Franny and Marcie.

About two years after the hailstorm, I arrived home from school to discover an enormous bouquet of deep red roses on my dining room table. A note from Earl, hand-lettered in all upper case, leaned against the vase. It said,

MARY: WOULD YOU BE INTERESTED

IN GETTING MARRIED?

LOVE,

EARL

I laughed out loud. The note was so true to Earl. It had been five years since he'd asked the first time, and by now, I knew we were both mature enough to handle the demands of married life.

But I had an important question to ask first.

I called him at his clinic. "Before I answer, I must know: will you adopt Pruney?"

Without hesitation, he said, "Yes." I had been reasonably certain he would, but if his answer had been no, it would have been a deal-breaker.

"Well, okay, then yes, I'm interested in getting married."

Despite our traditional courtship (unlike many of our contemporaries, we'd never moved in together), I didn't want an engagement ring. Wearing any kind of ring is not a good idea when you're teaching physical education, and rings get lost in the most unusual places in animals.

I knew that Earl, who was extremely shy, didn't want a traditional wedding. I was sure my father would just gripe about the cost of a wedding, and I didn't want a fancy wedding without my mother. We weren't sure exactly how or when we'd actually tie the knot, but we were officially engaged.

The following year, we were getting ready for our third spring break trip to Hawaii. We were scheduled to leave on March 13.

On Thursday morning, March 11, Earl called me and asked, "Do you want to get married today?"

I thought about it for a moment. I did want to get married, but not on the anniversary of my mother's death, which was Friday, March 12. We'd be en route to Hawaii on Saturday. So today had to be the day.

"Today would be perfect," I said.

I called my principal and said I was sick with a headache and wouldn't be in. He admonished me about being sick so close to spring break. I apologized but didn't change my story.

Earl and I paid the seven dollars for our marriage license at city hall. Our friends Nancy and David, plus Earl's mom, Beverley, and his Uncle Jim, who had just been released from the hospital, joined us at the judge's chambers upstairs. I wore corduroy slacks and a Harris Tweed blazer. Earl wore khaki slacks, a clean shirt, a tie, and a blazer. Beverley brought a rose for me to hold while the judge did his thing. We signed the certificate, slipped the judge a twenty, and were now officially married. After a fake rice toss (we didn't have any actual rice), we had a delightful lunch at a nice restaurant, then Earl went to work, and I went to my regular biology lab class at CSU.

I know it all sounds anticlimactic, but it truly was the perfect wedding.

We'd planned on moving into the old family farmhouse once we married, but after being used as a rental property for more than a decade, the house wasn't in the best of shape. We'd spent the last year working on renovations.

I didn't move in until two months after we returned from Hawaii.

That was partly because of my pre-vet classes on top of my teaching job—I really didn't have time to pack everything up immediately—but also because I refused to move in until the bathroom was finished.

I helped Pruney get acclimated to her new digs by taking her on a leash to the ash tree to claw. After about a month, she was free to roam about the property. She'd always been a mostly outdoor cat who came in at night, and she had no problems with the busy street that ran alongside our property.

Pruney didn't have any problems getting used to Keli, our first puppy, either. Their relationship was more peaceful coexistence than best buddies, facilitated by Pruney's excellent jumping ability. If she didn't feel like being in Keli's territory (the kitchen or family room), she simply leapt over the baby gate and sauntered away.

She became my practice cat when I entered vet school. Learning how to physically examine any animal takes practice, and cats can be especially challenging. They usually have the upper hand; they bite and claw more than other mammals, and some cat bites can result in an infection within two hours. That's why the vet techs always wear gloves when they hold the cat being examined and why most vets will have at least one and often two vet techs assisting when they examine a cat.

Pruney helped me study too, curling up in my lap as I sat at the family room table, poring through books and lecture notes. Her purring and warm presence helped me relax; we soothed each other.

Pruney was thirteen years old when I entered vet school. My hope was that she'd live at least until I graduated. My junior year, when she was fifteen, she was diagnosed with chronic renal failure. During my final two years at vet school, I'd bring her into the school clinic for blood work, putting her in a cage in the wards and bringing her out for rounds. She'd walk on the table and visit my classmates, as mellow and sweet as always.

Despite refusing to eat the special diet prescribed for cats with chronic renal failure, she survived for another two years. We both made it through vet school.

She was seventeen; I was thirty-four.

Half of my life. All of my heart.

Paw Prints in the Snow

I stared at the letter.

I'd known there was a chance I wouldn't get in. I'd been prepared to feel disappointed if they rejected me, maybe even a little angry. But I didn't.

I felt—

Relief.

Relief bordering on joy.

I know that sounds peculiar, considering how hard I'd worked to qualify for vet school. The five years it had taken me to complete the pre-vet science courses with decent grades had been brutal. I'd sandwiched the classes in between and around my job teaching elementary school physical education. Evenings, weekends, and every summer for the past five years had been filled with classes, coursework, homework, studying, and more studying.

My rejection was a year-long reprieve: I'd be able to teach school without struggling to keep up with pre-med science classes. I'd have more time to exercise and to ride horses. I'd have time to enjoy my first year of marriage—Earl and I had been married for only a month when my rejection letter arrived. I'd reapply for admission the following year, but in the meantime . . .

In the meantime, Earl and I decided to get a puppy.

This wasn't an impulsive decision. We'd always known that we wanted a dog; it was just a matter of timing.

And now, we had the gift of time, thanks to the vet school rejecting my application for admission.

We even had a name picked out. We both loved Hawaii. We'd honeymooned there and, all told, spent eleven vacations in the islands. I joked that Earl worked so hard that the only way to make him relax and not think about work was to get him off the continent—hence, vacations in Hawaii.

Kelly is one of my favorite names, so we chose a Hawaiian name that reflected that: Kelani, Keli for short.

The timing was right for another reason too. Earl's job included tending the greyhounds at the racetrack most nights, leaving me home alone. I enjoyed being outside at night, and I wanted the company and protection a dog would afford.

We had a name, and we had the time. What kind of dog should we get?

Maybe a Siberian husky? My sister, Natalie, had owned several, and they were a lot of fun. Huskies are beautiful, athletic, friendly, silly, outgoing, enthusiastic, loving, and happy to meet people. They don't bark much, if at all; they sing. (There are some fine examples of singing huskies online, like "Husky Dogs Singing Gwen Stefani" on YouTube.)

They're also stubborn, hardheaded, and furious diggers. They'll excavate an entire yard unless they have a specific area where they're allowed to dig, such as their dog pen. Huskies will take advantage of any opportunity to escape and run—and they run *fast*.

So they're not for everyone, but Earl and I felt confident we were up to the challenges. In December, we heard about a reputable breeder named Donna and contacted her.

Time was on our side again: we wanted a female puppy, and Keli was the only female in a litter of five that had been born just a few weeks earlier, in November.

As Earl and I chatted with Donna, a curious five-week-old puppy trotted into the room, investigating these newcomers.

Earl and I were astonished—and smitten. Keli was a strikingly gorgeous black-and-white pup. Her mask (the amount and pattern of white on the forehead) was a cloverleaf, my favorite pattern. She had one blue eye and one brown eye with a spot of blue in it called a "marble eye." Odd-eyed huskies can be show dogs—the eye color is simply a normal variation for huskies, not a sign of a mixed breed— but either way, it was fine; we weren't interested in dog shows. Besides, between our horse, Marcie, and this pup, they had one pair of brown eyes and one pair of blue, so everything matched up just fine.

I scooped her up from the floor and promptly got a face washing and a strong whiff of puppy breath. *Yish!* I am always surprised by how many people love to sniff puppy breath. I'm not one of them!

Keli was too young to bring home yet, so after Earl gave her a physical exam and pronounced her healthy, we gave Donna—who promised to begin calling our puppy Keli—a deposit and headed home.

I wanted Keli to stay with her mother until she was seven weeks old so she'd be properly socialized with other dogs and people. That gave us two weeks to prepare ourselves and puppy-proof the house.

Huskies shed nonstop, so we focused on our kitchen and family room, the two rooms Keli would have access to. We picked up any-thing she'd be able to reach and get into her mouth. Shoes went into the closet; coats, onto the coat rack; miscellaneous clutter, where it belonged. Our family room had never been so tidy!

We put up baby gates in the kitchen and then spread newspaper on a section of the kitchen floor for paper training, a precursor to going outside for toilet time. We emptied the local pet stores of puppy toys and chew sticks, collars, leashes, and dog tags. We used an old saddle blanket for her first dog bed. We bought and read books on huskies, books on dog behavior, and magazines dedicated to Siberian huskies. We even set up her first veterinary appointment with a colleague of Earl's, a fine dog vet, to vaccinate and deworm her and check her out so we'd have a second opinion about what an excellent puppy she was.

Finally, the day to bring Keli home arrived. Earl's mother, Beverley, was visiting us, and since Earl had to work, Bev joined me for the drive. Donna's house was well north of town, and the closer we got, the more excited I became.

Donna welcomed us in, and the three of us stood around chatting for a bit, even though all I wanted to do was retrieve Keli. Finally, I paid the balance due, and we drove home.

That is, Beverley drove. There was no way on earth I could pay attention to the dicey winter conditions on those country roads with my beautiful new puppy in the car. I sat in the passenger seat of the Javelin and fussed over Keli. Keli sat either on my lap or on the car mat at my feet, wriggling and wiggling. I couldn't take my eyes off her. Usually, I get carsick if I'm not looking out the window, but not this time. Every cell in my body was reveling in the excitement of bringing Keli home.

The first few nights, neither Earl nor I got much sleep. Keli, separated from her mom and littermates for the first time, wailed and yipped, keeping us both awake. But she settled into her new home fairly quickly, figuring out the places she was allowed to be in the house and yard, as well as the new people she now owned.

Keli introduced me to worlds I'd never known before, beginning with the rollicking fun of puppy kindergarten. Class was once a week in the evenings.

Huskies are a very stubborn breed, and for husky puppies, kindergarten is crucial. It provides an environment where they can focus on their human partners, learning to override their instincts to run away and also learning to follow, instead of ignore, commands.

Getting accepted into kindergarten almost didn't happen.

Our instructor was Clarice "Claire" Rutherford who, with David H. Neil, had written the defining book on puppy training, *How to Raise a Puppy You Can Live With*. She didn't want to admit Keli; the class was nearly full, and Keli was a little too young to begin training. But early training is an absolute necessity for a husky puppy, I argued, and the next puppy class was months off. I felt like an overbearing New York trophy wife demanding that the prestigious preschool admit her off-spring before she ever got pregnant, but in the end, I prevailed. Claire even signed my copy of her book, which became my new dog bible. I still have it, now worn to tatters.

Kindergarten was delightful, with different breeds and mixed breeds of pups in various stages of development. Keli was by far the youngest puppy in the class. As she and her classmates learned, I learned too. There's a real method for properly teaching puppies to obey the commands of sit, wait, stay, and down.

My Keli was the class model one evening for the down lesson. I was so proud—she did it perfectly. That was the lesson where I learned that Keli would do just about anything for a tiny corner of a Kraft cheese slice and a high-pitched, sing-songy, "Thank you!"

Our last class was on February 28, 1983, the same night that the final episode of the long-running TV show *M*A*S*H** aired. This was before VCRs and DVDs; there was no way to record shows, so if you missed it, you missed it. By unanimous consensus, class ended early so we could be home in time for the show.

I clasped Keli's graduation certificate close to my heart. In my mind, she was the valedictorian of puppy kindergarten. I was as proud as any mother could be, confident that my brilliant and beautiful pup was exceptionally obedient and well-trained.

We strolled home in the crisp, fragrant winter night, past the college dormitories. A handful of students was outside, blowing off steam by jumping into a huge pile of leaves leftover from fall. I let Keli join in the play, delighted to watch her making friends and having fun. She dove deep into the leaves and tunneled her way through, nothing visible but her wagging tail.

I felt lighter than air as we headed for home. I framed her graduation certificate while watching the final episode of *M*A*S*H** and hung it in a place of honor on the family room wall.

Keli was still too young to run; we wouldn't start running until she was twelve months old. So for the time being, we walked everywhere—in the neighborhood, at the park, up in the foothills—all the while practicing what she'd learned in puppy kindergarten.

I discovered that she loved car rides too. All I had to say was "Go for ride?" and Keli would sail into my Volkswagen Super Beetle. It didn't matter where we were going; she was ready for any kind of trip. She sat straight up in the passenger seat. Other drivers would grin when they saw my fine passenger.

She proved to be excellent company, and I enjoyed hiking with her alone. When we went out, strangers would say hello, admire my magnificent pup, ask what her name was, and talk to me about their own pets. The most common question they asked was if Keli was a wolf.

Huskies may look like wolves, but they're useless as watchdogs. With their friendly, outgoing personalities and boundless energy, they're more likely to join in the fun than chase off a bad guy. If a burglar broke in and a husky could speak English instead of canine, it would meet the bad guy at the door with a grin, tail wagging, and say with great enthusiasm, "May I lead you to the good silver, sir?" or "Hold your flashlight for you while you search for Mom's jewelry?"

Keli was no exception. She was lying on the kitchen floor one day when a workman knocked at the door and came in. Keli turned her head, looked the newcomer up and down, sighed, then rolled over and went back to sleep.

So she wasn't a guard dog by any means, but I never felt afraid walking with my wolf-look-alike dog, even at night. Friendly conversations with nice people focused on puppies, not robbery, and I thoroughly enjoyed chatting with the folks we met along our walks.

The fall before Keli joined our family, I'd finished reapplying to vet school. I was annoyed that I had to totally reapply, repeating everything I had done the year before. It was the institutional hoop-jumping machine at work. But I had to do it if I wanted to be admitted.

The application involved massive paperwork—no personal computers, stored databases, or saved electronic files in the early 1980s, just the chore of using a manual typewriter and carbon paper. I sighed. Why couldn't the admissions committee have saved my stuff from the year before and just moved it from the "no way" to the "try again" pile?

I submitted the application in November and turned my attention to teaching physical education to four- to twelve-year-olds at the country school east of town and enjoying adventures with our new puppy. It would be spring before I heard back from the admissions committee.

The letter arrived in April, just over a month after Keli's graduation from puppy kindergarten.

I looked at the neatly printed addresses on the envelope. "Colorado State University College of Veterinary Medicine" was embossed in gold on the return address corner. Everything looked very formal. I felt a little apprehensive about opening it. What if I were rejected again?

On the one hand, this past year, when I hadn't been accepted, had been a wonderful year, focused on our animals, my work, and the first year of our marriage. It had been a great year, and I wouldn't mind repeating it.

But I didn't want to be rejected a second time from vet school either. I still wanted to be a veterinarian someday.

I later met a student who'd been rejected eight times before she'd finally gained admission. I don't think I would have been able to push through that many tries; I think two failed applications would have been a Higher Spirit telling me that the universe had other plans for my life.

Finally, standing in the middle of the family room, I sliced open the envelope and slid out the letter.

My eyes widened as I realized it was not a rejection—the letter was welcoming me to the College of Veterinary Medicine Professional Veterinary Class of 1987, to begin the following academic year. I was in! I'd done it! *Wow*! *Woo-hoo*!

All that time in organic chemistry, which was not only difficult but downright scary, had paid off. After my first O-chem exam, I'd noticed my first gray hair. I'm sure it wasn't a coincidence.

To my surprise, calculus had seemed like a breeze. I had actually done well in it, although I couldn't have explained it, even if I'd been offered a winning Powerball ticket. I'd missed an A by a hair on a subject that not only was unintelligible to me but would have nothing to do with the practice of veterinary medicine. I've always thought calculus was a class designed to weed out the not-so-smart students from the truly smart ones. I think I was in the former group, despite my decent grade.

And I never did figure out why we had to take biochemistry as a prerequisite for vet school; med students took biochem in their first year of medical school, not before.

But all that was behind me now. I raised my arms in triumph, like Rocky Balboa on the top step of the Philadelphia Museum of Art after his famous training run.

I called the elementary school where I taught and sang a ridiculous version of "Animal Crackers in My Soup" to the receptionist to let everyone know I'd been admitted. I could hear cheering in the background. I'm sure my principal was thrilled too—I was definitely not his favorite teacher, and he restarted his campaign to have me resign as soon as possible so, he claimed, he could fill my position. He'd done the same thing last time, before I'd known whether or not I'd been admitted. Just to be obstinate, I waited until the last possible moment, in July, before I officially resigned.

I was lying on the couch, holding the letter, when Earl came home from work. He saw the envelope and knew what it meant.

"What did they say?" he asked.

I threw the letter on the floor, turned my head to the side, and covered my eyes in a dramatic display of overwrought grief.

Earl didn't fall for it for a second and congratulated me with a big smile and lots of hugs and kisses.

Sunday rolled around, warm, mild, and filled with hints of new life beginning to sprout. In Colorado, spring is often more extended winter than a hint of summer, and we don't take such days for granted. Earl and I took advantage of the fine weather by working in the yard.

Even though she was only five months old, Keli had already learned that "Keli, do you want to sunbathe?" was her cue to go outside to be tethered to the ash tree.

She loved "sunbathing." It didn't mean Coppertone and a beach towel; it meant being outside to sit, watch us, enjoy the nature of the back yard, and sleep while safely tethered to the tree. Her dog pen had plenty of space—it used to be my sister-in-law's playhouse—but the tree was a nice change of pace, a way for her to relax outside without being confined to the pen. She was free to move around as long as she didn't pull on the lead, and we were always nearby—we never left her alone when she was tied up; that wouldn't have been safe.

Keli was stretched out flat under the tree, napping while Earl and I worked. The day started to heat up, and I decided to take my cold-weather puppy inside, where she would be cooler.

Because the distance from the tree to the house was so short, about fifteen feet, and because she was a successful graduate of puppy kindergarten and because we'd practiced everything we'd learned frequently, I didn't bother putting her leash on when I untied her from the tree. I was confident she'd come with me.

Mistake.

I'd expected that I could control her by voice command.

Wrong.

She was curious about the world, and she didn't come with me to the house.

And even at five months, she already had the escape-and-run instinct of her breed.

Instead of following me to the house, she toddled like the gangly adolescent she was to the fishpond to investigate the water. She stretched her nose toward the fragrant water lilies.

I felt a little nervous. Where else would she go? Would I be able to catch her if she started to wander off? If an animal doesn't want to be caught, it isn't going to be caught.

She ignored my calls to come, confirming that she had the "selective hearing" huskies are known for.

What should I do?

Her little nose stretched farther and farther, trying to inspect the turtle and goldfish until—*plop!* She tumbled headfirst into the fishpond. She quickly surfaced, paddling her front paws a little, looking surprised.

I started to laugh.

Also a mistake.

I scooped my drenched puppy out of the shallow water and set her on the grass. I didn't even think about putting her leash on because I was laughing so hard at her—not with her, at her. Earl started walking toward us from the barn to see what was happening.

Keli gave herself a vigorous shake and seemed embarrassed, which just made me laugh harder.

Big mistake.

She didn't like me laughing at her, and she turned and made a beeline to the east—toward the main street and its heavy traffic.

I screamed her name in terror. I didn't use the enthusiastic sing-songy tone you were supposed to use for most husky commands. I was so scared I couldn't do anything but shriek.

What puppy would come when called like that? Especially one who'd been thoroughly embarrassed and was now in full-on husky escape mode? Hadn't I learned anything in puppy kindergarten?

I knew I wouldn't be able to catch up with her. I could only hope that she'd come back quickly on her own to get out of the heat.

But no, she ran through the spruce trees and bushes right into Shields Street.

A screech of tires, a dreadful thud.

Earl sprinted past me.

I was sure he would retrieve a crushed, dead Keli. I couldn't stand the thought of seeing my beloved first puppy as roadkill, but all I could do was stand by the fishpond, frozen by my fear and the knowledge that I'd killed her with my stupidity.

The driver had stopped to help and apologize. Earl assured him that it wasn't his fault.

Earl, clearly shaken, carried our limp puppy back to the ash tree. Her head and all four limbs hung down from his arms. I stumbled toward him, sure she was dead.

But Keli was conscious!

Earl gave her a thorough emergency head-to-toe exam under the ash tree and pronounced her uninjured.

Not a mistake! She was fine.

I was in shock.

I stared at her in wonder as she chowed down a huge bowl of puppy food and drank an entire dish of water, completely revived.

The shock wore off and was replaced with guilt. Being Jewish, I can assure you I know all about guilt, but this was guilt on steroids. I wanted to curl up and hide forever.

The next morning, I still felt sick to my stomach from the guilt and anxiety, even though Keli was fine, and I'd definitely learned my lesson. But no matter how I felt, it was a workday, so I headed to school.

I walked into the office and couldn't believe my eyes. The entire front of the elementary school office was covered in divine chocolate delights, homemade by the staff, in my honor. They'd planned a "Chocolate Monday" to celebrate my admission to vet school because they all knew I was a serious chocoholic. (I presume my chocoholism is a genetic trait. My dad's record for eating Oreos was twenty-two at one sitting. When my parents were still married, they would whack a five-pound Hershey bar with a hammer and eat the entire bar together.)

A huge double-chocolate cake was front and center, surrounded by cookies of any recipe that had chocolate in it, many types of fudge, chocolate-covered nuts, pecan turtles, brownies sprinkled with powdered sugar, brownies dripping with chocolate frosting—just about anything you could think of that had chocolate as an ingredient graced the table.

Any adult on a diet tossed the diet out the window that day to gorge on the bounty. I wondered if the kids noticed that staff members leaving the office were licking their fingers or surreptitiously wiping away a chocolate mustache. By the end of the day, nothing was left but scattered crumbs and a few crumpled napkins.

I was thrilled to be honored with such a special party, but I was still so upset from Keli's near miss that I couldn't eat a bite. I confess I felt a little sad that others who were not going to vet school ate all that lovely, luscious chocolate, but my body insisted.

A few weeks later, the school year wrapped up, and for the second time since finishing my vet school prerequisites, I took the summer off.

I spent the summer psyching myself up for the start of vet school in August but mostly relaxing with Earl (who, as a full-time veterinarian, did work summers) and pets Pruney, Franny and Marcie, and, of course, Keli.

I did put one rule change in place, however. Whenever we needed Keli to go from point A to point B, no matter the reason or the distance, we attached our adventurous pup to her leash securely, and we gripped that leash firmly. I never forgot her curiosity or her breed's instincts, and I would forever be mindful of the potential for disasters.

Keli's next class was "novice obedience training," although, as I was slowly learning, "husky obedience" is an oxymoron. Still, she did well in that class, which was taught by a retired police officer. He got Keli's stubborn little rear end to sit by smacking it.

I thought he was a little rough on her, but once home, she followed the sit command well from then on. I wasn't a pushover, but Keli knew I belonged to her, and she figured that she didn't have to listen all the time—but by golly, she sat when commanded. She even sat at every corner before we crossed the street, another skill we learned in the obedience class.

Learning to sing wasn't part of obedience class; that trick was one I taught her myself. I'd learned how from Natalie.

"Keli, can you go *ah-woooo*?" I'd say, howling with great enthusiasm. When I hit that *ah-woooo* note, she'd join in. She quickly caught on and would sing as soon as she heard me say, "Keli, can you go . . . ?"

She was a gifted singer and became quite proficient, learning a vast repertoire of songs. Before I left teaching for vet school, Keli and I recorded some Christmas and Hanukah songs, just for grins. I kept giggling during the duets, and I am embarrassed to say that my dog sang better than me. At least my students thought so. They groaned and rolled their eyes, clearly trying to convince me that this whole dog duet thing was totally stupid (and, of course, it was), but they enjoyed the silliness too.

Later on, when I was in vet school, I think I had fewer anxiety attacks than my classmates who didn't have a dog at home. Some of that was simply from the unconditional love of a great dog, but Keli helped me learn canine anatomy and medicine too. She was my very own study guide, a living specimen for practicing palpating canine anatomical structures in the comfort of my own home.

I felt like a real vet when I practiced giving her a physical exam. A veterinarian friend taught me how to examine an animal by starting at the head and working toward the rear. Head-to-toe repetition is important so you don't miss anything. The first year of vet school was all about the normal animal, because you have to learn what "normal" is before you can identify "abnormal" in examining and diagnosing. Keli let me practice all I wanted. If I wanted variety, I'd practice my new skills on my cat, Pruney, or the horses.

When Keli grew old enough to go running with us, Earl and I discovered that we both loved the sensation of running with a dog who had the genetic trait to go really fast in a straight line without stopping. My running limit was three miles interspersed with walking breaks, but Earl, who enjoyed distance running, took Keli on fifteen-mile runs once her bones were mature enough.

That fast-and-straight running instinct wasn't restricted to fair-weather running. Colorado might not be as cold and wild as the Arctic Circle, but we still get plenty of snow.

Snow is heaven for huskies; the more, the better. Huskies are a lot like foxes, which can smell their prey under the snow. They jump up, then plunge nose-first into the snow to catch a critter for supper. Keli had that husky hunting instinct, and when we were off leash out in the country, she'd nosedive into the deep snow, often catching rodents and gobbling up the tasty morsels.

At home, she rolled and frolicked in the snowfall, leaving paw prints in every inch of the fresh snow and digging "husky holes" out of the snow and dirt in her dog pen. She'd snooze in her snow caves, sheltered from the wind, even though she had the old playhouse, complete with a porch, as her huge doghouse. No matter the weather, she preferred to sleep outside, and we let her, unless the temperature dropped below ten degrees Fahrenheit; then we insisted that she sleep inside.

When she was about three years old, I bought Keli a harness so she could go cross-country skiing with me. Huskies are bred to pull, and they love to work. Keli's harness was similar to a dogsledding harness but less detailed. I figured it would be enough; after all, we weren't training for the Iditarod. It shouldn't be too hard to learn how to hook her up and have her pull me across our city's trails. I'm a relatively small adult, and Keli was certainly strong enough for the job.

I loaded up our gear and drove Keli the Mush Dog to City Park. I got all the equipment on us in good order, if not in an especially timely manner. Keli, attached to me by her leash and harness plus a safety leash attached to her collar, ran ahead, pulling me on my skis behind. I crouched low, racer-style with my poles tucked. We headed for the wilds on the south side of the park, where other skiers had already packed down a trail paralleling the busy street.

It was glorious! A perfect Colorado day, sky so bright blue and snow so sparkling white that I'd have been blinded without my sunglasses.

Keli galloped ahead, and we shushed around a slight curve and onto the straightaway. We were flying! I glanced across the short distance to the street, grinning at the drivers stuck in their chugging cars.

Keli ran faster. I hung on.

She ran full out. It was no use—I couldn't keep up—and—

Splat!

Face-plant in the snow, my arms spread wide like airplane wings, my hands still clutching my ski poles and the leashes, my feet and skis splayed awkwardly across the snow-packed trail. Keli kept pulling for a few seconds before turning around to look at me. I swear she was laughing at me—probably payback for the fish pond.

How embarrassing, I thought—ten feet away from Mulberry Street and all those people in their cars. I looked; people were actually slowing down, pointing at me, and laughing.

I sighed and rolled over, exposing my vital organs (a sign of submission to Keli, clearly my superior), ski tips pointed skyward. A fuzzy dog-face blocked my view of the heavens: Keli, coming to see what the holdup was. She pranced around as though to say, "Get up, Mom! This is too much fun! Let's go!" Her panting, snow-covered face and lolling tongue were adorable, and I was laughing too hard to be embarrassed for long. I grabbed her in a bear hug, and soon we were rolling and wrestling in the deep snow, skis and all.

Between cross-country ski mushing, charity fun runs, long-distance runs with Earl, and doggie Olympics, Keli had developed into quite an athlete and a stellar training partner. She had her share of sneaky dog antics, but all in all, she was turning into a polite and beautiful companion.

Little did we know that we had a killer dog among us.

It was a summer weekend, the sun not up yet.

Five o'clock. Still too early to feed the horses.

Piercing screams shocked us awake. Ungodly, unrecognizable, incredibly loud. The only thing we could tell for sure was that they were coming from Keli's dog pen.

Hearts racing, we rushed outside.

In the barely waxing light of early dawn, we saw them: a juvenile raccoon, bloodied and dead, on the ground in the dog pen and overhead, balanced high up in the apple tree that shaded the pen, its littermate hanging on for dear life and screeching that unearthly scream at the top of its lungs.

Keli trotted forward, tail wagging, to give us her usual morning greeting.

She looked like central casting's idea for the canine version of *The Texas Chainsaw Massacre*.

She grinned. Even in the half-light of early morning, we could see red glistening on her muzzle.

"Cujo," I whispered to Earl as we slowly backed away.

We gave her a bath, followed by steroids for any possible swellings, a penicillin shot in case she had bite wounds, and a rabies booster.

Raccoons are tied with skunks for land animals with the highest incidence of rabies, and although rabies in a juvenile raccoon was unlikely, it's better to be safe than sorry. We called Animal Control to notify them too, but they said the health department wouldn't be interested in testing the corpse for rabies. We buried it in the orchard.

After that, we fed the horses and went on an uneventful ride, enjoying the cool morning weather and the placid horses after the morning's excitement. When we returned, the sun now bright overhead, we saw that Keli's white face and mask were pale pink; we hadn't managed to wash all her victim's blood out of her fur. So we bathed her again, using plenty of dog shampoo.

That wasn't Keli's only run-in with wildlife, though aside from the occasional mouse plundered from under deep snow, it's the only time she caused damage.

From the moment she put her young puppy paws on the trail, Keli loved Pineridge Natural Area. Dirt trails crisscross the grassy foothills terrain and rocky outcroppings of this city-owned open space, weaving through a ponderosa pine forest and winding around the perimeter of a modest-sized reservoir.

In those days, when the town was smaller and the park wasn't so crowded, dogs were allowed off-leash at Pineridge. Keli would run full tilt, chasing imaginary prey. When she got hot—usually fairly quickly, thanks to her being an Arctic dog—she'd slow down but keep moving.

It didn't take long for her to discover the shoreline. Good thing she had tough paws designed for running on snow and ice; the shore was dry, cracked mud, with lots of rocks and sharp stones. Husky paws have tiny spikes that give them the traction they need to run on ice, the way cleats on football or baseball shoes give ballplayers traction on the field. She could clamber around all she wanted.

Soon, she was sniffing the air near the water. *Such intriguing smells,* I'm sure she thought. The next time we went to Pineridge, she stood at the water's edge and stretched forward to sniff the water itself. I could tell every sense was functioning on high alert, detecting all kinds of interesting data: the heat of the day, the temperature of the ground, the strength of the breeze, the tantalizing odors of as-yet-unidentified plants and animals.

A few hikes later, she put her paws in the water. Earl and I strolled along the shoreline path, and Keli followed, sloshing in the water close by, enjoying the new sensation on her soggy paws.

When she was a young adult, she finally took the plunge, literally.

It was a warm sunny day in midsummer. Not much wind; the surface of the lake was calm and quiet. Keli trotted over to the lake, the same as she always did, but this time, instead of turning to follow the water's edge, she kept walking straight out into the lake. She kept walking until her feet could not touch the bottom of the lake, and then she simply began swimming!

Not all huskies like to swim, but Keli was a natural and was clearly having a grand time. From then on, every time we went to Pineridge, Keli swam. And every time she swam, her swimming improved.

After the first few times, she never hesitated; as soon as we arrived, she'd run straight for the lake and plunge into the cold water. Her swims lasted longer and took her farther and farther away from shore. I could tell she was having a blast, but I was a little edgy, because there was no way I could rescue her if she got into trouble. I worried: if she went too far out, would she be able to make it back? Or would she sink like the *Titanic*?

The one thing I didn't worry about was Keli getting cold. Huskies have a double coat. The topcoat is the long, beautiful fur you can see. It's a mostly weatherproof coat that helps keep their bodies dry in snow or rain. Their undercoat is a soft, fine insulating layer that keeps them warm in cold weather, similar to the way a down jacket keeps humans warm. Those two coats are so thick that I suspect Keli never got wet all the way down to her skin.

Keli discovered she wasn't alone on the pond: there were mallard ducks! They floated serenely, apparently unconcerned that a dedicated hunter was sneaking up on them.

Keli paddled closer, a silent submarine surfacing, nearer and nearer.

Would she turn into Cujo again?

Before I could call her back, the ducks slid just a bit farther away from Keli the Curious Huntress.

Keli kept swimming, intent on her prey.

The line of ducks slid away again.

Were the ducks teasing her? I suspected so—they could have zoomed off into the clear sky anytime they wanted, leaving Keli far behind. But they stayed, quietly gliding along, a beautiful line that curved and curled on the pond's quiet surface, paced exactly close enough to Keli to hold her interest and far enough ahead of her that she couldn't catch them. They reminded me of our World War II battleships zigzagging to avoid the Japanese navy.

From then on, every dip in the pond involved synchronized swimming, Keli's head jutting out of the water, eyes focused on the tantalizing critters who were always just out of reach, ducks and Keli in an elegant line following the lead duck. She never captured a duck, thank heavens, but it was a joy to watch her try.

Eventually, she would tire of duck hunting and would swim to shore, where she'd shake herself off—soaking me in the process, of course—looking utterly satisfied. Then, cooled off from her swim, she was happy to go running. No wonder that, ten seconds after hopping into the car to head home, she'd fall fast asleep.

Earl and I had twenty-seven wonderful years of marriage, and from the day we brought Keli home, ten months after our wedding, until Earl's death, we always had a dog: Keli for almost fifteen years, then Tipper, also a Siberian husky, who joined our family as a pup soon after Keli's fourteenth birthday, for almost that long.

One morning during an unusually hot summer, Keli, almost

fifteen, was sleeping in the family room on her dog bed. Eight-month-old Tipper was snoozing nearby. They were both inside because it was much cooler inside the house than outside.

Earlier, I had cleaned up four small reddish stains around the family room, but I didn't think anything of it. I was busy in my cat clinic, which was next to the family room. The door between the clinic and family room was closed because the cat cages faced the door into the house, and I didn't want my patients scared if they saw the dogs.

In the afternoon, a new client, Bryan, came in. While polite and respectful, Bryan was clearly in distress. His cat, Mickey, who was his closest friend, had a dead tail that needed treatment.

Other vets in our town had turned away this gentle young man due to his obvious inability to pay. Bryan had developmental disabilities. He was dressed carefully, but his clothing was old and worn. The wages he earned from his job at a fast food restaurant would never cover the three-hundred-dollar cost of a feline tail amputation.

I agreed to amputate the scarified, hairless tail. Bryan, in a halting, grateful voice, promised to pay me as best he could over time, perhaps five dollars here and there. I knew in my heart that I would never see payment for the procedure, but I just couldn't let Mickey and Bryan go out the door without treatment.

My belief was that the cat needed care. Bryan had been turned down by everyone, probably making him feel like a less capable human being. He was doing the best that he could with the cards he'd been dealt, and I felt it would be a *mitzvah*—a good deed with no expectation of payback—to help him out and treat him like the kind adult he truly was. So I decided to make an exception to my rule about not working for free.

Many people think veterinary medicine is overpriced. I don't agree with them, but I understand where this belief comes from. They're used to going to their "real doctor," paying the co-pay (which is much less than the actual cost of the appointment) required by their health insurance provider, and walking out the door. In addition, many think that vets should work for less because they love animals.

Veterinarians go through training and education every bit as rigorous as medical doctors, and our supplies are the same price as human medical supplies. It takes time and skill to perform our job, just as it takes time and skill for physicians to treat their human patients. Vets charge a fair price for their services; the difference to the clients is that the money for the vet comes directly out of their pockets. Loving animals and our work doesn't make the expenses involved any less.

But once in a great while, just about every vet will treat a beloved pet for free. And this day, that beloved pet was Bryan's Mickey.

I checked on the dogs; they were still sleeping in the cool house.

I spent late afternoon operating on Mickey. When he was in recovery, I went into the house to let Tipper out. I stepped through the door into the family room and spoke Tipper's name. Her head perked up, and I put her on her leash to take her to the dog pen.

I came back inside to get Keli. She hadn't moved. In fact, I realized, she was in the same position she'd been in before I'd begun Mickey's surgery hours ago. I called her name, but she didn't respond.

I tentatively stepped over to her. I tried to move her; there was no voluntary movement. I lifted her forelimb. It was warm but limp. I let it go, and it fell back onto the cushion with a soft *plop*.

With a sinking feeling in my gut, I checked her mucous membranes by lifting her lip and pushing on the gums to see how fast the color would return to red.

Her gums were pale pink, and the capillary refill time (how long it takes the gums to turn red again) was slow.

My heart dropped to the floor. This was not just an old dog asleep. Keli, my sweet pup, was in a coma.

My hands shaking with fright, I picked up the phone to call my old classmate and friend Anna. Anna had returned to CSU to study for a PhD in anatomy after seven years in veterinary practice in Arizona.

She lived across the street in the farm's chicken house, which had been converted long ago into a house we usually rented to vet students.

I cried hysterically into the phone, trying to explain. Anna came over immediately. I called Earl, who was working in Denver, and, in a shaky voice, told him what was going on. When I realized there was no way he could be with us, I started to cry.

Anna and I carried a limp fifty-pound Keli out to the backyard and placed her under her favorite tree, shaded from the late afternoon's roasting heat.

A simple blood test revealed internal bleeding. We ran through the possible causes and decided it was one of two things—neither of which could be treated successfully, particularly in a fifteen-year-old comatose dog.

While Mickey recovered from his tail amputation, Anna and I prepared to put Keli to sleep under her ash tree.

I tried to raise a vein with the syringe full of euthanasia solution so I could euthanize my own dog, but my hands were shaking so hard as to be nonfunctional, and I couldn't see through the flood of my tears.

Anna managed the injection while I cradled Keli's head and supported the forelimb that held the vein Anna was going to use, whispering softly to her until she drifted away.

We let Tipper come out to say goodbye to her. Then I put Tipper back in the dog pen and went to Keli's body to hold her lifeless paw.

That night, the retired dentist who owned the local pet cemetery and crematory picked up Keli's body for cremation. He didn't usually make house calls after hours; he never said, but I think it was kindness as well as professional courtesy—and probably practicality too. It was broiling hot, so leaving her body beside the tree was not an option. Her body was too big for our freezer (never look in a vet's freezer), and the only other possibility was for Anna and me to take Keli's body in the dark of night over to the anatomy cooler at the vet school, undoubtedly raising the suspicions of the campus police.

After that, I was left alone at home with a heavy heart. I called my father to tell him that Keli was dead. He and my stepmother had met their granddog three years earlier, on their final visit to Colorado. Dad had never been an emotional man, though it was always obvious to me that he was a dog lover. Now he was seriously ill with heart disease, and he must have been thinking about his own mortality, because he called me back later to say how bad he felt about Keli and that he had been thinking of her all evening. Our conversation eased my tears a little while I waited for Earl to come home.

That was Friday night, but it wasn't my last encounter with Keli; she came back to say goodbye.

Sunday morning, I had a seven thirty tee time with my golf buddy, after which we went for a late breakfast while our husbands slept.

By midafternoon, I was napping on the couch. Tipper was spread out along the length of the couch on the floor below me, sleeping. You know that period when you know you are asleep but not in a deep sleep? That's when I felt a poke on my arm.

Keli used to poke us with her nose. Keli was also what I call a "face dog," meaning we could do a face-to-face hug. My eyes were closed because I was dozing, so I didn't see anything. I put my arm around her fuzzy neck as she stood by the couch, not quite knowing what was happening. I felt furry pressure on the side of my face.

I woke up immediately. Only Tipper was there, and she was still sound asleep. Besides, Tipper never poked anyone.

I remembered bringing Keli into the house via the cat clinic door one time when my tech assistant was bent over, looking through the microscope. Keli beeped her dead center in her rear end, much to the tech's embarrassment and my delight.

So I knew it had been Keli standing at the couch before she went to the Rainbow Bridge. It was Keli saying goodbye. Of this I am certain.

Earl and I considered spreading Keli's ashes on our favorite Hawaiian island of Kauai but ultimately decided we wanted to keep her close by. Her ashes, safe inside a lovely heart-shaped, lacquered paper box, rested on a shelf in the living room, reminding us of her long life and gift of companionship, love, laughter, and paw prints in the snow.

A Syringe and a Lariat

Vet school orientation day came at last—only a year later than I'd planned. But I was finally here, the sting of last year's rejection replaced by pure enthusiasm. I'd practically skipped the whole way from home to the anatomy building. It wasn't far—less than a mile— and the beautiful weather matched my mood.

I stared at the titanic stack of books and course notes and instruments. The stack was taller and heavier than I was.

I had assumed that orientation would just involve meeting kindly professors and their teaching assistants, then finding the cubicle and seat I'd be assigned to for the year. It never occurred to me that I'd need a forklift to haul a hundred pounds of bone-crushing study paraphernalia home. Fortunately, a friend I'd met in pre-vet science classes took pity on me and gave me and my gigantic load a lift home in her van.

Orientation barely hinted at what was to come.

Veterinary school was like being in a ring with a rodeo bull. I had trained hard to be there, I wanted to be there, but the unrelenting rush of information was terrifying. Sometimes, it was so scary that I felt like I was about to be—or had already been—thrown off the bull, with no rodeo bullfighters to distract the beast.

And it was exhilarating. Lots of my classmates lived on caffeine and not enough sleep. I don't use caffeine, and, with a few notable exceptions, I slept just fine. I felt the stress as much as anyone else, but with the hard work, I felt a peculiar type of joy.

I'd been a teacher for nine years before entering vet school. At the ripe old age of thirty, I was considered a nontraditional student, a "nontrad." That extra bit of life experience made a huge difference.

I'd spent all my free time over the previous five years fulfilling the prerequisite science classes, so I was used to the struggles and challenges of the hardest classes in the undergraduate curriculum and to balancing that coursework with the responsibilities of daily life, marriage, and a career in teaching.

A bigger factor was that, with the exception of my own nightmarish middle school experience, I loved school and learning. Being in school as a student beat "working" any day.

But I'd left behind a secure tenured teaching job—a job I'd enjoyed and had worked hard to get—to begin this new adventure. Would this be worth it? Would I succeed? Or would I go down in flames, with no job to fall back on?

Veterinary medicine is one of the most demanding programs at Colorado State University. Our professors and teaching assistants did what they could to ease the stress, but the student had to have the intestinal fortitude to go for it. You wouldn't make it if all you did was quake in fear. You had to find a way to survive.

And pass.

You couldn't squeak by with a D average either. Too many Ds was called "D-ing out," and you'd be bounced from the program. The admissions committee would decide whether or not you would be allowed to restart the program the following year.

I felt the blood drain from my face when Dr. Banks, our head anatomy professor, proclaimed with great authority that the grade we got on our first test, no matter what class it was in, would be the grade we'd get on every test at vet school. Despite my experience as a teacher and my joy in being a student, I've never been a great test taker.

Five days later, I huddled in the microbiology lab, writing the answers to an epidemiology quiz—my first official test at vet school.

Grades were posted the next day, taped to the window near the cubicles and the TAs' office. I approached the window with trepidation and ran my finger down the list of student ID numbers until I found mine and the grade next to it: a D.

"D for Doomed," I muttered, feeling as if a heavy weight were crushing me.

I remembered the first time I'd tried the balance beam in gymnastics. I was thirteen years old, and I shook so hard with fear that if it hadn't been for my spotters, I would have fallen off. But I didn't fall, and eventually, I learned to walk that narrow beam.

I gritted my teeth and swore that I'd learn this too.

A week later, we had our first true exam—not a quiz, but a full-fledged anatomy test. The textbook was by none other than our own intimidating Dr. Banks.

Exam protocol was more complicated than in-class quiz taking. While half of us sat in our cubicles and worked our way through an extensive multiple-choice test that would be graded by computer, the other half went from station to station in the gross anatomy laboratory, clipboards in hand, identifying and answering questions about pinned structures. When the time was up, the groups swapped places.

Again, I approached the results posted on the window. Again, I ran my finger down the list until I found my student ID number. This time, my grade was an A.

I refused to fail, no matter what the Dr. Bankses of the world predicted.

We saw Dr. Banks daily in the lecture hall. Students were silent during the lectures, aside from occasional questions. Some of that silence, especially during the first few weeks, was fear and uncertainty in navigating the foreign environment of professional school. Our class was small, compared to typical undergraduate settings—only 140 students. You couldn't hide from instructors among a mass of peers. Anonymity was impossible; Dr. Banks had a talent for learning our names from our student ID "mug shots," and by the third week of the semester, he knew everyone.

Add to that his imposing presence—he was a large man with a once-athletic build now shifting to obesity—his bombastic voice, and his rapid-fire wit, and it's no wonder we cowered before him.

But we didn't cower for long. Being with the same group every day, united in our common purpose and the demands of the coursework, molded us into a family. My cubemates even called me "Mom." As we settled into the new routines of vet school, the in-class silence became more about fascination and dedication.

The family feel also meant that exchanges between instructors and students were more informal and often unfiltered. Dr. Banks's humor was frequently crude and occasionally lewd, and he could make a joke out of almost anything. He could also skewer you if he thought you were a smartass.

In 1983, wristwatches that could be programmed to beep at a specific time were the latest cool technology. Dr. Banks's pet peeve was the scattered sounds of these watches beeping at ten minutes before the hour, when the lecture was supposed to be over. He made it clear that he would not tolerate the devices.

One day, students who owned these watches synchronized them so they would all chirp at the same moment. At the appointed time, a chorus of electronic alerts began to trill like blackbirds in a marsh. Dr. Banks whirled about, his lip curling in anger. He quickly realized the jest and laughed. He could (most of the time) take as good as he gave.

The courses and labs during the first two years of vet school took place on CSU's main campus, not far from my house, so I walked or rode my bike every day, in all kinds of weather.

I returned home for lunch every day too, for a bit of downtime and de-stressing. I ate lunch and watched my soap opera, *All My Children*. I'd been a fan since the series began in 1970, and I discovered that the show was popular with lots of vet school students, both men and women. We couldn't just study nonstop; everybody needed a break.

Before heading back to campus, I took Keli for a walk and held Pruney in my arms for another minute or three. Then I hugged and kissed the horses so that I could smell their comforting aroma all afternoon.

The first year of veterinary school involved mostly anatomy and physiology—where we learned normal animal structures and their functions—as well as a course called Agents of Disease. The latter included everything from bacteriology, mycology, and parasitology to the nutritional requirements of all species of animals. Thursday afternoons, a guest lecture series called Perspectives brought in speakers who presented real cases.

Strangely named diseases paraded through the presentations and into our brains for consideration: fistulous withers, balanoposthitis, lumpy jaw, wobbler syndrome, wooden tongue, cryptorchidism, left displaced abomasum, pyometra, and Sweeney. What the hell was Sweeney? Certainly not the Demon Barber of Fleet Street!

The answer arrived in the form of Dr. Simon Turner, an equine surgeon from Australia, at the first Thursday lecture. Sweeney is the dysfunction of the equine forelimb due to injury to the suprascapular nerve that supplies impulses to some of the muscles of the scapula. It shows up as atrophy or wasting away of the muscles located in the horse's shoulder area.

Each student had an assigned space in a locked part of the anatomy building called the cubicles, or "cubes." Each cube was a room, with assigned seats along a countertop work surface and shelves for supplies and equipment, such as microscopes and slides. My place was

D-5: cube D, seat five. We all had keys to the building so we could study or dissect our specimens anytime, day or night.

I generally stayed away from the building during the off-hours; I studied better at home, after dinner, when Earl was in Denver working, the dog asleep on the floor, and the cat sacked out on the couch. When I needed a short break, I went out to the barn and visited the girls. That was much better than trying to concentrate in the palpable tension of the anatomy building.

The only exception was Friday nights, when my classmate Heidi and I played badminton with the Pakistani club. After badminton, we went to our respective cubes in the anatomy building and studied for a while.

One Friday evening about ten, I left through the gross anatomy laboratory, nicknamed the "gross lab," where dissections took place. The students from Hawaii were busy dissecting their assigned dog and swigging beer, clearly having a grand time. I don't know if it was the extra study or the beer, but they were among the top students in the class.

Students weren't the only ones in the anatomy building at odd times. Dr. Banks was known to roam the halls in the wee hours. If you had the gumption, you could approach him and get clarification about the topics he covered in his lectures.

The topics were crucial to our understanding of veterinary anatomy, but his lecture notes were practically undecipherable.

I wasn't willing to wander around at three in the morning on the off chance that I'd run into him, so I ventured into his office one afternoon during normal working hours. I did my best to hide my nervousness as I told him I was having difficulty understanding the difference between hydrostatic pressure and colloid osmotic pressure. Could he please explain the difference for me?

He glared at me. "Did you read the lecture notes?"

I nodded. "Yes, but I didn't understand them."

"Read them again, and read the textbook," he growled. "Don't come back until then."

I fled, tail between my legs, but I did as he demanded. Then, still uncertain that it all made sense, I worked with three of his teaching assistants until I was sure I understood. It was a harsh lesson but a successful endeavor; I've never forgotten the difference between the two types of pressure in the vascular system.

My classmates and I would have been in serious trouble when we hit the neuroanatomy section if not for a secret weapon.

Dr. Banks's lectures on the anatomy of the nervous system sounded like an utterly alien language, even for jargon-dense vet school. His lecture notes were as unintelligible as his lectures. This wasn't teaching as I knew it; it was torture.

I wasn't alone in my frustration. Almost everyone in the class was floundering in a confusing sea of terms, structures, and concepts.

By the dark of night, we rendezvoused in the lecture hall and gathered before our secret weapon, my cubemate Anna. I didn't know how or why, but Anna understood this puzzle, and more importantly, she understood how to teach it.

Anna stood on the lecture hall stage and drew elegant pathways of each cranial nerve. Cranial nerves are the nerves that emerge directly from the brain and exit through foramina—spaces—in the skull. Olfactory, optic, facial—there are twelve pairs in all. Anna explained the structure and function of each one and clarified which nerve exited through which space in the skull. She transformed us from a pack of confused students who had tried and failed to understand the professor's gobbledygook to students who thoroughly understood cranial nerves. Now *that* was teaching.

Dr. Banks wasn't our only instructor, of course. Dr. Robertshaw, a well-dressed English gentleman with a ruddy complexion, lectured on the physiology of the digestive system, explaining how the system works in various animals.

One lecture, presented in his serious, upper-crust British accent, was on *deeee*-fecation, or solid waste elimination, and how animals accomplish this. You and I call it defecation.

Okay, it was a lecture about animals taking a crap.

At first, it just seemed a bit strange, watching this man in a tweed suit, vest, and tie speak in that sophisticated accent about the process of pooping. But the mismatch grew even more pronounced as his discussion continued. This was clearly his favorite subject.

Feces are pushed out of the body by bearing down on the abdominal muscles in order to release stool, a process called the Valsalva maneuver, named for Antonio Maria Valsalva, a seventeenth-century Italian physician.

The Valsalva maneuver can vary in intensity. There can be weak pushes or strong pushes. Dr. Robertshaw pointed out that people can actually die sitting on the toilet if they do the Valsalva maneuver too hard and long without breathing. The maneuver can stop the heart. He spoke at great length about constipated Grandma dying on the can. By the time he reached the Grandma example, the lecture hall was filled with quiet snickering, my own included.

Like most of us, I'd thought of death as dying peacefully in bed, surrounded by loved ones. Here was a distinguished British fellow talking about how Grandma died on the pot trying to alleviate her constipation. Perhaps she'd been taking a stool softener, and she'd settled her creaking bones onto the cool porcelain throne, praying to the Almighty for a pleasantly soft poop while reading a romance novel. But, being constipated, she pushed so hard trying to get her rock-hard stool out of her rectum that she'd died of sudden cardiac arrest.

By the time we reached the end of the lecture, the snickers had become giggles, then, as we escaped into the hallway, outright laughter. Some of the humor was because we'd never heard of the Valsalva maneuver before and hadn't thought about what was involved in such a basic biological function. Some was the weird-to-us pronunciation of *deeee*-fecation and the juxtaposition of proper Dr. Robertshaw and the improper discussion of bathroom activities. Or maybe that's too much rationalization; maybe it was just that we'd never outgrown potty humor.

Dr. Robert Kainer was the head anatomy instructor for freshman spring semester. He was a gifted anatomist and an excellent teacher. Later, he became my employer and friend.

Dr. Kainer had been lecturing for days on the structural anatomy of the equine hoof. Day after day after day, he spoke in exquisite detail about its microscopic layers. We watched a seemingly infinite parade of slides of the same image with different colored stains illustrating the various tissues that were so important for us to learn. Even I eventually began to nod off.

One day, from the far back of the lecture hall, a student raised a weary hand. "Dr. Kainer," he said, clearly suffering from a severe case of information overload that had short-circuited his common sense. "Why do we have to learn all this stuff?"

The lecture hall instantly became as quiet as a tomb. The only sound was the *whoosh* of the ventilation system.

Dr. Kainer glared at the offending student for a long moment, then replied in a clipped tone, "Well, young man, I guess all *you'll* need is a syringe and a lariat, and you'll be ready to practice."

His response broke the tension, and the entire class cracked up. We understood what Dr. Kainer meant: we'd better get on board with a medical education filled with the accurate details we needed to properly diagnose and treat animals. Learning the normal structures is crucial to the ability to identify the abnormal. Learning what was normal, from the largest overview down to the tiniest detail, was our job and our responsibility, and it was really what freshman year was all about.

Soon after, exams wrapped up freshman year. I was by no means near the top of the class, but I had a decent enough grade point average, and I was thankful to have it.

Sophomore year, pathology replaced anatomy as our major morning course. Disease systems courses began after lunch.

Dr. Patty Olson taught our first disease course, Diseases of the Endocrine System, which entailed the study of all the disorders of the endocrine glands in the body. These are the ductless glands that secrete hormones or other products directly into the blood, and the information about abnormalities applies to all species. The course covered the effects of the over- and under-secreted hormones from those glands.

We'd studied the normal structure and function of the endocrine glands the previous year, and I'd done fine with it. But the endocrine diseases course was a mixed-up jumble for me. I was confused all the time. My concrete sequential style of learning in an orderly fashion, A-B-C-D-1-2-3-4, failed me.

Animals don't have symptoms as humans do. They have clinical signs.

A human who tells his doctor, "Hey, Doc, I have a bad bellyache and some diarrhea too," is describing a symptom. An animal who is lethargic and off its feed is displaying clinical signs.

We learned step-by-step pathways to discover what disease was presenting, but animal patients don't necessarily follow the algorithms we learned. Animals don't read their lab work, and they can only tell you what is bothering them by the clinical signs they manifest.

Clinical signs were the key to diagnosis. Simply memorizing—like learning the name and function of a shoulder muscle or regurgitating Anna's lessons about the cranial nerves—didn't work. I had to have the thought patterns to get the knowledge. It's the biggest difference between book learning and the laying on of hands. It would be another year before I began clinical rotations; for now, I had to focus on the causes, clinical signs, diagnoses, and treatments of abnormal endocrine function and real diseases.

I was in serious trouble. To succeed, I had to overcome my natural learning style and find a new way to think. I needed to develop a more abstract learning style. There were times when I thought my head was going to explode.

I would wake up in the wee hours in a cold sweat, convinced that my diabetic patients were going into ketoacidosis. Diabetic ketoacidosis is a life-threatening complication, insanely difficult to treat, and it can quickly kill the patient.

I soldiered on, despite my starring role in the Walking Dead Vet Student Night Terrors. I wish I'd known at the beginning what Dr. Olson confessed to me just before the final exam: she never graded anyone lower than a C unless the student was truly a dolt, and I was not, she assured me, a dolt.

I was never happier to get a C in my life.

Pathology, which met in the mornings, was challenging but not as nerve-racking, at least for me. In anatomy, we'd studied normal structures. In pathology, we learned the consequences of disease, the morphology that told us what made the animal sick and how and why it died.

Dr. Jaenke, one of our pathology professors, told the story of a dinner party he and his wife had hosted. The main course was roast leg of lamb (a personal favorite of mine). As he sliced into the meat, the carving knife opened up an abscess the size of a tennis ball. Viscous grayish-white pus poured out of the meat and onto the platter.

Fortunately, none of the guests saw the disgusting river of infection. He quietly disposed of the meat and called for Chinese takeout.

I'd never eaten liver, and after the class in veterinary pathology, I swore I never would. The huge portal vein that drains the intestines goes directly to the liver, bringing along any disease-causing organisms. The liver tries to remove them. Nasty-looking abnormal livers paraded past us in the lab and on lecture slides. Liver and onions? Not in this lifetime.

At the beginning of the semester, Dr. Jaenke asked for volunteers to come in early on Fridays to set up lab specimens. These were from cases that went to the necropsy lab during the week for diagnosis, after which they were returned to the Veterinary Teaching Hospital for the afternoon's one o'clock pathology rounds. The volunteers set up the specimens so they could be broadcast along with explanations via closed-circuit TV into the lecture hall. Afterward, students could examine the specimens in the lab. I was chosen to be one of the volunteers.

It was interesting work; I got to see the specimens up close while preparing them for viewing. I felt rather like a funeral director preparing a body for visitation. I also thought there might be potential for a little comic relief with the "organ recital."

I discarded my first impulse; decorating specimens with parsley and crackers would be both tacky and disrespectful. But it didn't take long for a better idea to surface.

I recorded the theme song to *All My Children*—my beloved soap opera, which most of my classmates watched too—and made a book cover with the title *All My Innards*. In the lab, we played the theme song, and as the camera beamed the music and image to the lecture hall, we opened the book cover the same way the soap opera began, and then the professor presented the various organs and case histories.

The transmission was only one-way, so my fellow volunteers and I couldn't hear the reaction of our classmates. But later, friends told me that the entire class had erupted in laughter, not just at the comedy but because they knew exactly who had perpetrated the joke. I think it helped everyone relax a little bit. I know it helped me; I slept better that night than I had all semester.

During spring semester, we had eight classes. The veterinary ethics course had an option: instead of attending class, you could write a paper. Juggling the studying for seven classes would be tough enough; I opted for the paper, wrote "Understanding Grief and Pet Loss" during the winter break between the semesters, and attended only two of the actual class sessions. I got an A on the paper and thus in the class.

To my surprise, the professor suggested that I submit my paper for publication. Not only did *Intervet*, the national veterinary school publication, accept it but it awarded me a hundred dollars for the best article in that issue.

I dove into the rest of spring semester's classes, reveling in the fascinating topics our professors presented.

Well, most of them.

Dr. Kessel, with her wild and windblown hair, long peasant skirts, and Birkenstocks, looked like a refugee from a 1960s hippie commune. She was a researcher, working with laboratory animals in a secured building next to the pathology building. Her primary area of research had something to do with rabbit diseases.

I'd come down with a nasty case of bronchitis and was doing my best to pay attention, despite what was (to me, anyway) a stultifying lecture on rabbit research.

My surgery partner, Steffan the Obnoxious, was sitting beside me. When Dr. Kessel said something about having to slice up dead rabbit tissue so she could study her results on slides, Steffan leaned over and whispered that she chopped them up using a new machine called a "Rabbomatic."

I pressed my hand against my mouth, trying to keep my giggles from escaping. Steffan stepped it up a notch and kept going on and on about the Rabbomatic, just to make me laugh harder. My shoulders shook and tears ran down my face; I could barely breathe. Then my bronchitis kicked in, and I started to cough too, that deep hacking cough typical of bronchitis. I fled the room before I could cause any more disruption and sat in the hall outside the door so I could hear the rest of the lesson. I was glad to have escaped without

Dr. Kessel realizing that it wasn't just coughing that had caused me to rush out.

As the end of sophomore year wound down, another pathology professor said, "It goes fast from here." He was right. It was time to get our hands on some patients. It was time to move to the hospital.

Sick Pets and Summer Olympics

Summer Olympics, 1984—and the women's gymnastics finals!

I've been an avid fan of the Olympics my whole life. You might think it's because I'm an ex-gymnast myself, not to mention a former physical education teacher, or because my cousin Dave competed in the Olympic steeplechase trials, though he didn't make the final cut for the 1984 Olympic team.

But my fascination began with my mother's friend Elizabeth "Betty" Robinson Schwartz.

Betty won the one-hundred-meter dash at the 1928 Olympics in Amsterdam. It was the first time female track-and-field athletes were permitted to compete in the Olympics, and Betty had won the gold. She'd added a silver medal as a member of the American relay team that year too.

She'd been only sixteen years old, and even more amazing to me, she hadn't even trained as an athlete. Charles Price, her high school biology teacher and the assistant track-and-field coach, saw her sprinting for the commuter train—she was late but made it to the train—and was amazed at her speed. The rest, as they say, is history.

She'd been slated to compete in the 1932 Los Angeles games, but in June 1931, she and her cousin had almost died in a plane crash near Chicago. In 1936, after rehab and surgery that left one leg half an inch shorter than the other and unable to bend enough to kneel in the classic starting position, she returned to the Olympics, winning gold again, this time as a member of the American relay team—in front of Hitler—beating out the much-favored German team.

Betty and my mother had worked together in Wienecke's, the Glencoe hardware store, where I'd worked during my undergraduate summers. I'd loved hearing her stories, loved the fact that most of those North Shore matrons imperiously barking out demands had no idea that their salesperson was a famous athlete who'd won gold medals not once but twice. I've never forgotten the feel of holding her Amsterdam gold medal, as if I were sharing the glory of being the fastest woman on the planet.

Of course, I didn't have the luxury of spending the entire day watching the Olympics on television. I had chores to do, beginning with feeding the horses, and then there was Keli's "respay" appointment. But my plan was in place, and I was confident that I'd be done in time for my favorite Olympic events.

When Keli, our first Siberian husky, had been spayed as a puppy, a tiny bit of ovary had been left behind. It's a relatively common problem; the ovaries can be hard to see in their entirety. The left-behind piece secretes hormones, which cause the dog to go into heat (also called estrus). She can't get pregnant, but dogs don't know that, of course!

And humans don't know that the bit of ovary has been left behind until the dog goes into heat despite being spayed. Estrus only happens twice a year, so it can be a while before the problem is discovered.

During estrus, the ovarian tissue enlarges and is easier to see, so as soon as you realize your dog's in heat, you want to respay as quickly as you can get an appointment with your veterinarian. Otherwise, you wait another six months for the animal to go into heat again, to find and remove the offending tissue.

I'd suspected that Keli had been in heat once before because she'd been acting "bitchy" (pun intended!), but it wasn't until one lovely August morning about a year and a half after she'd been spayed that we confirmed her diagnosis.

I awoke, rolled out of bed, and opened the curtains. There was Keli down in the dog pen, locked into the distinctive canine mating position with a stray dog. She was facing north; her sex partner was facing south—the position is called a "tie" and can't be broken until ejaculation—and I swear Keli had a satisfied grin on her face that no amount of her beautiful cloverleaf mask could disguise.

I, however, was not amused that my virgin husky had been deflowered. I stomped downstairs to find my five-iron, nearly breaking my toe in the process when I slammed it against the wicker couch. By the time I'd recovered and stormed outside, the evil cur had run off. Game over for Keli! And time for me to schedule an appointment with the veterinary surgeon who had spayed her the first time. She'd need to do an exploratory laparotomy and, once she found the recalcitrant bit of ovary, remove it.

"Respay day" ended up being the same day as the women's gymnastics finals. I scheduled Keli's surgery for first thing in the morning. We'd all be home by midafternoon, and soon after, Earl and I would be cheering for our favorite Olympians.

But first, there were horses to feed.

Earl and I lived on the family "farm"—a large house with a yard, a corral, and a few outbuildings in what was now the middle of town. Earl's grandfather had sold the rest of the original farmland to a developer long before I'd met Earl. What remained was a little piece of the rural West hidden away behind student housing and older suburban homes.

I walked to the barn and measured out the grain for each horse. I dispensed enough flakes of grass hay to last them until suppertime.

Horses live to eat, but this morning, Marcie wasn't eating her breakfast. She had a look in her eye that I'd learned meant trouble. Something was definitely wrong.

I examined her carefully and discovered an inch of a nail sticking out of the very center of her abdomen.

"How did you get a nail *there*?" I asked her, shaking my head in disbelief. Most likely, she'd rolled onto it in the corral, but even that scenario didn't completely explain such bad luck.

I couldn't tell how long the nail was, and I certainly wasn't going to remove it. I was only a rising second-year vet student, not an expert nail puller.

So much for my neatly planned morning.

Earl and I hitched up the trailer to the pickup truck and loaded Marcie into the trailer. Earl drove Keli to the surgeon for her respaying, and I drove Marcie to the Veterinary Teaching Hospital, where she was admitted as an emergency patient.

The equine medicine resident pulled out the nail, yelling "Ouch!" for dramatic effect. The nail was six inches long, rusty and corroded, clearly an antique from times long past. Why it had surfaced now, no one could say.

There's a significant danger of systemic illness with this type of injury. "Systemic" means any infection that could spread through the body, and the doctor treated the wound aggressively to prevent that. After numbing the area with a local anesthetic, he made a slit in her abdomen and checked for the discharge that would indicate infection. Fortunately, there was none; Marcie's body had encapsulated the infection (formed a kind of protective bubble around it, like an internal scab), and she never became systemically ill.

As soon as the immediate crisis was over, I left Marcie at the hospital and drove to the surgeon's office to see how Keli was doing. The surgeon invited me to take a look. I remember staring at Keli's exposed liver and thinking, *From rusty nail to Keli's liver . . . what a strange day.* The average dog owner never sees her dog's liver, let alone an engorged remnant of functional ovary destined for the trash.

We brought Keli home, where she slept on the floor near us while we watched Mary Lou Retton win the Olympic All-Around Gold Medal in women's gymnastics.

Marcie stayed in a hospital stall to continue her recovery under the watchful eyes of the fourth-year vet students, who were on duty twenty-four seven to learn equine medicine.

Although I wasn't a student at the hospital yet—that part of my training wouldn't start until my third year—I routinely attended the large animal rounds in the vet school barn in the summer, and I was there the Friday after Marcie was admitted. The senior student who presented Marcie's case did a fine job.

Marcie was a good patient, quiet and cooperative, unlike some horses that would just as soon kill you as look at you. Initially, I wasn't sure of the senior student who cared for Marcie because I didn't know her, and she wasn't enamored of horses. But she won me over; she did a first-rate job, with both treating Marcie and communicating with Earl and me. I learned later that Marcie was the favorite of all the students who were on the equine medicine rotation during her stay.

After Friday's large animal rounds, I asked one of the equine residents for the nail that had been removed from Marcie's abdomen. He refused.

I knew that every vet kept a collection of bizarre objects found in patients, but the nail was my property. He still refused; he wanted it for his personal animal foreign body collection, and it didn't matter what I wanted or to whom it belonged.

I eventually asked the clinician who was in charge of this resident to please retrieve the nail and return it to me, which she did. And yes, I still have it; I keep it in my desk drawer, part of my own "bizarre objects" collection and a reminder that my careful plans for the day have to stretch and shift to accommodate the surprises that surface.

Although I was more than a year from being a student doing clinical rotations at the Veterinary Teaching Hospital, Marcie's recovery gave me a taste of what it would be like to be available around the clock, caring for a seriously ill equine patient.

As happens from time to time, there was a bacterial outbreak in the vet hospital's barn. In this case, it was *Salmonella*, a species of bacteria commonly associated with food poisoning and spread through contaminated food or water. Its source was a patient's intestine; the bug was flourishing and making its way around the barn.

Although Marcie still needed ongoing treatment, we had her discharged and brought her home.

Since our barn had three stalls and we had only two horses, we'd already set up the larger stall, which had a stone floor, as a "just in case" hospital stall. It was large enough for us to work around a horse, but small enough that the horse didn't have enough room to lie down. The stone floor would have been uncomfortable to lie on too.

It was important that Marcie not lie down, because horses can get "cast" in stalls (and other places)—they lie down, get stuck, and can't get up again. They can injure themselves as they struggle to stand.

Once home, Marcie was on "stall rest," the equine equivalent of bed rest. We wouldn't give her full run of the corral until she'd finished all her treatments and we were sure she was fine. We tucked her into the makeshift hospital stall and fastened the chain across the entryway.

Her medication was the same as at the vet hospital: twice a day, I crushed the huge antibiotic tablets, mixed them with molasses, and filled a big syringe (the tip cut off, and no needle) with the molasses and medication sludge. Then I reached up (and up; I'm a lot shorter than Marcie), positioning the syringe as far back into her mouth as I could, and pressed the plunger, aiming for the interdental space or as close to the back of the jaw as I could. Marcie swallowed the goop down without complaint.

I checked on her frequently during the day and evening. Earl took the night shift, since he worked nights and was up in the wee hours.

Within a day or so, she was feeling fine, so we let her eat a little bit more each day, though she was still restricted to her stall. Finally, after several days of intensive care in the barn, we allowed her to join Franny out on the lawn to eat grass. I was glad to see her in the yard again; she and Franny made great lawnmowers and saved us a bundle on the cost of hay.

A couple of mornings later, I stepped outside the house and nearly had a heart attack. Marcie was lying flat out on the lawn. From where I stood, she looked dead.

I ran to her and checked: she was breathing. I ran back to the house and called the student who had taken such good care of her in the vet hospital.

She was kind enough to not laugh at my panicked description. "Marcie's fine," she reassured me. "She's just decided to take a siesta on the comfy grass in the warm summer sun."

When my heart rate finally dropped back to normal, I stretched out beside Marcie on the lawn. Keli gave an approving "*Ah-woooo!*" from the dog pen. I agreed; plan or no plan, the day was a perfect ten.

It's All in How You Talk to 'Em

The Veterinary Teaching Hospital—VTH—was the temple of veterinary medicine at Colorado State University.

We had arrived.

Well, mostly. As juniors in vet school, we shifted from days filled with lectures to mornings filled with fascinating clinical rotations at the hospital, where we got to *do* medicine and surgery instead of just reading and listening to lectures about them. Classes on more disease systems filled our afternoons.

The mantra of veterinary procedures is "See one, do one, teach one." On clinics, each junior student worked with a senior partner; the senior had the responsibility, and the junior watched and learned. Clinicians oversaw everything.

I admired the "See one, do one, teach one" method. I may not have been number one in my class, but my teaching skills were still razor sharp. I'm the one who taught our class valedictorian how to place a central venous line into a dog in the ICU.

After clinics and before classes, I still went home for lunch every day, except for the day of the Incredibly Long Cat Spay.

On that day, I was the anesthesia student for two of my junior surgery lab classmates. My job was to manage anesthesia and monitor the vital signs of the patient while my classmates spayed the cat. Close monitoring is crucial; without it, the patient could die or wake up in midsurgery.

My record time for a cat spay was eighteen minutes. I doubt I was fastest, but after being Steffan's partner in junior surgery lab, I had pretty fast skills for a student.

These guys were at the other end of the spectrum. They achieved our class record for the longest cat spay ever: three and a half hours. We worked over clinic time, through lunch, and showed up late for class, still dressed in scrubs and covered with surgical gowns.

Most of the topics we practiced were organized into one- or two-week blocks called "rotations." Dr. James Ingram, nicknamed Grim Jim, was a popular and respected veterinary neurologist who led us, literally, through our neurology rotation. He had a reputation for slipping away, so the students would lose him. Or, more accurately, he would lose the students, on purpose, maybe because he never liked the moniker Grim Jim.

Students arranged themselves like ducklings following their mother to stick with him. Earl told the story of when he'd been at vet school ten years earlier, the "duck patrol" had actually followed Dr. Ingram as he'd sauntered out of the hospital and across the parking lot, all the way to his parked car. They didn't break formation until the good professor drove away.

We had a "gunner" in our class named Dane. Gunners are students who will do anything to gain recognition and prove they're superior. They show up in every professional school and graduate program, and the game is always the same. The gunners monopolize class time, trying to show how smart they are by arguing with the professor or asking questions they already know the answer to. The other students pass the time playing "Gunner Bingo," guessing (and sometimes placing bets on) how many questions the gunner will ask, then comparing results later in the day to see who won.

This particular day, Dane spent ten long minutes asking Dr. Ingram his question. The question was elaborate, exquisitely crafted, and filled with extensive detail.

Silence filled the room as we waited for what would surely be an equally elaborate and important answer.

Dr. Ingram slowly pushed his gray hair back, took off his glasses and cleaned them with a plain white handkerchief, wiped his face with the handkerchief, returned the handkerchief to his pocket, settled his glasses back on his nose, and looked Dane intently in the eye.

"No."

No? That was his answer? Yes, that was it—all of it. Dane's face flushed bright red as the rest of us crumpled into laughter.

Each spring, four piglets were put in a stall on the food animal side of the barn so we could learn how to handle them and practice doing procedures on them. They weren't sick; they were there simply for our practice. Their final fate was noted on the stall's "reason for admission" card, which proclaimed in large, clear letters, "BBQ."

Pigs are a particularly obstinate breed of farm animal. Boy, can they bite! In one of his books, James Herriot tells the story of a snooty, first-in-his-class visiting vet student trying to draw blood from pigs for necessary blood tests. By the time the student had finished, he was covered in porcine excrement from the enraged patients. Like that student, I never did learn to draw blood from a pig; I still panic when I think about my screwups and the deafening squeals of angry pigs.

Although I didn't much like pigs, I loved the barn. The smell of hay was sweet, as was the fragrance of horses on the equine side of the barn. The smell on the food animal side wasn't as nice, but it was still a place of comfort for me.

One morning, my classmate Bullet Bob and I were on barn duty on the food animal side. Robert and I had been cubemates our first year and had become good friends. He was a good ol' cowboy from the eastern plains of Colorado, a big guy who plodded his way through school as if he were a slowpoke. But he was no dummy; he opened his own practice immediately after he received his license, the first of our class to do so. He set up shop in the eastern plains, a vast, semiarid region not usually considered for Colorado tourism ads. There wasn't another vet within a hundred miles, so Robert practiced on all species. He was the first among us to earn a six-figure income.

On that morning, while Robert and I were on barn duty, the energetic piglets escaped their stall.

Jailbreak!

We did have the presence of mind to close all the barn doors, but darned if we could catch those little piggies.

They sprinted up and down the wide aisles of the barn, squealing and grunting. They fell and rolled over and over after trying to negotiate ninety-degree turns. We'd chase; they'd flee up and down the aisles, back and forth across the barn.

The only thing we got for our efforts was sweaty. Robert was intent on catching the piglets, but I ended up laughing, utterly useless to the task at hand. Nothing in my childhood in the upscale, predominantly Jewish suburb of Highland Park, Illinois, had prepared me for this. All I could do was watch the piglets race around, laughing at their silly-sounding and incredibly loud vocalizations.

Robert and I were coated in sweat and dirt. The piglets showed no sign of slowing down, let alone returning to their stall.

Finally, after what seemed like forever, Dr. Smith, the food animal professor in charge of all pigs great and small, came in. He was a short, slight man, not much bigger than I am, and a native of Alabama with an accent to match.

Oh no, I thought, *Robert and I are going to be in big trouble.*

Dr. Smith ignored the thundering Four Porkers of the Apocalypse (who also ignored him) and stepped into their stall. Then he let out an ear crushing, "SOO-EY PIG! SOO-EY PIG!"

To my utter, open-mouthed amazement, the pigs ran at top speed right into their stall.

That was enough to put me on my knees, cackling hysterically.

I thought Dr. Smith would be angry with me for my helpless laughter and for being so useless.

But he casually closed the stall door and, with a twinkle in his eyes, looked at me and drawled, "It's all in how you talk to 'em."

Senior year began the day after junior year finished. There could be no gap in the care of the patients; the former seniors had graduated two days after their last day on clinics, and we were the new seniors. One day we were junior students; the next, we were in charge of the cases. It was a little daunting.

At the time I attended veterinary school, seniors were on a trimester program, with fall, spring, and summer trimesters. Each student was in school for two of the three trimesters. Most students spent their "off" trimester working in some capacity in veterinary practice outside the university.

I chose section B so I could have large animal rotations during the summer trimester (outside in summer was better than outside in winter) and because I already had a job with Dr. Kainer as an anatomy teaching assistant for the fall trimester. My small animal rotation would be during spring trimester.

Senior year was certainly no less stressful than the first three years, but I enjoyed it—the professors, the patients, and my classmates, even some of the odd things we were required to do—much more. The close relationships that developed between students and professors, made possible because we worked together in small groups of five or so during the weekly rotations, made all the difference.

The equine and food animal rotations were in four-week blocks, each followed by a huge exam. These block tests were fraught with fear. Other rotations included ophthalmology, radiology, anesthesiology, electives, and more. I continued to make it home for lunch every day, except for the last two weeks of my vet school experience. Those two weeks were my small animal surgery rotation, and there simply wasn't enough time to make it home and back again. I brown-bagged two slices of Little Caesar's pizza for a quick and tasty lunch every day—and packed five extra pounds onto my normally 102-pound frame. Twenty pieces of pizza in two weeks will do that.

My first rotation was an elective I'd chosen, equine medicine. Attending barn rounds on Wednesday and Friday mornings was required for all seniors on large animal rotations. I was already used to them; I'd begun attending them the summer after my first year.

The clinician on duty that week was Dr. Bennett. My first patient was a marginally sick horse. Because it was such a minor case, I asked Dr. Bennett if I would be presenting during rounds. He said, "No."

When we gathered for Wednesday's barn rounds, Dr. Bennett called on me first to present my patient. Ack! I was totally unprepared and stumbled through my case.

That was a lesson I never forgot.

From then on, I carried the information about each case in my head, lab work values and all. I didn't use a cheat sheet; I presented from memory, whether I was explaining the overall issue with my patient or answering a question about a specific detail. If someone asked me what the blood glucose value was for my equine patient, I could tell them, exactly, what that value was without referring to any notes. I drew from my experience as a teacher too; I had years of practice with public speaking, and I was comfortable pulling up information I'd prepared whenever I needed that information.

During that first week, one of the patients was Superbear, a gorgeous American paint horse stallion from Arizona.

Superbear had been in an exclusive paint horse show in Denver, where about half the horses had come down with colic (belly pain).

Colic can lead to laminitis, which is a dangerous inflammation of the hoof wall. Laminitis, in turn, can lead to founder, where the bone that goes into the hoof rotates away from the hoof wall, crippling the horse. (Thank goodness I'd paid attention to Dr. Kainer's lectures on the structural anatomy of the equine hoof!)

None of the other horses had been as sick as Superbear; they had been treated successfully at VTH and released the week before my rotation had begun. Dr. Bennett assigned Superbear to me.

I fell in love.

Although I look upon stallions with trepidation, Superbear was my all-time favorite equine patient because of his sweetness, his gentle beauty—I have a fondness for paints—and his will to fight his dreadful illness. I think he knew we were trying hard to save him. I even dreamed about him at night.

Superbear was a well-known stud horse, so his sweet disposition surprised me. Stud horses can be nasty. After all, they have only one thing on their minds: a pretty little mare and Barry White on the stereo.

Superbear was hospitalized all summer, isolated in his own hallway. No other horses were allowed in his section of the barn due to the possibility of spreading his infection via the diarrhea caused by his disease.

I cared for this sweet beauty under Dr. Bennett's supervision, doing everything I could except for feeding, which the barn employees did. When Superbear went down with his illness, unable to stand, I cleaned his stall myself, and I devised a berm of wood-shaving bedding to prevent his mess from getting out of his stall and endangering the other patients.

One day, I was shoveling out Superbear's stall, dumping the heavy, soiled wood shavings in the bin outside, when Dr. Ball, the bovine practitioner whose rotation I'd be on soon, drove up in his food animal ambulatory truck. A bunch of my classmates were in the truck, and as they all looked on, Dr. Ball belted out the lyrics from "Old Man River": "Tote that barge! Lift that bail!"

I grinned and sang back, "Get a little drunk, and you land in jaaaaiil!" A nice bit of humor and humanity for a sweaty, smelly job on a hot summer day.

I'd see Superbear again at the end of the trimester, during my required equine medicine block, but this time, he wouldn't be my patient. Dr. Bennett thought I'd become too attached to him. He was right.

Soon after my first equine rotation, I began the food animal block rotation, initially assigned to Dr. Ball's ambulatory truck for dairy herd medicine. Ambulatory trucks bring veterinary care out to the country to treat animals, since ranchers and farmers can't bring an entire herd to the hospital. The truck seated three in the front and three in the back; as the smallest person in the group, I got stuck in the "death seat," front seat center.

Dr. Ball was tall and lanky, with arms long enough to reach a cow's tonsils by going in through the rectum. That was an important talent; pregnancy testing is a significant part of herd medicine, and Dr. Ball's skills were legendary. Golden Arm Ball could tell by feel practically the exact date and time when a cow had gotten pregnant and when she would deliver her calf.

The procedure sounds (and is) messy, but it's necessary. First, you must remember to remove your wedding ring; many rings have gone missing up a cow's rectum. Next, you pull a plastic rectal sleeve over your nondominant arm. Then you reach into the rectum and palpate, feeling for the cervix, uterus, ovaries, and uterine arteries through the rectal wall.

We students were supposed to learn that skill too, but I never did. The business end of those large, roomy black-and-white Holsteins was literally out of my reach; I can reach only as far as the cervix. My arms are simply too short for bovine practice. Not that Dr. Ball didn't try to persuade me otherwise. He offered to lift my five-foot-nothing body up and hold me parallel to the ground so I could stick my arm up the cow's rectum to feel for a pregnant uterus. Thanks, but no thanks!

Before our rotation had begun, I'd seen Dr. Ball's classic prank that he played on students learning the preg-testing procedure. Before actually feeling for a fetus, the examiner has to empty the rectum. Dr. Ball was as gifted at cleaning out a cow as he was in determining its pregnancy status and progress.

Cow feces have the consistency of foul-smelling pudding; they're not like the fragrant "road apples" horses leave behind. With his arm still in the cow's rectum, Dr. Ball would aim a shot of bovine feces at an unwary student, covering the entire front of the student's coveralls with a sticky slurry of pungent cow shit. Other students put up with this malodorous trick, believing a clinician could do whatever he wanted to.

Not me; I had no intention of playing this game. The first day of the rotation, in my best "nontraditional student who used to teach K through 12" voice, I quietly told Dr. Ball that if he ever pulled that stunt on me, we were going to have a little go 'round.

Perhaps he remembered how tough teachers have to be; perhaps it was simply because I was assertive enough to talk to him straight-on about it. Whatever the reason, he honored my request and never took aim at me.

Dr. Johnson was another food animal clinician I worked with during the food animal rotations. I knew him from my physical education teaching days, because his daughter had been one of my students. I'd known he was a veterinarian before I'd met him because Jeruesha had come to school one day nursing a sprained ankle, which he'd wrapped in the veterinary medicine version of an Ace bandage: Vet Wrap, a sticky, brightly colored wraparound bandage material.

One morning, Dr. Johnson and our group headed out in the ambulatory truck to a sheep feedlot on the high plains east of Fort Collins.

I like sheep. They're easy patients to work with when they need vet care or shearing. They are definitely not the rocket scientists of the animal kingdom. All you have to do is prop the sheep up on its bottom, with its forelimbs up—the same posture as a dog begging—and the sheep sits stock-still. It doesn't even try to move.

We reached the feedlot, but instead of meeting a kindly rancher who needed us to work on his Suffolk or Hampshire sheep, Dr. Johnson drove us to the far back of the lot.

We got out of the truck and stared at a four-foot-high, ten-foot-wide pile of dead, flyblown sheep that lay reeking in the hot sun.

"Go find out how they died," Dr. Johnson said.

We had learned through word of mouth the "four S's of ovine medicine": Sick Sheep Seldom Survive. The usual diagnosis is shipping fever, which happens when the sheep are so stressed by transport that they get sick and die.

I walked off a little to the side, away from my classmates, looked into the bright blue heavens, and said, "Mom, do you see what your nice little Jewish girl is doing now?"

It was a gross, grisly, and, yes, disgusting task, one of the worst things I had to do that summer. My classmates probably thought I was nuts, because I kept smiling as we opened up carcass after rotting carcass. But all I could think about was my late mother, wherever she was, equal parts chagrined and amused, shaking her head at what I was up to.

Later that week, Dr. Johnson and our crew of students visited an SPF pig farm. SPF stands for specific pathogen free, which means that the herd is free from disease and must be carefully protected.

As part of that protection, we had to "shower in" and pick clean clothes from the farmer's supply to wear before seeing the pigs. After finishing our work, we "showered out" and returned to the truck wearing our own clothes.

The shower-in, shower-out requirement was one of the reasons I chose section B, with its large animal rotation in the summer. The day we visited the SPF farm, it was ninety-five degrees Fahrenheit, and a couple of showers felt pretty good. I had no desire to be naked on a pig farm outside in February, when temperatures would be in the thirties, if we were lucky.

Of course, none of the clothes in the farmer's stash fit me. Everything was huge. I had to use both hands just to hold up my borrowed pants, as if I were wearing a denim barrel with no shoulder straps.

Without asking, Dr. Johnson grabbed the front of my borrowed jeans at the waist, pulled the belt loops (and me with them) close to him, and secured the loops with adhesive tape from the truck. He spun me around, grinning.

After I'd gotten over the initial surprise, I grinned back. Cover Carlson with tape, and she's good to go! And hats off to a creative clinician for finding a solution to my farm fashion problem.

We also visited an indoor swine facility with Dr. Johnson. It wasn't an SPF facility, so we kept our own coveralls on, although we did have to sanitize our rubber boots going in and out. That's an easier process; just step in and out of the tub of sanitizing solution.

Sows and boars are vicious, and they're one of the worst-smelling animals in creation. We spent a long time examining the sows and their adorable youngsters. By the time we were finished, we smelled almost as bad as the pigs.

When we returned to the VTH, the other students bolted to the locker room showers, but I headed straight home. I doffed my clothes and left them in a smelly heap beside the washing machine to deal with later, crept up the stairs in my birthday suit—Pruney and Keli must have thought I was nuts, not to mention foul smelling—and stood under the hot shower for a long time. I scrubbed, I washed, I scrubbed again, but no matter how long I washed, I could still smell the swine aroma wafting off me and up to the ceiling in the steam. I didn't care how lucrative swine herd management could be; a porcine practice was not going to be in my future!

My final rotation of the summer was the equine medicine block. It included two weeks of equine medicine, followed by two weeks of equine surgery.

Just the thought of equine surgery rotation put knots of anxiety in every student's stomach. Equine surgeons were considered Masters of the Universe. It's incredibly difficult to land postgraduate residencies in this field. You have to be at the top of your class, with superior recommendations. Most of us believed equine surgeons were obnoxious prima donnas, and the students whose goal it was to become equine surgeons were up-and-coming obnoxious prima donnas.

My attitude right from the start was "No one is that good to be that obnoxious, no matter how brilliant or famous they are." I was willing to challenge it or ignore it, if need be. But I never had to; I got along well with the surgeons and had a great two weeks.

My first week, I lucked out and was on Dr. Stashak's service. Dr. Stashak was a nice person, as well as a good teacher and surgeon. He knew that I owned horses, and thus he considered me to be a "horse person."

I just shrugged and got on with the work, but to be honest, I objected to that label. The people I knew who referred to themselves as "horse people" were self-aggrandizing, and I didn't want to be lumped in with them. My classmates certainly didn't think of me as a "horse person," even though many of them had been to my house, seen my horses, and had even practiced palpating them back during freshman year.

One morning, Dr. Stashak operated on Wrangler's Rocket, a young paint gelding. Rocket was a "wobbler," a horse with a neurological problem in its neck vertebrae and nerves that prevents normal movement. Riding a wobbler can be dangerous, and they are never used for breeding stock. Surgery is difficult and performed only when the neurologist thinks there's a better than decent chance that it will help. The surgery went well but had a poor prognosis. Dr. Stashak and I hand-recovered Rocket after the operation.

The darkened, closed recovery stall had mats on all sides and a large, soft mat covering the entire floor. Dr. Stashak and I sat together beside Rocket, waiting for him to regain consciousness. When he began to stir, Dr. Stashak gave him a small dose of sedative so he wouldn't thrash around and stand up too quickly, which would disturb the site of the delicate neck surgery.

The time alone with Dr. Stashak, sitting on the cushioned stall floor together, helping Rocket recover, gave me a chance to talk with him about equine practice. I fretted that my small size meant I couldn't be successful in equine medicine.

He reassured me, telling me gently, "Mary, the clients are paying for your knowledge, not your size." He nodded toward Rocket and said, "And there's little difference to the horse between a hundred-pound person and a two-hundred-pound person."

My second week of the equine surgery rotation was with the most feared professor on the staff.

Dr. McIlwraith was world-famous in the field of equine orthopedic surgery. He'd pioneered the technique of arthroscopic surgery in horses, a technique similar to the procedure used in human medicine.

Veterinary-to-human and human-to-veterinary medical breakthroughs happen more often than many people realize. My father-in-law, Dr. William D. Carlson, CSU vet school class of '52, transposed human radiology into veterinary practice, launching the field of veterinary radiology. CSU vet school's own Dr. Harry Gorman designed the first artificial hip joint for dogs; later, it was adapted for human use. As the happy owner of my own hip replacement, I owe the late Dr. Gorman an extra dose of gratitude.

Dr. McIlwraith had traveled the world to operate on the horses of the rich and famous. He'd pioneered arthroscopic surgery and performed it on the racehorse Spend A Buck in 1985, in time for Spend A Buck to win the Kentucky Derby that year. The Sultan of the United

Arab Emirates had flown Dr. McIlwraith to Dubai to operate on the Sultan's prize racehorses.

My experience with Dr. McIlwraith so far had been a positive one in junior year classes. I found both his lectures and his course notes clear and easy to understand, but I'd heard through the grapevine that he was mean and nasty to students and staff during clinics.

I'd also heard from someone—I no longer remember whom—that Dr. McIlwraith held a PhD in anatomy too, and if we had a slow week, on Friday, I should ask him to take us to necropsy and show us the surgical anatomy of a horse's leg. I asked him, and he agreed. He went through the entire forelimb, pointing out which injuries occurred at various locations and dissecting out the anatomy, showing us where the procedures were done. It was a wonderful end to a marvelous week.

Block tests, the big exams that follow the four-week large animal block rotations, are notoriously difficult; more than one student has gone down in flames. I always struggled, always worried that this time I'd fail the big test big time.

I worried this time too, but much to my relief, I aced the equine block test—a great ending to an enjoyable summer.

I spent the fall trimester working as Dr. Kainer's anatomy teaching assistant, and when spring trimester rolled around, I was on Dr. Ingram's neurology rotation, the same Dr. Ingram of duck patrol fame. He and my father-in-law had been classmates in the class of '52, and Earl had been his student, so Dr. Ingram and I were on pretty friendly terms from the beginning. I even knew where he hid when he wanted to escape the duck patrol.

It's a tradition for the seniors to make a video for the junior–senior banquet held near the end of the year, and Dr. Ingram agreed to star in our vignette that poked fun at him and his duck patrol.

In the video, he slipped away from his trailing line of students (including myself) and entered an empty room. He uttered the immortal words, "Beam me up, Scotty!" and disappeared in a shower of flashing sprinkles. I still have a copy of the video; if the Academy of Motion Picture Arts and Sciences awarded Oscars to vet school films, our masterpiece would have been a shoo-in.

Senior clinical rotations were graded weekly on a 0 to 12 ranking system. Each Friday afternoon, we would pick up that week's grade sheet from the clinical sciences office.

Since we shifted to different practitioners each week, we usually didn't follow the same patient beyond the end of that particular week. As luck would have it, I had the opportunity to follow one patient over two weeks, from diagnosis and surgery through recovery and dismissal.

The week before I served with Dr. Ingram, I'd been on an elective neurology rotation with a different neurologist, Dr. LeCouteur. One of our patients had been a twelve-year-old golden retriever named Boo-Boo. Boo-Boo's owners had brought him in because he was weak and was walking on his whole feet instead of just the paws.

Dr. LeCouteur had taken one look at the critically low glucose level in Boo-Boo's blood work and sent him directly to surgery to remove the tumor he knew was there. No ifs, ands, or buts: it was an insulinoma, a fairly uncommon cancerous, insulin-secreting tumor of the pancreas.

Yes, an endocrine disease. At least I knew how to care for Boo-Boo without giving myself night terrors.

During my regular week on neurology, this time with Dr. Ingram, I continued to treat Boo-Boo, who was recovering from surgery. When it was time for Boo-Boo to be released, I met with his owners.

When clients come to the vet hospital to pick up their animals, we leave the patients in the wards so their owners can focus on what we tell them, without the distraction of greeting their beloved pets. The student, who in this case was me, explains to the owners what the illness is all about, what the treatment involved, what medications are going home with the patient, and how to administer medications and other at-home care. The student also gives the prognosis, which in Boo-Boo's case was not a good one.

Boo-Boo didn't have a lot of time left, but he would go home to be comfortable with those he loved.

It's always hard to deliver that kind of news, but it's important. It's crucial to allow enough time for the clients to understand everything and to ask questions.

Dr. Ingram listened to me chat with the clients and answer their questions. Later, he complimented me on my discussion with Boo-Boo's owners.

When I received my grade for my week with Dr. Ingram, my score was 11.96 out of 12. I knew that many of my classmates would have raced to the professor to demand where they'd gone wrong or to argue about the missing 0.04 points, but I smiled; 11.96 was so like Dr. Ingram.

I wasn't worried about my grades—I had a 4.0 GPA that trimester—but I couldn't resist the temptation to pester him. I marched into his office, trying not to grin too much, and asked him to tell me just where, exactly, I had missed 0.04 points.

He leaned back in his chair with his hands behind his head and laughed.

To this day, that's the only weekly grade score I remember.

My last patient as a vet student and my all-time favorite canine patient was a Dalmatian coach hound named Bullet, who belonged to a beer company. He'd fallen off the company's horse-drawn beer wagon and gotten hung up with his leash on, which left him dangling by his neck. I assisted in the delicate, dangerous surgery to remove the dens (the piece of his second cervical vertebra) that had snapped off in the accident.

The surgery went through lunch; I was so hypoglycemic that I bumped into the surgeon, who promptly snarled at me. After the surgery, I spied a classmate eating an orange in the hallway and begged for a few segments. I sank down to the floor and reveled in the delicious sweetness, temporarily revived.

Bullet survived, despite having a major bout of bleeding during the surgery. He had to be treated very gently. I couldn't put a leash around his neck, so I wrapped it under one shoulder. I took him everywhere I went around the small animal side of the VTH as physical therapy.

As he improved, I would say to him, "Bullet, hug!" He would rise up on his hind limbs and rest his front paws and head on my shoulders, giving me a full-body hug while I wrapped my arms around him. We looked like odd lovers, a Dalmatian and his married girlfriend. Other classmates tried to get a hug from him, but Bullet was a faithful dog and would hug only me.

After graduation and before the state board exam, there wasn't much to do except prepare for the exam. I relaxed, worked in the garden, and (of course) watched my soap opera, which is what I was doing when Dr. Ingram called to tell me that Bullet was coming in for a follow-up exam. Would I like to come to the hospital to see him again? I said yes, absolutely.

When I arrived, Dr. Ingram teased me about sitting around watching soap operas all day, then noticed my swollen right hand. It was about the size of a baseball, thanks to an angry yellow jacket I'd encountered in my garden.

That didn't stop me from going into the exam room to see my best canine patient. He had recovered and was well on his way back to working on the beer wagon during parades.

I was well on my way too. Soon, I'd be a licensed, practicing veterinarian.

9

What's in a Name?

My own cat clinic! Earl, his dad, and I converted our one-car garage into Blue Spruce Cat Clinic, the only feline-exclusive practice in Northern Colorado. It was wonderful to practice veterinary medicine from my own home.

Fort Collins is a college town with a more diverse population than the average small city, and I had all types of clients and cats. "Regular folks," college students, and professors (including vet school professors)—both locals and those from far-flung countries—brought their kittens and cats to me for care. I did free exams for the local shelter when cats were adopted, which helped both the shelter and the cash-strapped coeds who'd fallen in love with a feline sweetie. The Veterinary Teaching Hospital often referred clients to me when their clinicians were stumped. I researched diseases, presented lectures, and wrote for journals and magazines too. It was exciting, fulfilling work.

But during my senior year in vet school, I had discovered that I missed working with kids. I'd always wanted to be a teacher, and teaching was my first career. So I added it back into my life, teaching junior high school science—initially part time, then expanding to full time—while also running my feline-exclusive veterinary practice.

It was quite the rat race and made for long and often hectic days.

I rarely had time to visit with my friends in the teachers' lounge. Occasionally, I'd pop in long enough to eat lunch and listen to the school chatter.

One afternoon during office hours, Ashley, a new client and beautiful young college student, carried a tiny kitten into the exam room for his first visit. She was clearly thrilled with her new buddy, and no wonder: he was an adorable black-and-white tuxedo boy.

Ashley fretted because she hadn't come up with a name for him yet. As I examined the endearing mass of kitten fur, I reassured her. "Sometimes, you have to wait for the cat to tell you its name," I explained. "Based on my experience with my own pets, I suspect you'll discover his name within a week or so."

I gave the unnamed kitten his first deworming medicine, his first round of vaccinations, and his feline leukemia and FIV tests. I discussed the basics of proper kitten care with Ashley, including my advice to never use hands and feet to play with her kitty—that's how people get scratched, bitten, or ambushed.

As Ashley was leaving, she spied a photo on the clinic bulletin board. "Who's that?" she asked, peering at the image of a middle-aged man holding a gigantic black-and-white tuxedo cat.

I grinned. "That's my husband, Earl, and our twenty-pound cat, Alexander."

Ashley looked like a light bulb had suddenly turned on in her head. She tried out the name: "Earl . . . hmmm . . . Earl!"

And that was it: her new kitty became known as Earl.

Ashley returned a few weeks later. Kitty Earl had managed to get a fishhook stuck through his upper lip. Although removing the hook would be relatively straightforward, it would require general anesthesia. Since Earl was now big enough, it would make sense to neuter him at the same time. That would save him the risk of a second round of anesthesia and save Ashley a nice stack of money too. Ashley agreed, and Earl had surgery to remove the fishhook and his ability to reproduce.

The next day, I dropped into the crowded teachers' lounge for a quick lunch. As I was getting ready to go back to my classroom, a colleague asked what was going on in my life.

One foot out the door, I said, "Well, yesterday, I neutered Earl."

The entire room fell silent. Teachers stared at me, expressions ranging from puzzlement to confusion to alarm. Finally, someone said, "That's nice, Mary," and as the door swung shut behind me, they erupted into laughter.

Wandering in the Outback

My graduation present to myself as I headed into my final trimester of vet school was a brand-new Subaru station wagon. I'd driven my 1973 VW Super Beetle one hundred thousand miles during the fourteen years I'd owned it. It had served me well, but I was ready for a car that could handle a house call practice and anything the mountains, plains, and unpredictable weather of Colorado could throw at me.

I'd driven that Subaru for nine years, crisscrossing the country between home and Washington, DC, cruising west to Utah and north to Wyoming, and climbing into the Colorado high country. My "Sube" and I had even made it to the top of Colorado Yule Quarry in Marble, Colorado. That's the quarry where the marble for the exterior of the Lincoln Memorial and the Tomb of the Unknown Soldier came from. That drive had convinced me that the reason Subarus were (and still are) one of the most popular brands in Colorado is because they're part mountain goat.

By the time I was ready to retire my first Subaru and replace it with a new model, I'd opened my home-based cat clinic and returned to full-time teaching at two junior high schools, one in the morning and the other after lunch. My usual routine was to teach all morning, then zip home to check on my patients and the horses and, after eating a quick lunch, head over to the second school to teach my afternoon classes.

It was 1995, the year of the first Subaru Outbacks. I bought a sapphire-blue model with silver trim—so pretty! The tech teacher at school noticed my new machine in the staff parking lot and recognized it as the sports utility wagon of the future.

A few days later, I crossed the parking lot to my new beauty. It was a lovely spring day, warm and sunny. I was looking forward to spending a little time enjoying the fine weather during my short lunch break at home.

I slid into the driver's seat and fired up the engine.

Oh no! What was that strange bumping noise coming from my brand new engine? What was wrong with my car? It was brand new; nothing should be wrong!

The Subaru dealership was nearby, so I drove there straightaway. All the sales and service guys there knew me. I'd always brought my first Subaru to them for service, and they'd taken good care of my Sube and me over the years. Of course, I'd purchased my new Subaru from them too.

They popped open the hood and *yowl*! A young coal-black cat exploded out of the engine compartment. Airborne for a second or two, it hit the floor and vanished behind a barrel in the corner.

I knew exactly what had happened. In cold weather, cats like to crawl under car hoods to enjoy the warmth of the engine. Worst case scenario, when the engine starts, the cat gets chopped up by the fan. On cold days, you should bang on your car's hood, just in case there's a cat hiding out on your engine. But it was a warm April day, and the possibility of a cat curling up on my new Sube's engine had never occurred to me.

The poor panicked cat dashed around the garage like a cat version of rodeo barrel racing as the guys tried to catch him. The more they tried to herd the cat, the more the cat dodged and ricocheted around the room. One of the young women who worked at the dealership started chasing the cat, shrieking, "Get that cat! It's got to go to the vet!"

I said, "Let it calm down a little, then you'll be able to—"

She screamed again, "It's got to go to the vet!"

Whereupon all of the guys shouted in unison, "She *is* the vet!"

Finally, we managed to corral the feline youngster into a carrier I keep in the car for wounded animals on the roads. Engine problem solved; now it was time to tend to the cat.

I took him home to my clinic. It was well after noon, and I had to be at my afternoon school by two. My business partner, Dr. Patton, was on duty, and together, we examined the little guy. Fortunately, he'd escaped major injury; all he had was some soreness and a dose of pure fright. I administered fluids and steroids for shock and put him in a cage to rest. Dr. Patton would watch him until I returned home after school.

No time for lunch or anything else; I made it to my afternoon class just as the bell rang.

Back home after the day's classes were done, I examined the cat again. He seemed fine. He didn't have a collar or other identification, so I called the local newspaper to tell them what had happened and ask them if they'd put an announcement in the paper so the owner would know where their cat was.

True to the reporter's word, the article appeared in the next morning's paper. But it wasn't a simple announcement; it was an article about how the town's cat doctor had found a cat stuck in her own car engine.

I felt doomed, a victim of the First Amendment. The facts were accurate; I couldn't argue with the story, regardless of my embarrassment.

That afternoon, Roger, the reporter from 9 News Northern Bureau, called to ask if he could interview me to follow up on the story. I'd had two years of TV experience when I'd served on the school board, so I figured sure, no big deal, and we agreed to meet at the clinic.

Roger stood at the ready with his camera as I opened the hood of the Subaru. There was fur everywhere. Roger gasped, then tried not to laugh as the camera rolled.

We went inside the clinic, and I presented the cat, whom we'd dubbed "Outback," showing that he was, in fact, fine.

The story ran on the news twice that night, at six and ten. The six o'clock newscaster giggled into the camera and said, "Do you believe it? She actually *drove* that car!"

Every village needs an idiot, and today, it was my turn. But it was only the local evening news. *This, too, will pass*, I reminded myself.

The next day, a man from North Carolina called the clinic and offered to adopt Outback.

North Carolina? How did he even know about this cat and its misadventures?

The next call was from Arizona; could Outback be the cat she'd lost a year ago?

Not possible; Outback was barely old enough to be her lost cat. And this was years before social media and viral internet videos, so how did she know?

The network affiliates, always on the lookout for quirky, bizarre, or funny stories, had picked up my "Outback in the Outback" story and run it all over the country. It was just too funny to pass up.

The news spread even farther. The day after the calls from North Carolina and Arizona, one of my students said, "Hey, Dr. C., I saw you on TV last night, channel three."

Good grief! Channel three was CNN! I didn't know whether to be appalled that the story had hit the big time or delighted that this teen-ager—a rough kid who claimed gang connections—actually watched CNN.

I resigned myself to accepting that I was the town's feline vet who'd saved a hidden cat that was taking a siesta in her car engine *and* the doofus who had driven with a cat stuck in deadly machinery.

No one called to claim Outback. After a few days, we noticed he had a slight limp in his forelimb. The X-ray showed a minor greenstick fracture of the radius. I put a cast on the limb, and Amy, one of my school colleagues, took Outback home to care for him.

She returned the next day, holding the cat in its carrier in one hand and the cast in the other. I used a different bandage to protect Outback's leg—he was fine—and sent him back home with her again.

Amy tried to adopt Outback, but he had other ideas. Even though I'd neutered him, he ran away from Amy's house, never to be seen again. Some cats just like to live solitary lives, I guess. I'm pretty sure Outback was a feral cat, but he was a sweet one, not the more common vicious-feline-rascal variety.

I wished him well, wherever he was, and hoped that he remembered to stay away from engines, regardless of make and model.

And I always bang on my car's hood, no matter the weather.

Sex Changes and the Amazing Testicle Hunt

I felt a wonderful sense of anticipation when meeting new clients and their cats. Being professional meant that I had to be ready for the diversity of all who entrusted me with the care of their feline friends. It was like Forrest Gump's box of chocolates. I never knew what I was going to get.

I always enjoyed seeing guys come into my clinic by themselves. Manliness was the order of the day, especially when the guy in question was the owner of the cat. People often think of women having cats and men having dogs, just as they think dogs are masculine and cats are feminine. This is not necessarily true.

One scruffy college student named Finn brought in his tiny four-month-old jet-black kitten, Kitty Monster. Kitty Monster was adorned with a wide black leather collar with silver-colored spikes sticking out of it. That collar really complemented Finn's Goth look of hair dyed black and styled bristly with lots of gel, black jeans, a torn black T-shirt, and black boots. Teenage Finn may have thought his style was fierce and intimidating; I thought they were both totally adorable. I insisted on taking a picture of them for the clinic bulletin board before I gave Kitty Monster his exam, deworming, and shots.

Another client, Max, was a huge motor-head, complete with a long ponytail, scraggly beard, tattoos, and Harley. Max owned an adult brown tabby cat called Slash, named, I presume, for the potential damage the cat could inflict. But Slash was no vet killer, despite the mental images that whirred through my mind of a kitty sidecar on Max's Harley for the annual Sturgis roundup. He was a pussycat, one of the sweetest patients I ever had.

I expected clients to bring their cats safely to the clinic. My staff and I discussed this with new clients on the phone before their appointment rolled around. I once had a client bring two cats to the clinic in the trunk of his old beater, without the safety of pet carriers inside the car. The instant he opened the trunk, out flew the terrified cats. I normally won't chase cats, but my clinic was on a busy street, and the cats ran away after fleeing the trunk. We did eventually capture them, but when I insisted that the owner buy two cardboard cat carriers from me to go home, his attitude made it clear that he wasn't interested in safer transportation for his terrified pets. I declined to take him on as a client after that first visit.

Fortunately, Max drove Slash to the clinic safely in a cat carrier in his car, not strapped to the back of his Harley. He was such a charming man—one of the tattoos on his forearm was a likeness of Slash within a heart—and so careful with Slash and mindful of his proper care.

I have also done many sex changes in the office, often during that first visit.

Sex changes?

Yes, really!

It's not as difficult as you think. Bonny's a good example of the procedure.

Bonny's older owner, David, brought her in. When David left a short time later, Bonny had become Sir Bonny, no muss, no fuss. Well, not much fuss.

How is this possible, you ask?

The exam began simply enough. I positioned the cat on my exam table. Cats were pretty comfortable on my table, because instead of the usual cold stainless steel surface, my beautiful cat-sized exam table was a converted antique Singer sewing machine stand. Its oak tabletop was covered with a pad and towel so my patients wouldn't slip or slide.

I rolled the friendly adult cat over so it was belly-side up. And there, right where you'd expect it to be, was a scrotum containing two testes.

Bonny was definitely a male. Instant sex change!

As politely as I could, I asked David if he had looked for the scrotal sac. He turned bright red and stammered, "I didn't see anything hanging." This is a pretty common scenario, and I always imagine myself replying, "Cats don't hang, sir." But I know better; my clients are already uncomfortable enough as it is.

So, very gently, I pointed out Bonny's male genitalia and explained that cats, even lions and tigers, have scrotal sacs very close to their abdomens, which can make them difficult to recognize. Bulls hang, rams and buck goats hang, dogs hang a little, but not cats, nor horses for that matter.

Talking about testicles to a guy is dicey. To ease the embarrassment, I often shared the story of El Toro, the Brave Black Bull.

El Toro is a life-sized anatomically correct sculpture of a bull and matador outside a Mexican restaurant in Tucson, Arizona. El Toro is amazingly well endowed—so well endowed, in fact, that it has become a tradition to paint the hanging scrotum in a seasonal theme, such as Santa and his reindeer at Christmastime, shamrocks for St. Patrick's Day, or the University of Arizona's signature *A* during basketball play-offs, depending on the time of the year. There is a long waiting list to be allowed to paint that bull's huge privates. There is no vandalism on this statue—it is art. This story is true and ridiculous enough that my clients can laugh about hanging versus not hanging and girl cats suddenly becoming boy cats.

Owners are not allowed in the surgery room, but they are welcome to stay in the exam room for treatments. Some clients walk out of the room when their cats get vaccination shots; others are fine no matter what procedure needs to be done. No one is required to stay, of course, but guys like me to know that they can handle observation of medical treatments.

One young man, Callum, brought in his adult long-haired cat, Lionel, who had an abscess on his back from the bite of another cat, a common reason for a trip to the vet. I diagnosed this before the cat ever got to the examination room. The feline mouth is a cesspool of bacteria, one species in particular, *Pasteurella multocida*, which is instantly identifiable by the putrid smell the moment the cat comes through the clinic door.

Fortunately, Lionel's abscess still had a scab. This could be treated in the exam room and not compromise the antiseptic cleanliness of my operating room. I could just pull the scab off and squeeze the pus to the outside, thus avoiding general anesthesia, a surgical incision, and a drainage tube stitched in.

I gave Callum the option of waiting in the reception area if he wished. Callum said no, he was a pre-vet student, and he'd like to stay in the exam room and watch.

I told him that it might be unpleasant for him and warned him that it's different when it's your own cat on the table, but he insisted he'd be fine and he could handle it.

He was a nice guy, but I wondered if he could take what was coming.

When I pulled the scab off Lionel's side and started gently squeezing the swelling, pus oozed out everywhere—I mean on my gloves, down the side of the cat, onto the exam table and my lab coat, overflowing to the floor, and splattering onto my shoes. That small, lumpy abscess turned out to be a volcano of infection that yielded over a cup of stinking, gooey yellowish pus mixing in with Lionel's long fur. Good grief! Half that cat's weight must have been pus.

As I milked the abscess, I glanced at Callum. He was as white as a sheet. His mouth hung open. His face was sweaty, and he was breathing hard. Then his complexion turned green, a portent of sickness to come. I told him quickly to lean over, put his head between his knees, and take slow, deep breaths. I couldn't catch him if he fell over; I had a patient on the table and was covered with pus. Besides, I'd rather smell cat abscess than human vomit any day of the week and twice on Sundays. I told Callum he would be okay; it's just that some inexperienced people can handle watching treatments and some can't. Not to worry, nothing to be embarrassed about.

As I finished treating Lionel, Callum still needed a few minutes to recover. It was a while before my next appointment, so I let him hang out in the chair, head down, while my staff cleaned up the room around him. Eventually, he was stable enough to stand up and no longer looked as though he had been run over by a truck. After taking care of the bill, he shook his head, grinned sheepishly, and said, "Jeez, what a gross and disgusting way to earn a living."

Indeed. Being a vet isn't all about cute and cuddly; some days, it's about having pus pour down your lab coat and praying that no one, human or animal, throws up on your shoes. I knew that Callum's queasiness that day might—or might not—matter by the time he got through the rigors of undergraduate work.

"Pre-vet" isn't an actual major; it's more of a declaration of intent. Vet school prerequisites—medical-level organic chemistry, genetics, and calculus, for example—can be part of any major and many career paths. Once he finished these courses and others, he could apply to vet school, or he could pursue any one of the hundreds of other science-based careers out there. Add a teaching licensure program, and he could have a great career as a teacher.

I'd begun as a physical education teacher and returned to college to take the veterinary prerequisites during summer semesters and, when my teaching job was part time, in my free time during the school year. I loved my new career, but it's not for everyone.

Even those who are confident in their career choice will succumb to the "green around the gills" phenomenon in the right circumstances. It's a physiological reaction, biology at its most basic. The remedies we learn address that.

One of my best employees was a freshman pre-vet student. Steve, who was a big kid, first started with me as a teenaged member of a high school project in business class. Steve later told me he'd felt embarrassed when he'd held cats for me because his hands were so huge they'd covered the entire cat. He was worried that clients thought he was hurting their cats. I found that concern charming. Steve made it into vet school and continued to be a caring, gentle employee.

While Steve was assisting me in surgery and learning how to monitor the patients, he kept excusing himself to leave the room. He almost fainted several times.

I told Steve not to lock his knees, which almost every rookie in the OR does. I told him to breathe slowly and deeply and to move around a little while being mindful not to touch me or the table, which could compromise the sterile technique we were using. For weeks, he jogged gently in place during surgery in my small OR, training his body to tolerate the sights, smells, and sounds that are routine in surgical procedures. It worked, and he ultimately completed vet school. After graduation, he became a feline practitioner in Utah.

I was not immune to this challenge. My first experience with it in animal care was one summer long before I went to vet school, when I was helping Earl in his clinic. It was a hot day, and I was wearing a cap, mask, gown, and gloves for the first time. I was standing—knees locked, of course, since I didn't know any better—under the light of Earl's towering surgical lamp, becoming increasingly hot and uncomfortable. I started to feel light-headed, and then everything went black.

I didn't faint—I didn't collapse, and I was fully conscious—but I was blind. I recognized this as something I'd experienced before, once as an undergraduate and once in high school.

I fumbled my way out of the OR, sat down, and lowered my head until I recovered. I realized later that it wasn't looking at guts that triggered this reaction; it was wearing a mask over my nose and mouth and standing with knees locked under a hot light on a hot day.

During junior year in vet school, learning to cope with a mask was part of our training. A surgery professor gave each of us a mask and encouraged us to wear it as much as possible at home and in the hospital, just to get used to it before ever going into an operating room. Even with practice, each year at least one junior surgery student fainted dead away to the floor in the student OR. Unfortunately there's no one to catch them—everyone is in sterile clothing, busy with procedures, and can't break sterile technique.

Of course, vet students and wannabes aren't the only ones who get queasy when it comes to procedures. Many otherwise responsible and intelligent men turned interesting shades of green or flushed red when the subject of neutering their cats came up. Often, on their first visit, they refused to discuss the topic at all. When I finally could get them to talk, we'd have to wade through a lot of misinformation.

More than one client relayed that they'd heard you weren't supposed to neuter cats until they "knew everything." Knew what? How sex worked? Where kittens came from? What tomcat urine smelled like?

Kittens reach sexual maturity at about eight months of age. It may be tough to look at that little furball and think, *It's time*, but delaying or avoiding the procedure is never a good idea. The kitten's urine starts to reek of the horrible, beyond-pungent odor of the mature tom. And the cat starts using this substance to mark its territory, spraying it to tell other toms that there's a new sheriff in town. It doesn't matter if there aren't any other toms; the territorial marking behavior is hard-wired into the intact male cat. One-half regular Listerine mouthwash to one-half water in a spray bottle can help with the odor when cleaning surfaces such as a cage a tom has occupied, but in homes that have an adult intact male cat, the house and cat reek horribly of tomcat urine.

A beautiful tomcat named Mikey, who lived in a rural area not far from my home, was a classic: huge tomcat shape to the head, muscular physique, and massive testes in his large scrotum. He was kept outside to deal with the rodent population. However, looking for a feline girlfriend is pretty much all that toms want to do. Eating is secondary.

Add that to the problem of pet overpopulation and the number of unwanted cats that fill up animal shelters, not to mention the decline in the songbird population thanks to outdoor cats hunting birds, and there is a real problem with having outdoor intact toms.

When I broached the topic of neutering their cats, I think men involuntarily projected an imagined experience of their own castration onto their cat. I never used the word "castration" with them; it was just too close to their virility, and I didn't want them to collapse on the floor, moaning about losing their own manhood. I also knew that I couldn't just say, "Hey! We aren't talking of neutering *you*, just your kitten."

I had to be very diplomatic on such a touchy subject. I learned early on that everything would work out as long as I could educate the guys about their cats. That included taking their reluctance regarding neutering seriously, thus lessening their self-induced trauma. Once they realized that their own manliness would be intact—and so would their cat's, except for the cat's ability to breed—the light bulb would go on in their heads, and they'd understand the importance of having the procedure done, and done correctly.

I recommend all feline males be neutered at five months, or sooner if there is something there for me to grasp. If I can't palpate the testis— if I can't feel it in the scrotal sac—I have to hunt for it.

Cats are born with two testes. If only one or none are palpable, the cat is termed cryptorchid, and you wait a little longer to see if the testes will continue on their journey out of the abdomen, under the skin and other tissues, and drop into the scrotum. If they don't descend, they still have to be removed, which can involve major surgery. It's important not just because you want to be a responsible pet owner; retained testicles can also lead in later life to a cancer called Sertoli cell carcinoma.

Kirk, a brilliant English teacher and good friend, brought his cat in for routine dental care but mentioned that his previous vet had told him that three-year-old Tigger had been born with only one testicle. Kirk thought Tigger was special because Tigger had only one, which the vet had removed. But Tigger was not special, medically speaking.

Cryptorchidism is fairly common among male cats. I'm sorry, but God gives the male cat two testes. Having only one is so rare as to be unheard of. If you can't find the missing testis, you have to go hunting for it. The veterinarian has to know this and know how to resolve the problem.

I put Tigger on his back and pushed my finger over his abdomen on one side, where the testis leaves the inguinal canal via the cord that takes it out of the abdomen and under the skin to go into the scrotum. As I moved my finger over the abdomen, I saw and felt a large lump. It was the testis, right under the skin. It just hadn't made it all the way to the scrotum, missing it by two inches.

It's common to see in practice and, in this case, was easy to remedy. I anesthetized Tigger as planned for his dental work, popped out the misplaced testicle, put in a couple of sutures, and then cleaned his teeth.

Other times, the hunt for missing testes isn't so easy. Jason brought in a new patient, a drop-dead gorgeous purebred Birman kitten named Jasper, which his parents had bought him to have as a companion at college.

The Birman, also called the "Sacred Cat of Burma," is a longhaired, color-pointed cat typified by a silky, fluffy coat, deep blue eyes, and white "gloves" or "socks" on each color-pointed paw. It looks similar to the Siamese, but there are no longhaired coats or white socks on Siamese cats.

I confess that my first reaction when a client brings in a purebred cat is to insist that the client not tell me how much the cat cost. While I love to see beautiful purebred cats, I've never owned one. I'm a firm believer in adopting cats from the animal shelter. However, I had to admit that while my three tabbies were beautiful cats, Jasper was breathtaking.

Different people have different wishes and needs, which quality breeders fulfill. And Jason was a good kid. He loved Jasper and was a topnotch cat owner. He listened to what I said and followed all my advice about his fluffy Birman buddy.

Jasper, as it turned out, was bilaterally cryptorchid. Cryptorchid cats can't be used for breeding, as the trait of undescended testes can be passed along to male offspring. That should be pointed out to the buyer, who shouldn't have to pay such a high price for a purebred cat that won't be able or allowed to breed.

At six months of age, when I should have been able to find the two testes in Jasper's scrotum, there were none. I told Jason that sometimes purebred kittens need a little more time. We would give Jasper until eight months to see if the testes would descend.

A few months later, at nine months, Jasper came in for a checkup and a second round of vaccinations. There was still no sign of the testes. I've seen purebred cats with undescended testes at eighteen months of age, but I didn't want to wait that long. The results would be the same. Wherever they were, it was time for Jasper's testes to go. We scheduled the operation.

And so Jasper went to surgery. For the life of me, I couldn't find his gonads. But God still gives them two, so they had to be there somewhere.

First, I tried the usual way to find testes, opening the scrotum by making an incision on each side, then exploring the inside. Nada.

The next step is to explore the area where the testes leave the abdomen to be under the skin and fat on their way to the scrotum. Now Jasper had four incisions: the original two in the scrotum, plus one on each side of the lower abdomen, running diagonally from the inguinal ring area to the scrotum. I explored the path the testes are supposed to take on their migration from the abdomen to the entrance of the scrotum. Nope.

I reviewed in my mind the absolute last thing you do if you can't find the testes: a very long incision, similar to the short spay incision on a female cat, midabdomen, straight down to the genitalia. A cat spay incision is maybe an inch long for me unless the cat is pregnant or infection is present. Jasper's incision was five inches long. I reminded myself of the pearl of wisdom a surgery professor had once given me, "Incisions heal from side to side, not end to end."

Eureka! There they were, two little squashed, alien-looking structures right next to the bladder on either side. Victory was mine!

These testes would clearly be nonfunctional with that structure combined with the heat of the abdomen. Temperature control is why the testes are outside of the body cavity.

A couple of sutures to the mashed testes' attachments, then closure of the long incision, and Jasper was officially neutered. Although his suture-covered abdomen looked like a road map, his long, luxurious fur would cover the scars as soon as it grew back. He would again look beautiful.

I kept Jasper overnight to observe him and administer pain medicine if needed. That's the benefit of having an in-house clinic.

Jason and Jasper had a happy reunion the next day. Jason took him home, no worse for the wear. I had no doubt that Jasper would be in good hands with his best buddy.

Summertime is kitten time, and my appointment book fills with new patients and their humans. I grinned as Gil, the electrician who'd rewired our house the previous year, made his way carefully from the waiting room to the exam room. A snoozing white-and-gray kitten nestled entirely in Gil's massive left hand. The kitten woke and yawned wider than wide, as if practicing for future leonine roars.

Gil, as concerned as any new father, gently handed the kitten to me for its first exam.

Boy or girl?

Almost time for the talk.

Tipper the Wonder Husky

Our house was perfect for dogs, and after Keli joined us, we couldn't imagine living without one.

A dog inside, even one who shed nonstop and "blew" her coat twice a year, wasn't a problem, because the layout of the house made it easy to cordon off a "dogs allowed" area. Outside was ideal too. The big playhouse and surrounding land, once a playground for Earl, his sister, and their friends, now served as a fine dog house and pen, with plenty of space for digging husky holes.

In the fourteen years since Keli's graduation from puppy kindergarten, I'd learned how to be a good dog owner. And my work world meshed well with husky ownership. My cat clinic was attached to the house, so Keli and I could keep an eye on each other while I cared for my feline patients. I'd returned to teaching junior high school, and she'd often join me there too.

But Keli was showing signs of old age. She had more white on her face, she was slowing down, her muscles weren't as prominent, and she was not as eager to run fast. We no longer skied.

She was healthy; she ate and drank well and still preferred to sleep outside in the cold of her dog pen. She was clearly happy being a dog, but I worried. Fourteen is old for a big dog.

What would we do without our Keli dog?

As hard as it was to imagine life without Keli, it was harder still to imagine life with no dog at all. In early November, 1996, the month when Keli turned fourteen, we decided to get a puppy so it could benefit from Keli's wonderfully outgoing personality and friendly charm. And of course the new pup would be a husky.

We had reconnected purely by chance with Donna, Keli's breeder, a few years earlier. I was serving on the school board, which was considering closing an ancient school located out in the country north of town. The board held a meeting at the school one evening to hear what the parents involved with the school had to say. Earl and I went out to dinner, and then he accompanied me to the meeting. Afterward, we started chatting with a lady about huskies. I have no idea how or why we started on that topic, and at first, we didn't recognize each other—then suddenly, we realized that, yes, this was Donna, and yes, we were the people who had brought Keli home all those years ago.

Donna had moved since then, but she was still breeding huskies. She wanted to know what kind of dog Keli had turned out to be and everything she enjoyed doing. There wasn't enough time in the universe to tell her all that! We stood outside, doing our best to ignore the freezing cold, and talked for a long time about the many things we'd been up to since adopting Keli. Donna gave us her card and invited us over to see puppies anytime we wanted to.

At the time, we weren't thinking about another puppy, husky or otherwise, but we kept her card. Now, even though we'd made the decision, it took us a few weeks to call. Would she have a litter? Would there be a pup we'd love as much as Keli? Was that even possible?

Finally, we called.

She had a litter, barely four weeks old, born on November 27. Keli had been born on November 24. Earl and I grinned; such close birthdays felt like a good sign.

Donna suggested we drive out to take a look at the puppies, despite how young they were. A few days later, we loaded up Keli—who still loved to go for a ride anywhere, anytime—into the back seat of the Javelin and set out on the snowy roads to Wellington, Colorado, and Donna's new home.

When we arrived, we left Keli in the car to avoid potential conflicts with the protective mother husky. Donna met us at the front door, delighted that we'd brought Keli. We were more than happy to show her off.

Donna led the way back to our car and immediately spied Keli, who was in the back seat, poking her grinning face through the open window. Despite that welcoming face, I doubt Keli had any idea who Donna was; after all, she hadn't seen her for fourteen years.

When we let Keli out of the car so Donna could get a closer look, Donna immediately recognized Keli as one of her pups and remembered who Keli's dam had been, thanks to the reddish spot on the top of Keli's tail. All of Alika's puppies had a red spot there, Donna explained. Not only that, the new pups we were here to see were Alika's great-great-grandpuppies. The puppy we chose from this litter would actually be related to Keli!

Reintroductions done, we put Keli back into the car and followed Donna to her basement. Husky puppies were everywhere, playing, lapping water, running around, coming up to us to investigate, running around some more.

We were in heaven!

We noticed a red female pup that was tremendous in size for a four-week-old. We couldn't hold her—mom was still very protective of her brood, and when I carefully tried to touch the pup, mom nipped my hand. The nip wasn't a big deal; vets are used to getting bitten. She didn't break the skin, so I knew I was okay.

That nip didn't stop me from examining the litter with a critical eye as the puppies romped around the room. I watched the huge red girl closely, thinking she might be the one. Earl and I dubbed her

Moose and told Donna we were interested in her. We'd come back when Moose was older and her mother wouldn't get upset with a little handling. We'd see how Moose was getting along then and make our decision.

Two weeks later, we made our way to Donna and the puppies. This time, we could handle them without upsetting the mother.

I turned Moose over to examine her tummy and discovered a large umbilical hernia. These hernias are pretty common, and they have an easy fix. When spaying the dog, you simply make a longer incision than usual, then spay the dog, prepare the skin bordering the hernia, and tuck the hernia back into the abdomen where the contents, such as the small intestine, belong. A long incision sounds scary, but I always remember my surgery professor talking about them: all incisions heal from side to side, not end to end.

Unfortunately, Donna wouldn't pay for the hernia repair, so we decided not to take Moose.

I scanned the room again. Would another female puppy catch our interest?

There, off by herself, playing with some insulation left on the floor, was a wolf-gray puppy with two crystal-blue eyes, a cloverleaf mask, and a cute little upturned nose. We played with her and quickly fell in love.

We also noticed that she had an extra dewclaw on her right hind leg. I remembered seeing her sire, an astoundingly gorgeous and friendly red husky named Sir Nicholas. He too had an extra dewclaw on each of his hind feet. This is a heritable trait, so he should never have been a breeding sire; he should have been neutered instead. Even though we weren't interested in dog shows or becoming breeders ourselves, this meant the puppy could not be considered defect-free. Yet Donna was charging full price for her pups, whether or not they had a defect. And that was on top of the increase in puppy prices—our new pup's price was double Keli's.

But we were madly in love with her, faults and all. We didn't quibble over the price, and Donna promised to cover the cost of the dewclaw removal, which would happen at the same time we spayed our new puppy. When the time came, she didn't, but we knew by then that our purchase was a good one, and we weren't going to argue.

Before we left, we went over every inch of the puppy, using our stethoscopes to check out her heart and lungs, an otoscope to examine her ears for parasites, and an ophthalmoscope to examine her eyes for birth defects. Other than the dewclaw, she was perfect. Vaccines and deworming would be all that she would need at the appropriate age.

We put a deposit on the little puppy with the turned-up nose and headed for home. We'd be back in just over a week to retrieve her, when she was seven weeks old.

We chattered all the way home about the new addition to our animal family. How would Keli react to a new dog in the house? What about the cats? We were buying a winter puppy again, and we knew the cold and snow made housebreaking more difficult. We had our work cut out for us.

We puppy-proofed the house again. The new way to train puppies included crate training, so we bought a crate, which turned out to be a godsend. The dog thinks the crate is its wolf den, and it won't soil its home.

We investigated the local puppy kindergarten schedules to make sure we could sign up for a class with the teacher I wanted, Dr. Gail Clark. Her license plate read, "K9SHRINK." I knew her through teaching her two kids in PE when they were little.

Finally, the seven-week mark arrived—in the midst of one of the harshest Januaries ever. Donna called and said not to come, because the long driveway from the road to her house was impassable, and the road wasn't much better. She promised she'd deliver the dog to us as soon as she could.

Days passed, ferocious storms pummeling us one after the other.

Finally, Donna called to say she was coming to town, bad weather or not.

My vet tech and I were in the exam room with a patient. It was late afternoon, already dark outside. I heard the clinic door open and shut. The tech and I grinned at each other; we knew who it had to be. I wrapped things up with my client and her cat as quickly as I could.

I opened the door to the reception area and there was Donna, holding a puppy in her lap, waving the puppy's little paw at me.

Whoa! Back up the delivery truck! This wasn't our puppy! I didn't recognize her at all.

Donna pointed to the dewclaw, and then I remembered her, and everything clicked into place. Yes, this really was the right puppy, our new gorgeous, ridiculously cute puppy, with that sweet nose and those crystal-blue eyes.

I scooped her up, paid Donna the balance due, and she was ours.

As part of our puppy preparations, I held a puppy-naming contest among my students. The kids submitted some pretty cool names.

The day after Donna dropped her off, I ignored veterinary convention and took her to school with me to introduce her to the students. She was so tiny I tucked her into a cat carrier for the trip. The kids were thrilled with the puppy, but we agreed that none of the names quite suited her.

Because she had tips of color on all of her fur, Earl and I decided to call her Tipper until we could come up with something better. It's a common dog name, utterly unoriginal. What I hadn't expected was how many people assumed we'd named her after the wife of then-Vice President Al Gore.

I tried and failed to come up with a unique name, so Tipper it was, and Tipper it remained. It didn't take long before we realized it was the perfect name for her after all.

She was a rambunctious little puppy who ran circles—literally—around and under a very patient Keli. Her personality was bright and upbeat and often silly. A more serious name wouldn't have fit this little tyke.

Tipper often joined me in my classroom, to the delight of both dog and students. She was so young and active that she needed a rest every hour or so, so we set up a small crate for quiet timeouts.

There's an old saying, "Never turn your back on the ocean," that my teaching colleagues and I used as a reminder to keep a close eye on our middle school students. Tweens and young teens could shift from gentle waves to exuberant surf or crashing tsunami in a heartbeat. Having huskies requires the same attention; it's like having an entire room full of my middle school students. After Keli's mad dash from the fishpond into the street, I was always on guard for a runaway pup.

I posted a sign on the doors outside my classroom saying, "Puppy inside. Please keep door closed." I warned my kids to keep the classroom door shut and to watch for a puppy escape if anyone needed to leave the room.

One afternoon, a boy left the room without checking to see where the puppy was. Tip was right there, and by golly, true to husky behavior, she zoomed out of the room and raced for the open back door to the parking lot. I panicked, remembering Keli's close call as a puppy.

I learned somewhere that if you drop to the ground, wave your arms and legs, and howl crazily, "Oh where, oh where is my puppy, *ah-woooo!*" the runaway pup will return out of curiosity. I fell to the floor in the hallway in break-dancing movements, howling for all I was worth.

It worked like a charm.

Tipper skyrocketed back and started licking my face. Two colleagues were standing nearby, watching the whole episode. They had never seen such bizarre silliness in their lives. They burst into laughter—and so did I, still lying on the hall floor, with my puppy safe in my arms.

Tipper went to puppy school too, of course. She made it through puppy kindergarten just fine, but the novice obedience course was a different story. She was "retained" to repeat the course. As a teacher, I knew what that meant: she'd flunked and wouldn't be allowed to advance to the next level unless she retook—and passed—the novice class. I was pretty sure repeating the course wouldn't do much good.

The one takeaway she got from her formal training was a trick where she'd high jump over a raised dowel rod for a snack. I called it the "Pupperoni trick," after the name of the snack. I thought it was a hilarious thing to show visitors because it was so incredibly stupid. Tipper didn't think so; she was a willing participant.

The visitor held the dowel rod straight out in front. I stood on one side of the rod, holding a bag of Pupperoni treats. Tip was on the other side.

"Pupperoni?" I asked; then I'd tell her to sit. She sat stock-still. Then I said, "Wait!"

She quivered in anticipation, her paws ready for the command she knew was coming.

"*Jump!*"

And she'd sail over the rod and sit down right in front of me. I'd give her a small piece of Pupperoni—which she quickly gulped down—and then I'd tell her, "Go back!"

And *boing*! She jumped back over the rod and sat down again, ready for another go 'round. Two tricks for the price of one!

Despite failing novice obedience class, Tipper did learn a decent repertoire of tricks, most involving food.

One of my vet techs, Manda, taught her to guzzle a Slushy from a straw.

Earl and I trained Tipper to shake one paw, then the other paw, then both paws at the same time, a trick Keli had learned early on too. Then Earl added what became known as the "banana trick": both paws on the couch, head down, good doggie. Then he'd give her the first piece of banana and eat the rest himself.

They repeated this trick every single morning. Years later, I had the couch reupholstered, and it finally dawned on me that the large discolored area on the middle cushion was where Tipper had always put her paws and head to get her precious bit of banana.

Tipper loved fruit. When I ate an apple, she stared at me the whole time. I always gave her the apple core. Okay, I confess; under that unblinking gaze, I would bite off chunks of apple and give those to her as well. And yes, sometimes I'd give her a whole apple. I was well trained; all she had to do was sit and give me the husky stare, and I'd give her the treat. It was a good trade; watching her eat a whole apple was a source of great amusement to me.

One of the most valuable lessons she'd learned in puppy kindergarten was the "wait!" command. It's an important command in its own right, but it's also necessary for the "biscuit trick," one of the hardest tricks to learn and one that most dogs don't master.

I would balance a Milk-Bone dog biscuit on Tipper's long nose and command her, "Wait!"

She would hold her head very still until I said, "Okay!"

Then she'd turn her head and snap the biscuit from midair right into her mouth. What a genius! Who needs novice obedience training when you've mastered such an advanced trick? She was such a superstar that we began calling her Tipper the Wonder Husky.

Like Keli, Tipper was a gifted singer. I used the same training technique I'd used with Keli, crooning to her, "Tipper, can you go *ah-woo*?" and she'd join right in. Two singing dogs; if we'd adopted another two, we could have had the world's first canine barbershop quartet.

Tipper's signature song was "Ragtime Cowboy Joe," the fight song of the Wyoming Cowboys, University of Wyoming's football team. Earl was a rabid UW fan who never tired of the Tipper and Mary Duet serenading him with his favorite song.

All huskies have a big smile when their mouths are wide open. They just do; they are happy dogs. Some dogs, Tipper included, can smile with their mouths closed, with just their choppers showing. This isn't something I taught her; I just happened to notice it one day when she was sitting in the family room. She had a big grin without snarling when she lifted her upper lip to show her teeth. It was hysterical, and she soon learned to do it on purpose. "Smile, Tipper, smile, smile!" I would sing to her. Her nose would come up, and there were her closed front teeth, a shining white grin.

That grin changed over time because Tipper had trouble with bad teeth, leading to many dental surgeries. During one of these, she had all of her upper incisor teeth extracted. Her toothsome grin was no more; it was all gums. I called her Banjo Dog as though she were a redneck from *Deliverance*, but I was happy that she could still smile that open-mouthed husky smile.

Not every trick was one we taught her; she came up with a few herself.

When I came home from school, I noticed the couch in the family room was warm. Who was warming up the couch? No humans were home. Surely the cats weren't big enough to leave that much heat. That left Tipper—but she wasn't allowed on the furniture, and she knew it. Or at least I thought she knew it. Was she being a *b-a-d d-o-g*?

One fine day, with the last of the autumn leaves on the ground, I arrived home earlier than usual. *Aha!* I thought. *I will sneak up to the window and look in! I will catch that criminal canine in the act.* I placed my purse and school bags softly by the driveway. I crept along the ground, tiptoeing to avoid the crunchy leaves. I approached the window like a CIA operative spying on an international criminal.

I peeped into the window.

There she was, my dog child, lying spread out her entire length on the couch, joined by the cats, all sound asleep. I knocked on the window, waved, and said, "Hi there, Tipper!"

She looked at me with those crystal-blue eyes without a hint of guilt. I could imagine the wheels turning in her canine brain, figuring out what to do about finally getting busted.

I scurried around to the back of our house, unlocked the four locks on the two doors, and pushed my way in, anticipating catching my dog in the act of couch surfing.

No such luck.

In the time it took me to unlock the doors, not only was she inside her crate, she was faking sleep and looked surprised to be awakened! What could I do? Two points for The Wonder Husky.

The Hundred-Dollar Horse

Tracy, burbling with glee, sat proudly in the saddle on Marcie's back. Tracy's dad, Scott, walked beside them, holding on to Tracy to keep her secure, while her mom, Linda, led Marcie slowly around the corral. I was proud of them, especially Marcie, who was so gentle and giving.

Tracy had been born with multiple severe handicaps; she was mostly blind and deaf, didn't speak, and was developmentally delayed. To walk, an adult usually needed to be alongside, holding her hands.

She adored horses, but even though she was now an adult, the local special needs riding programs would not allow Tracy to participate for two reasons: helmets and shoes. She couldn't tolerate wearing the mandatory helmet and constantly picked at it to get it off her head. She could manage socks but refused to wear shoes (not surprising, considering how much information she had to gather through sense of touch alone), and it's risky to be in a barn with nothing but socks to protect your feet.

Her parents were fellow teachers and friends of mine, and I'd suggested that we try having Tracy ride Marcie. We wouldn't worry about helmets and shoes; I wouldn't worry about liability, beyond the usual notice posted on our property that states the Colorado revised statute about the liability of a horse professional and how people can't sue a horse owner for any accidents.

The three of them arrived one sunny morning for their first lesson. They learned how to saddle Marcie, what to do to help Tracy ride safely, and where we stashed the key to the corral. Tracy and her folks now had our permission to saddle up Marcie and help Tracy ride whenever they wanted, whether Earl and I were home or not.

Tracy's way of telling her parents that she wanted to ride was to bring them her jeans. After helping her change into her "riding clothes," they headed to the corral and saddled up Marcie and then, outside the corral, settled Tracy into place. Usually, you'd mount up inside the corral, but inside meant horse manure and occasionally hardware on the ground—no place for stocking feet. As soon as Tracy was mounted comfortably on Marcie's back, they'd enter the corral and ride. Throughout every session, Marcie stood and moved quietly; she was very gentle with Tracy.

Marcie was a great teacher for people without disabilities too. Her calm demeanor allowed me to let almost anybody ride her, especially in the corral. When we had houseguests who wanted to ride, Marcie was their horse. She was mellow enough to help those who were nervous around large animals get comfortable with her and patient enough to let future veterinarians poke and prod her. On top of all that, she was gorgeous.

Not bad for a hundred-dollar horse.

She was our bargain "extra," purchased for an extra hundred dollars when Earl had bought Franny, the little sorrel mare who'd captivated his heart. She'd been known as our hundred-dollar horse ever since.

She was also known as The Pig, The Snout, and Miss Piggy—and eventually (though not often) as Liberty Sunshine, her formal registered APHA name. By the time we learned her "official" name, we'd been calling her Marcie—the name Dr. Greene used and, coincidentally, also the name of one of my stepsisters—for so long that anything as fancy as Liberty Sunshine didn't seem to fit.

As for those nicknames—The Pig, The Snout, Miss Piggy—they came from her winter appearance, not her behavior or eating style.

Marcie was a palomino dun American paint horse. She was a little stockier than Franny and a bit taller, about 14.1 hands. In the summer, her coat was grayish-gold with bright chrome (white) paint markings, and her face was bald (which means white, not hairless).

In the winter, her chrome stayed bright white, but she grew a longer, much lighter coat and such long muzzle hair that her white nose looked like a pig snout. That first winter, Earl dubbed her The Pig, and we shared many happy times calling her The Pig from then on.

The rest of her paint pattern was overo, the second most common paint horse pattern (tobiano is the most common). In addition to her bald face, Marcie had one solid-colored leg, a white pattern of hair that rose up from her abdomen, and no white on her back. She was also a dun, with the characteristic dark dun stripe down the center of her back all the way down her tail, plus the distinctive zebra stripes on the backs of her legs.

On the left side of her face, she had a little gold hair, and her left eye was brown. All the hair on the right side of her face was white, and her right eye was blue.

The genetics of horse coat colors and patterns are complicated, usually confusing, and make for lots of interesting reading, discussion, and arguments for those so inclined. But regardless of what anyone called her pattern, Marcie was a gorgeous, colorful animal.

Before Marcie and Franny, my riding experience had been fairly limited. Chico, Earl's cantankerous old nag, was the first horse I'd had total access to. I met Earl, and Chico, my senior year of college.

Chico had never been properly trained and was cranky and hard to manage—a butthead, Earl and I both agreed.

Franny and Marcie had spent their first years on the wide-open range as members of a herd. Left on their own, they'd be a handful and then some. We wanted horses that were easier to ride than Chico, and that meant expert training right from the beginning.

After they'd finished their initial training at a ranch near us in Fort Collins, we brought them home and began riding them in the corral and on the nearby trails. At first, I rode Marcie even though she was bigger, because I was scared to ride little Franny, who was so full of pep. Riding Franny was like driving a Mercedes—smooth, fast, and responsive, but you better pay attention every minute!

Marcie was a Mack truck—solid and dependable—but for the long haul, you might need to sit on a rubber doughnut to protect your backside. When Marcie trotted, I learned to ride either standing up in the saddle or in a posting trot, where, with each stride, I rose up out of the saddle for a beat and then sat back down for the next beat. That's easier on the horse and a lot more comfortable for the rider too.

When Marcie was four years old, we began jumping lessons, and on the advice of our instructor, I switched to riding Franny most of the time. I was a more confident rider by then, and I discovered that Franny was, with all that peppiness, great fun to ride and jump.

Marcie was a determined jumper, no matter the setting. She did well in both indoor and outdoor arenas, but one of our favorite places to play was the beautiful open cross-country jumping course at Lory State Park, in the foothills west of town. The course had lower jumps as well as high fences, which I appreciated because I insisted on a two-foot limit on my jumping—due to my fear factor, not either horse's jumping ability.

Jumping in the open course was a lovely change from arena riding. I especially liked the section where we jumped into a little corral, then jumped out the opposite side without breaking stride: in and out, no stopping in the middle. Marcie always kept good form, knees tucked up tight, sailing over the jumps with room to spare.

Marcie helped others learn to jump too. Twelve-year-old Shira was mad for horses, as many preteen girls tend to be. She'd taken basic equitation, and now she wanted to learn to jump. Marcie was willing to oblige.

Earl accompanied Shira and her parents to her first jumping lesson on Marcie, with Franny in tow. Shira's mom kept Franny in Marcie's line of sight so Shira (and Marcie) wouldn't have to deal with the horses' separation anxiety. They all did fine.

After that, for many years' worth of lessons and shows, Shira's mom drove their SUV to our place, hitched up our trailer, loaded up Marcie and Franny, and drove off to wherever Shira's next lesson or competition was. Marcie was a good teacher; Shira became a good jumper and won many ribbons.

Marcie continued jumping until she was twenty-nine years old. She was still willing, but we both knew jumping was too hard on her aging bones. So we learned pole bending, a rodeo event.

Marcie charged the poles just like a pro rodeo horse (though at a trot, not a run), weaving in and out and then running full-out straight home to the finish line. She wasn't the fastest horse ever at her age, but she was certainly the most enthusiastic. Pole bending was sheer delight for both of us.

Anna, my classmate and across-the-street neighbor, moved her horse, Aria, in with Marcie after Franny died. Aria had been unhappy alone in her solo pen, and Marcie had missed Franny. We'd expected that putting them together would help both horses.

What we didn't expect was that Marcie would become the Notorious Barn Diva.

Despite being smaller than Marcie, Franny had always been the boss mare of our little herd. Now that Franny was gone, Marcie was finally in charge, and she made sure Aria knew it. She and Aria got along well, but Aria was clearly subordinate. If they were both in the aisle of the barn and things were a little crowded, Aria immediately backed out, yielding right of way to Marcie.

Marcie sang like a bad opera diva too, always at four in the morning. She'd done this occasionally before, but now that she was the
Notorious Barn Diva, she screeched almost every morning. Hours
before breakfast time, she'd let loose her high-pitched whinny that
could crack your eardrums and shatter wine glasses. We worried that
the neighbors would complain about our equine rooster, but they
reassured us that they preferred the Diva over having student housing
high-rises next door.

Being Barn Diva didn't solve the problem of Marcie missing Franny
on our rides. We finally hit upon a solution that worked: Earl rode his
mountain bike on the road in Lory State Park while I rode Marcie on
the trail that paralleled the road. It worked beautifully, and after a few
bike-plus-horse rides, Marcie was good to go with me on her own.

My idea of heaven is riding Marcie on a hot summer day in Lory
State Park—brilliant blue sky above us, rolling foothills around us.
There is a special kind of peace riding alone on horseback in such
beauty.

She and I often rode the wide circle of trails that looped through
the park. On one of those hot, sunny days, we were high up on the
west side of the park when a loud roar shattered the quiet. Marcie
didn't panic or bolt, but her head and ears went straight up, and,
uneasy, we both looked for the source of the roar.

I was pretty sure we'd heard a mountain lion, but I tried to convince myself that it was only a powerboat revving up on Horsetooth
Reservoir, which was east and downhill of us. Acoustics can play
tricks on the ears in mountain country; surely there wasn't anything
to worry about, I reassured Marcie.

We picked our way down the trail, pretending (at least on my part)
to be nonchalant as we made our way with controlled swiftness out of
mountain lion habitat. As we arrived back at our rig, a boat engine,
readily recognizable, started up. Its deep whir sounded nothing like
what we'd heard up on the trail. I loaded Marcie into the trailer, feeling

a mix of awe that we'd heard a lion—it's rare to hear or see them—and relief that we'd *only* heard one.

Marcie and I enjoyed a lot of surreptitious rides too. At my junior high school, teachers were required to be at school half an hour before school began and to stay half an hour after classes let out at two thirty, to handle parent meetings and phone conferences or to work with kids who came in for extra help. Many teachers used that time for prep and homework grading, but I enjoyed working from home and did most of those tasks there, sometimes in between patient visits or while recovering a cat from surgery.

I'm a morning person, and I was usually the first teacher to arrive. I enjoyed the peace and quiet of school before the kids came, and I loved to see the school buses arriving, loved watching the halls fill up with energetic kids every morning.

On most days, I followed the rules and stayed until three, but some days were so beautiful that, if I didn't need to stay for students and parents, I sneaked out of the building, telling only the receptionist that I would be out and that I had my cell phone, in case someone needed to reach me.

I'd be home by a quarter to three, change my clothes, load Marcie into the horse trailer, and be in the saddle at Cottonwood Glen Park, four miles from home, by three thirty—plenty of time for a ride in the undeveloped land beside the park before supper. Even in the waning light of winter's short days, we could squeeze in at least a forty-five-minute ride.

These rides weren't just goofing off. When you ride a horse, you must focus entirely on the horse. You must be aware of anything that might spook the horse. Marcie taught me early on to stay focused on her while we rode. That meant I had to let go of worries about every-thing else. Riding demanded that I keep my mind clear of school issues, work that I had to do, and anything else that didn't have to do with being on Marcie, riding, right now, where we were. My focus had to be one-hundred-percent on riding my mare. Others might pay thousands of dollars for therapy to help them learn mindfulness and how to deal with the stress of daily life. I had my hundred-dollar horse.

When we'd finished our ride, I was relaxed and reenergized. By the time we got home, it was time to feed the horses their grain and hay, check the water level in the trough, and sweep out the barn. After that, I'd enjoy a nice hot shower, fix dinner, and spend a pleasant evening with Earl.

Being a diva didn't change Marcie's willingness to teach. A few years after Franny died, Marcie landed a job as teaching assistant for CSU's new veterinary acupuncture program.

The acupuncture classes involved a series of five four-day weekends. Students came from far-flung places as well as our immediate region. The course needed "sub animals"—animals that could substitute for real patients so students could practice locating the points where acupuncture needles would be inserted.

Dogs were readily available, so students had plenty of canine practice for identifying meridians and acupuncture points. But in the early days of the program, sub horses were hard to find. I became the dude wrangler, bringing Marcie to the lab classes, along with Scootsritealong, the young paint gelding we'd bought three years after Franny died.

Initially, I didn't intend on taking the course myself. I was teaching school full time and had more than enough to keep me busy.

I was also teaching a human anatomy class at Fort Collins High School. I'd been bringing in guest speakers every Friday, drawing on many of my professors and colleagues to talk about various aspects of comparative anatomy. When I realized that one of those Fridays coincided with an acupuncture course weekend, I contacted my friend and old classmate Marybeth, who would be staying at my house while she was in town as a teaching assistant for the course. Would she be willing to talk to my students about animal acupuncture and how it related to understanding the anatomy of the patient?

She agreed. I warned her that high school kids were hard to impress, but that, so far, they'd enjoyed the guest speakers.

I volunteered Tipper the Wonder Husky as her sub dog for the presentation. Tipper was, as always, hyper, happy, and delighted to be back in school, where hundreds of kids could pet her and admire her beauty.

Marybeth demonstrated an acupuncture point located on the top of Tipper's head, called GV-20. It's a "relaxing point"; GV stands for Governor Vessel, one of the meridians. The point number on that meridian was number 20, hence the name, GV-20.

Tipper, grinning and practically vibrating with excitement, stood, tail wagging furiously, beside Marybeth at the front of the small science lecture hall. Marybeth explained that acupuncture needles don't hurt, and then she slid the needle under Tipper's skin, talking slowly to the kids as the needle made its way to GV-20. The kids watched in silence.

Tipper slid gently down, glassy-eyed, onto her side.

Relaxed? If she were any more relaxed, she'd be dead.

The kids gasped, and their excitement was palpable. It was "way cool" to watch a hyperactive dog fall asleep after having one needle placed in the top of her head. I think I was most thrilled of all, but I kept quiet, enjoying the high school students' enthusiastic responses to learning something totally new. They asked questions nonstop until the bell rang.

After class, I went to the vet hospital to see the acupuncture course coordinator and said, "Count me in!" I knew there was a years-long waiting list, but she bumped me to the next available class, probably because I provided the horses.

A year later, I had passed the grueling three-part international examination on the first try, completed my internship—first in

Colorado and later in Florida—with Marybeth, and become a certified veterinary acupuncturist. I was chosen to be an equine teaching assistant for the acupuncture course and ultimately taught many veterinarians how to find acupuncture points on horses. By then, CSU had its own "teaching horses," but I continued to practice my labs at home on Marcie. Horses are still my favorite patients for acupuncture treatment.

As a full-time teacher and vet who worked Saturday mornings in my clinic, I treasured my Saturday afternoon luxury of a long nap on my Uncle Tom's ancient couch. It's the same couch my sisters and I slept on when we were kids visiting him in his little one-bedroom house on Mountain Avenue, the same couch I used when I lived in that house before I married, the same couch I still have, twice-reupholstered, its time-rotted cushions replaced. It's an excellent sleeping couch.

One Saturday afternoon in February when the weather was worse than nasty, the ringing phone woke me from a sound sleep. Groggy, I picked up the phone and mumbled a greeting.

It was Marylynn, our corral neighbor. Marcie was down on the ground, kicking with pain.

I rushed outside. My twenty-three-year-old gold-and-white beauty was writhing on the cold, soggy ground in the corral. She was soaked, completely coated with brown mud, and in the throes of extreme distress.

I didn't need to do a diagnostic workup in the mud; I knew what was wrong. It didn't take a veterinary degree to see that Marcie was seriously ill with severe colic, a condition she'd been plagued with all her life.

Colic is a generic term for abdominal pain. There are many causes for the pain, though we don't always know the specific cause. Marcie had more attacks of colic than I can count. Hers were always the spasmodic type, as opposed to a torsion, or twisting, of the bowel or a dead piece of intestine, either of which would have required expensive surgery.

Most of the time, we'd treat her intravenously with medicine and reduce her feed for a couple of days, and the colic would subside. Sometimes, she was so ill that we had to take her to the CSU Veterinary Teaching Hospital. Colic is a medical emergency; a horse can die from it.

Marylynn, Earl, and I watched out for each other's horses. Earl and I checked up on the horses all the time, both day and night. So did Marylynn. How long had Marcie been in trouble while I'd slept, oblivious to her agony?

I shook off my guilt and took action.

This was clearly an emergency; Marcie needed to get to the hospital as quickly as possible. But Earl was working in Denver that afternoon, and I hadn't yet learned how to hook up our horse trailer to the new truck.

Marylynn volunteered to haul my quivering, shaking Marcie in her huge stock trailer. I loaded Marcie into the trailer; Marylynn said to not tie her in as we normally would, in case she went down. I took my seat next to Marylynn, and off we went.

We pulled up to the large animal entrance at the hospital. I unloaded Marcie, and Marylynn returned home.

As soon as Marcie was admitted as an emergency, I called Earl and told him to get home fast; Marcie was extremely ill and might not make it.

Clinicians, residents, and students hustled to save her. Her blood chemistries were beyond abnormal. That, combined with being wet and cold, were the likely cause for her twitching and spasming muscles.

Staff and students ran liters of warmed fluids into her IV under pressure; drew blood for more analysis; and administered pain medicine, medicine to calm her gut, and more medicine to correct the abnormal electrolyte levels in her blood. They cleaned her up as best they could and covered her in blankets to keep her warm. They watched her closely for what seemed like hours before moving her into one of the stalls in the special colic cases section of the hospital.

The aggressive emergency treatment worked—Marcie would live!

She was, without exception, the sickest horse I've ever seen who survived.

When it was clear that she was going to recover, the students tried out the hospital's new horse-washing station on her. Marcie loved the warm water and attention. I think she felt better just getting all that mud off. Her fuzzy gold-and-white winter coat practically glowed. She was so shiny and clean that she looked ready for a horse show.

Soon after, she was able to come home and resume her normal life. As she got older, she had fewer colic episodes, and they were less severe. We attributed her improvement in part to a special diet Marybeth formulated for her and the monthly acupuncture treatments I gave her.

And in the end, colic, as dangerous and frightening as it was, wasn't what killed her.

Marcie and I had a relationship that went far deeper than most human-animal bonds. She seemed to realize my status as one learning to ride again as I healed from a shattered hip and subsequent surgeries. Marcie was so gentle with me during my recoveries; were it not for her, I doubt I would have ever been able to resume riding.

Walking was painful, but riding was a joy—once I got on the horse.

I'd lost a tremendous amount of range of motion, and it was difficult to mount horses for a long, long time. I had been a gymnast, flexible and strong, and a physical education teacher. Being relegated to "handicapped rider" status added to my misery.

First, I had to step with my uninjured leg onto a stool to reach her back. Next, I used both hands on the saddle to hoist myself up—definitely not cool—and haul myself into the saddle. Marcie stood patiently throughout the whole procedure, waiting in place until I gave her the cue to walk on.

As I began riding again, I definitely preferred Marcie over Scooter. She was the one horse I could take alone in the trailer and be as safe as a horseback rider could be. I could trust my senior horse who, at twenty-nine, was totally bombproof. Nothing bad would happen to me on Marcie. I liked to ride her alone, thankful for the day and that I was still alive to enjoy it, grateful that I was becoming a confident and joyful rider again.

I'd hoped to take Marcie on a ride to celebrate her thirtieth birthday, June 1, 2005, but it had been less than three months since my third and final surgery—this one for a total hip replacement—and I hadn't been cleared to ride yet. Fortunately, my cousin Gail was in town. A good friend of hers in Denver had just turned fifty, and Gail had flown out from Chicago to help celebrate.

And celebrate.

And celebrate.

I'd promised Gail's mom that I'd get Gail sobered up and home in one piece. I picked her up in Denver after the festivities were over and brought her back to Fort Collins so we could visit for a few days.

Gail ended up riding Scootsritealong—I teased her about Scooter being her love man—and Earl rode Marcie. I couldn't ride, but before they left for Lory State Park, I took plenty of photos. My favorite is one of Earl holding Marcie by her lead rope and patting her on the neck.

I finally was able to ride Marcie myself a few times before heading out on a long road trip in my Mercedes Roadster to Chicago to hang out with Gail and my other cousins and, after that, meet up with my best buddy, Jean, who was in Minneapolis for a vet conference. Jean and I headed west to tour the Laura Ingalls Wilder Homestead in De Smet, South Dakota. The 250-mile trip is usually about a half-day drive, but "traversing Minnesota" became what Jean called "getting hopelessly lost in the vortex of Minnesota." We did finally get there, glad we were in the roadster and not a covered wagon for all those miles.

When I returned home, I took Marcie up to ride on one of our favorite trails at Lory State Park. At first, everything seemed fine.

But she didn't want to trot, and then a greenish slime poured out of her mouth. Her breath sounds gurgled.

I led her to Horsetooth Reservoir a few feet away, but she wouldn't drink. I took the tack off quickly, loaded her back in the trailer, and drove her home.

The next day, Sunday, she looked a little off. Worried, I treated her with acupuncture and kept an eye on her all day. She wasn't colicky, but her gut looked empty. That meant it was something else; we just didn't know what.

On Monday morning, Marcie didn't eat her breakfast. She had that look in her eye that said it was time. Earl agreed with me, and I called the equine medicine department at the hospital.

"We don't take patients on Mondays," the receptionist said.

What? I repeated to her that we had a sick horse and that it would probably involve euthanasia. She finally gave us an appointment.

The clinician told us that it was most likely a dental or mouth problem. We already knew she had a dental problem—she had the teeth of a thirty-year-old horse, including wave mouth. Wave mouth is an uneven wear of the molars that makes the tooth crowns different heights, which, in turn, can prevent the jaw from moving freely, making it hard for the horse to grind her food properly. It's a long-term problem that requires routine management, and we already had an appointment for the dental team to come out later in August to work on all three horses. We didn't want to wait that long for Marcie; she was too ill for this to be just a tooth problem.

The all-day medical workup included endoscopy to examine her respiratory system, plus turning the scope around to take a thorough look at her teeth. Nothing abnormal showed up.

Radiographs of her neck and mouth showed the slightest hint of swelling. The clinician thought it might be a tumor in Marcie's mouth.

The head of the teaching hospital, an equine medicine doctor Earl and I both knew, was rounding with students near Marcie's examination room. I showed him Marcie's X-rays. Then, with my back to his students, I gave him a thumbs-up, thumbs-down gesture, then another thumbs-down.

He simply nodded his head.

I knew there was no hope.

Earl and I signed the papers for Marcie to be euthanized, and she died that day.

I try to remember that she had an amazing thirty years of life and that I was lucky that she lived her life for more than half of my own. I had Marcie longer than I had my own mother, who died when I was twenty-six. Marcie lived longer than my little sister, Natalie, who was killed by a drunk driver at twenty-seven. I remember all the students Marcie helped, the people who aren't afraid of horses thanks to her gentleness, and the kids who learned to ride and jump. I remember that it was Marcie who solidified the friendship between Earl and me and Marcie who helped that friendship grow into the joyous married life Earl and I shared.

Not bad for a hundred-dollar horse. Not bad at all.

A Matter of Respect

"What a sweet kitty," I gushed, stroking the gorgeous fur of Sienna, the seal point Siamese gracing my exam table.

Dee, the cat's owner, stiffened and said, "Dr. Carlson, this is not a kitty. This is a cat."

My face flushed with embarrassment. I was a new veterinarian, with my own newly opened cat clinic, and I'd just managed to offend one of my first clients. I backpedaled, trying to apologize without making matters worse.

This isn't something they teach you at vet school. Vet school teaches you all the technical and medical jargon. How to diagnose and how to treat.

Not how to talk to clients.

I was already pretty good at translating the technical medical gibberish into language clients could understand, but it had never occurred to me that calling a client's full-grown felines "kitties" could be offensive. It was true that Sienna and her companion cat, Daisy, were both well beyond kittenhood. I estimated their ages at twelve or thirteen years, which put them at late middle age to early old age for Siamese cats.

But my vet school classmates and I always used terms of endearment like "kitty." I called my own elderly cats "kitties."

At the same time, I understood that this was a matter of respect. To Dee, calling her stately Siamese pets "kitties" was disrespectful, as well as inaccurate.

Dee and her cats left, exams completed. I still felt chastened, and I was certain they'd never come back.

From the first day I opened my clinic, I introduced myself as Mary Carlson, not Doctor Carlson or Doctor Mary. I was proud of my degree, but I didn't feel the need to flaunt it; I'm more of a first-name-basis person. I also had each new client fill out an information sheet. One of the questions asked if they preferred to be addressed by their first name or their last.

Why hadn't I asked my clients their preferences for their adored felines?

Especially since one of my own pet peeves is a stranger calling me "honey" or "dearie" or "sweetie."

I remembered the phone call from the hospital's grief counselor after my mother had died.

Mom had been hospitalized for complications related to Crohn's disease. Unfortunately, she'd had a bad internist instead of a good gastroenterologist. Her intestine ruptured, pouring its bacteria- and pus-filled contents into her abdomen, causing fatal septicemia. By the time the hospital staff noticed that she'd stopped breathing, she was essentially brain-dead.

There was no reason for me to go to the hospital; the woman I knew as my mother was gone, even if life support was keeping her body functioning, and I had no desire to see my mother as a corpse. I told the doctor to discontinue her treatment and call me when she was gone.

He never called.

So when Mrs. Lyons, the counselor, called, my first question was simply whether or not my mother was dead.

Mrs. Lyons's voice was steeped in syrupy, somber tones. "Yes, dear," she intoned. "She's gone."

I have no idea what followed that; I only remember her overblown sorrow and that she called me "dear."

Later, I called her back to ask about Mom's possessions. I began the call by identifying myself: "Mrs. Lyons, it's Mary Elson calling."

"Yes, sweetie?" That same funereal tone oozed from the phone.

That did it. I said calmly, "Mrs. Lyons, we've never met. I am twenty-six years old. My name is Mary, not sweetie, not honey, not dearie."

There was a brief moment of silence, and then she replied in a businesslike tone, "Yes, Mary, what can I do for you?"

Much better, lady, I thought.

That phone call became family legend. I'd always been Mommy's Girl, and my small stature meant people often treated me like a little girl. I think that phone call was the first time I'd advocated for myself and openly refused to be treated with disrespect.

In some ways, the moment I challenged Mrs. Lyons was the moment I officially became an adult. My insistence on being treated with respect translated into the strength to deal with all that follows a parent's death, from notifying friends and family to filing a wrongful death suit against the hospital (the same hospital where I'd been born and where my father had admitting privileges).

So I understood Dee's point about cats, not kitties, and I vowed to never make that mistake again.

As it turns out, my fear that I'd lost Dee as a client proved unfounded. Perhaps, when, like Mrs. Lyons, I'd corrected my mistake after it was pointed out to me, Dee had decided to give me another try. I'm glad she did; Daisy was my patient through the end of her life, nine years later, and Sienna was my patient for the ten years I operated my cat clinic.

Teaching science, filling a seat on the board of education for several years, and running a solo veterinary practice at the same time meant hundred-hour workweeks more often than not. After ten years in solo practice, I decided to close the clinic and pursue teaching science full time. With my help, Dee and my other clients found new veterinarians for their pets. Sienna was quite elderly by then. I promised Dee that when it was time for Sienna to go, I would come to her home and put Sienna to sleep at no charge.

It had been two years since I'd seen Sienna when Dee called. It was a sunny June day, and I was hobbling around in a cast, nursing a stress fracture in my foot.

I collected my gear and drove to their home. Dee and her husband, John, met me outside in their garden. It was a beautiful setting, with lovely shade trees, blooming roses, and flowering shrubs. Dee gasped when she saw my cast and apologized profusely for causing me any discomfort. I assured her I was fine.

Dee and John wrapped Sienna in her favorite towel and carefully placed her on a garden bench. I noticed a recently dug hole nearby.

I administered anesthesia to Sienna, and we all spoke quietly to her until she fell asleep. Then I completed my task.

Dee brushed Sienna and snugged the towel around her. John placed the little bundle gently in the small grave. We each scattered handfuls of dirt into the grave, and then John buried her. Soon, Dee said, they would plant a new flowering shrub to mark the gravesite. Sienna's duty now was to support new life.

Dee and John no longer live there, but whenever I go by that house, I look at the flowering shrub and remember the cat that was not a kitty.

Eating Disorders of The Wonder Husky

A healthy diet makes for a healthy dog. I stared at the plastic ID badge, chewed beyond recognition, wishing Tipper the Wonder Husky understood that.

We'd fed her high-quality puppy food when she was little, three times a day at first, then shifting to twice a day and then to free choice when she was ready. We didn't feed her tidbits at the table, because begging dogs are bad dogs, and a regular diet of people food can turn a husky into a picky eater. I sighed and dropped the useless badge into the trash. Tipper was definitely not a picky eater.

When she was old enough, she'd graduated to adult dog food. Doting dog-parents that we were, we fed her occasional, but still healthy, treats, such as dog biscuits and small bits of fruit. That would have been enough for any dog—any dog except Tipper.

The day before, I'd completed training for my volunteer position at the hospital. As a freshly minted volunteer, I'd received three credit-card-like badges, which I'd put on the table in the family room.

During the night, The Wonder Husky had eaten one, chewed one to oblivion, and nibbled on the third. I called the volunteer coordinator, sounding like one of my junior high school students: the dog ate my ID badges.

The next week was Thanksgiving. On Tuesday, as I tried to teach through the haze of a monster migraine, an email for a drawing for two Rolling Stones concert tickets landed in my inbox. The tickets had been donated for a charity fundraiser; whoever won the drawing would pay for the tickets, and the money would go to the charity. The concert was in two days, on Thanksgiving Day. On impulse, I entered. If I won, it would be Earl's and my holiday presents to each other.

And I won! I paid for the tickets when they were delivered to the house that evening. I put them on the table, well out of Tipper's reach.

The next morning as I was getting dressed, Earl came upstairs and informed me that Tipper had eaten the tickets.

The kittens, brothers who usually restricted themselves to stealing pens and pencils and depositing them around the house, must have slid the tickets off the table, providing tasty and expensive morsels for The Wonder Husky.

Everyone who heard what had happened said that since we were veterinarians, we should just cut our dog open to retrieve the tickets. Thanks for the advice! This wasn't Red Riding Hood, where a simple slice to the belly would release Grandma whole and unharmed (ignoring for the moment that things didn't end well for the wolf in that story). The tickets were ordinary card stock; Tipper's stomach had already turned them into mushy gunk. I called the Pepsi Center box office in Denver and explained that our dog had an eating disorder. They graciously printed out new tickets for us to collect at will-call.

One Super Bowl Sunday (one of two the Denver Broncos won back-to-back—yes!), it was warm and dry. Seventy degrees in January in northern Colorado is a gift! I decided to take advantage of the fine weather to clean Tipper's dried-out dog pen. I raked and raked, making piles to shovel later.

I spied one doglog that seemed a little different. I looked closer. The grayish color turned out to be from currency in the dried feces. I went inside and asked Earl if he was missing any money. He said yes, eight dollars had gone missing from the table in the family room.

I pulled on a pair of exam gloves and broke the dried pile apart. Sure enough, there was a five-dollar bill and three singles—intact. Tip had grabbed the bills off the table and gobbled them down whole. They must have tasted pretty good for her to eat four bills. I was impressed with how rugged paper money had to be to make it through undamaged, at least where dogs were concerned. I'd fed a dollar bill to my horse, Marcie, once, to see what she'd do. She ate it and completely digested it. I was glad I hadn't tried that experiment with a fifty!

I washed the bills in the sink with Dawn dish detergent, dried the crumpled wad in the sun on a paper towel, pressed the bills flat with my hands so they would smooth out, and put them in a plastic sandwich bag.

Earl didn't want anything to do with the currency—it was only eight dollars, he pointed out—but the next day, I had to make a bank deposit anyway. So I included the four semi-smooth bagged bills that had gone completely through Tipper's alimentary canal. I attached a note saying what had happened, just to give a giggle to the bank employees, dropped the bag and note into the drive-up pass-through, and asked the teller for fresh bills.

The teller wasn't amused. She seemed puzzled. She paused for a few moments, then finally said over the intercom, "Uh, ma'am, I don't think we can take these from you."

I told her they were legal currency—clean, bagged so no one had to touch them—and that I had a right to exchange them. I told her that if she wished, she could deposit the amount into my account and send the bills back to the United States Treasury. I said, "There's no harm in a little money laundering," but I don't think she got the joke.

The teller sounded a little queasy as she asked me to wait while she talked with her manager. I imagined her holding the bag gingerly by its corner, as if afraid the contents would escape.

The answer came back: yes, she could deposit my, er, Tipper's money. I've wondered ever since if the bank added "What to do with currency found in dog doody" to the new teller training manual. I hope so.

Not all inappropriate eating has such an easy or funny ending.

Dog parks—public fenced areas where dogs are allowed off-leash to run around, play, and socialize—are loved by many people, including those who live in my city. Nowadays, almost all of our community park plans include one. Huskies are friendly and sociable, so it seems as though a dog park would be a perfect playground for them.

Dog parks are a great idea, but they are often good business for veterinarians. Mishaps—some minor, some major—are common.

At one of our local dog parks, a presumably kindhearted person left behind a lot of small, soft toys for dogs to play with. Tipper ate one so fast that I doubt she even chewed it. I took her home pronto and made her vomit up the toy so it wouldn't block her stomach or intestines. If I weren't a vet myself, I would have faced a substantial bill for veterinary services. As soon as I'd taken care of Tipper, I called the city's parks department to tell them of the problem, and they sent a crew out to pick up the soft toys.

Even without the dangers of misguided toy donations, taking Tipper to the dog park was not always a good idea. Huskies' high energy and exuberance combined with their wolflike looks can scare people, including other husky owners.

One Easter Sunday when Tipper was only two, we went to the dog park. It was a beautiful morning, and the park was crowded. One of the dogs was a husky mix.

It and Tipper came toward each other in a greeting I call "the husky crash and smash," which is when they stand up in the air and crash into each other's chests from a run. There is no aggression; it's just normal husky behavior.

The owner of the husky mix was a big, macho-type guy. We both went toward our dogs. I was going to get my dog, and I thought he was going to get his. Imagine my horror when he went to Tipper, picked her up, and slammed her body hard to the ground.

Oh, my God, I thought, *she's seriously injured and has broken bones.* But she was all right and ready to play again. Tipper the Wonder Husky, indeed.

I never tell anyone at a dog park that I am a veterinarian, but I started talking to the man about dog behavior, explaining that this was normal for huskies. I suggested kindly that he read some books and take care of his own dog.

He wouldn't listen.

Every word out of his mouth began with the letter *F* as he came closer and closer to me. Eventually I told him in a soft voice that if he came one millimeter closer, I would kill him.

Big guy, small woman, but there was no mistaking my seriousness. He retreated with his dog and joined others at the park. I leashed Tipper, and we sat down alone on a bench for over an hour, staring at him.

He'd turn around from time to time to see if I was still there. So would everyone else. Yep, there I was, staring. He kept his distance. I think I scared him. I certainly hope so.

That was Tip's last time at a crowded dog park. From then on, I knew her park time would be restricted to being on a lead and running with us, unless it was a day when there weren't many people and dogs at the park.

I've served many years on our town's Parks and Recreation Board, and we still recommend approval of dog parks when there is space available to include one in a new park, because people request them. But injuries from fights can happen to dogs, and people can get into a brawl as well and be seriously injured. Tipper and I were living proof of that danger.

Tipper ate weird things on our walks too, enough so that I worried she might have pica.

Pica is a condition where a dog consistently eats things that have no nutritional value. "No nutritional value" refers to pretty much anything that isn't food—rocks, coins, plastic bags, tissues, pine cones. People and cats can have pica too.

Sometimes pica behaviors are caused by an underlying medical problem. A dog with malnutrition or vitamin deficiencies might eat dirt, sand, or tile grout to increase micronutrient levels. Scary medical issues such as brain lesions, abnormalities in the circulatory system, diabetes, anemia, and parasite infections can also cause pica behaviors. And some behaviors (a mama dog licking her puppies and eating their feces to keep the pups clean) are quite normal. None of these is true pica.

Tipper checked out as one-hundred-percent healthy, with no underlying medical issues to worry about.

Other causes of pica include anxiety and boredom. For example, if a dog has separation anxiety and also eats the plastic grocery bags you've been saving to reuse the next time you go shopping, there's a good chance the anxiety and grocery bag snacking are connected to each other. A dog might eat yucky stuff just to get your attention or because he thinks you're taking something important away from him. If you're so determined to get that rotted tennis ball out of his mouth (so his canine reasoning goes), it must be important to keep it, so he swallows it. There's also a form of doggie OCD called Canine Compulsive Disorder that shows up as compulsive pica.

There's accidental pica too. That's when you don't get supper cleaned up quickly enough, and in your pup's haste to scarf all the leftovers before she's caught, she swallows the plastic fork along with the beef fried rice. That isn't true pica, though you'll be heading for your vet's emergency room when it happens.

Tipper definitely wasn't bored, and she got plenty of attention and exercise. She shied away from bicycles zooming by us during our walks, pressing a little closer to me, but her nervousness about bikes disappeared as soon as the cyclist passed us.

As we strolled the streets of our college student neighborhood, Tipper vacuumed up all kinds of litter—tissues, chunks of plastic, bits of cellophane, windblown papers—a little too fast on the uptake for her own good, despite my attempts to navigate around the worst of it. I warned her more than once that if she scarfed up a used condom, she'd either have to pass it on her own or go to surgery; I wasn't going to touch one of those, let alone pull it out of her mouth.

I sighed as I extracted the latest clump of unidentifiable trash from her mouth before she had a chance to swallow. Not pica, accidental or otherwise; the cause of this "eating disorder" was unbounded enthusiasm and insatiable curiosity.

There's no cure for that—but I wouldn't want one, even if there were.

Hike! Hike! Hike!

The wind in my face, raindrops blurring my glasses.

I was used to this. When you have animals that need care, you are out in all kinds of weather. Today was no different: cool fall weather, drizzling on and off.

Well, maybe a little different.

To broaden her horizons, when she was older, I took Tipper with me to school so she could visit the moderate-needs class during my planning period in the morning. I taught these developmentally delayed junior high kids all about dog safety and behavior, how to groom Tipper, and how they had to hold firmly onto her leash when they took her outside to do her business. After the lesson, Tipper usually spent the rest of Wednesday mornings in the moderate needs classroom.

Tipper was a big hit in their classroom, and we both loved working with the special-needs kids. The teacher rewarded the students for doing things well, and taking care of Tipper was definitely a reward. The proud student got to brush her or take her out for a break. The kids considered it a reward even when it involved picking up her solid waste. They followed all the leash laws too; Tipper didn't escape from these kids.

I held a pet food drive at the school to benefit the humane society during the holidays. My school was always very generous and giving, and most years, we collected close to a thousand pounds of food. The students from the moderate-needs class decorated the drop-off site, and they donated pet food too. The humane society required unopened bags of food and treats, but I will never forget one student who simply left a gigantic dog biscuit decorated with a festive ribbon and bow.

Around the same time, one of my best clinic employees, Manda (the same Manda who taught Tipper how to drink a Slushy through a straw), was applying to veterinary school. After several tries, she realized that vet school wasn't going to happen for her.

Even though I knew it would mean I'd lose an excellent employee, I urged her to apply for a job as an in-class aide in the special-needs program at Fort Collins High School, where I'd taught for a year. I knew working with special-needs kids would be a great fit for her, and I was right. She loved it. She continued working for me too, coming to the clinic in the late afternoons, entertaining me with stories from her days with the students. Eventually, she would attend the University of Northern Colorado and become a licensed special education teacher, immediately hired by the same school where she'd worked as an aide.

One of the students Manda grew close to when working as an aide was a teenaged girl with severe cerebral palsy. Kristy couldn't speak or move on her own and was confined to a wheelchair. Her dad had left the family soon after Kristy was born (something that is, unfortunately, an all too common occurrence for kids born with severe disabilities). She and her mom had been on their own ever since.

Manda thought Kristy would enjoy visiting the clinic and meeting my duo of cats, who were fantastically friendly to everyone.

And Tipper the Wonder Husky, of course.

Kristy and her mom, Terri, were delighted when Tipper greeted

Kristy with a joyous "*Aah-woooo,*" followed by a big doggie smooch on her face.

Manda and I floated an idea to Terri. What would she think if—?

Terri grinned and said yes.

Manda and I dug out the mushing harness Keli had used years ago to dump me in the snow when we were skiing in City Park. Tipper danced with excitement. What new adventure was this?

We clipped the harness into place on Tipper and then fastened the other end, along with an extra six-foot leash, onto Kristy's wheelchair. I held the end of another leash that we connected to Tipper's collar.

Manda took the "musher" position, standing behind the wheelchair and holding the chair's handles to control direction and help balance Kristy. In my finest sled dog command voice, I called out the official "go forward" command to Tipper: "Hike! Hike! Hike!"

We began an easy jog up Springfield Street, going slowly so Kristy could get used to things and we could make sure that this crazy setup actually worked.

As The Wonder Husky got fired up, we went faster and faster.

And faster! *Whoosh!* The fence and trees flew by as we ran full tilt, Kristy laughing with glee as we rounded the end of the block and sprinted back to the clinic.

Had Kristy ever felt the joy of rushing headlong with the wind and rain on her face before? Other kids had bikes or roller skates, something Kristy would never be able to enjoy.

Today, for the first time in her life, she was racing in the rain, immersed in the speed and exhilaration of being pulled by an enthusiastic Dog of the Frozen North.

Hike! Hike! Hike!

The Easter Gift

The jangling phone interrupted the quiet of Easter morning. I set my Rollerblade skates and helmet aside and picked up the phone. Mrs. Johnson, a client I hadn't heard from for a while, was on the other end.

"Dr. C., it's about Misty," she said, her voice quavering. "Can you come now?"

Misty was the Johnson family's elderly cat and one of my longtime patients. About six months earlier, when I knew I'd done all I could for her, I'd referred Misty to the oncology service at the CSU Veterinary Teaching Hospital. She'd been under their state-of-the-art care ever since.

Mrs. Johnson and I had both known this time would eventually arrive, and I'd promised her that when it did, I would come to their home to perform the euthanasia, at no cost. That's always been my policy; I never charge for euthanasia unless it's a first-time client bringing a patient in specifically for that. There are now many success-ful veterinary practices that specialize exclusively in euthanasia. They provide a useful service that has also changed the face of veterinary practice itself; now, very few clinicians do euthanasia, instead trans-ferring this task to the specialty practices.

I arrived at the small, modest home in an older subdivision and carried my vet bag into the house.

I'd expected Mrs. Johnson and her son, the two members of Misty's family I'd met, but to my surprise, the living room was filled with family members, all there to say goodbye to Misty.

In the corner of the room was a handmade, cat-sized coffin. I'd never seen anything like it before. Its beauty took my breath away. Its dark wood was polished to a high sheen. A bas-relief cross in a lighter stain had been carved on the lid. Light blue satin lined the padded interior.

I gently examined a listless Misty. The tumor on the side of her abdomen had expanded to the size of a baseball. A hard swelling typical of a cancerous mass took up most of the space. It was indeed Misty's time to be released from her suffering.

After injecting anesthetic into Misty's quadriceps muscle, I searched for a usable vein in the sleeping cat. Truly ill old cats have such tiny veins, the diameter of dental floss at best.

Euthanasia solution should be injected into a vein or, if the needle pierces the other side of the vein, into the liver, kidney, or heart, not muscle. The euthanasia solution is so thick it has to be drawn up into the syringe using a large-diameter needle, much wider than the vein. Once the syringe was filled, I changed needles to a size that would fit the tiny vein and then performed the procedure while Misty was unconscious from the anesthetic.

Misty went to the Rainbow Bridge with her family surrounding her, whispering softly to her and petting her.

I pulled out my stethoscope and listened carefully. I knew Misty was gone, but the ritual of the stethoscope is important for the family. It provides a closure of sorts to be able to officially pronounce the animal dead.

The family hugged her and prayed over her, inviting me into their circle of prayer too.

Then they groomed Misty's body and nestled it in the extraordinary coffin. As I packed my things into my black bag, each family member hugged me, moistening my T-shirt with their tears and thanking me for being there for Misty on this beautiful religious holiday.

By the time I reached my car, the impact of how powerful Misty's end of life had been hit me, and my own eyes filled with tears. No matter our beliefs or the faith we follow, euthanasia, releasing a beloved pet from suffering, is truly a gift we veterinarians have to give.

Best Cat

My name is Franklin Irving Carlson. You can call me Frank. I am fourteen years old. I am Best Cat of the Carlson household today, but it has not always been so.

My story started in a cold metal cage. Was this prison of steel bars a kitty jail? I was there with my brother. Our only crime was to be kittens.

We had been adopted by a family who'd loved us. But our people hadn't been able to afford keeping us, so they'd brought my brother and me back to the animal shelter. I understand now how lucky we were and how kind our family was to return us. But when I was a kitten, I didn't know those things. I felt sad because we weren't adopted any more.

We had soft blankets in our cage. The people who worked at the shelter made sure we had good food and fresh water every day. There were other cages in our room, with other cats in them. Most of the others were grown-up cats; there weren't many kittens.

People came into the cat room and stared at us as if we were animals at the zoo. For a long time, nobody wanted us.

But our fortune was about to change.

That afternoon, the cat room was pretty crowded. People jostled against each other, trying to get a good look at all the different cats. Rick, the animal control officer, yelled, "Look out! The doctor is in the house!"

People moved aside. A small woman walked toward us. Rick walked beside her, talking and laughing.

She came up to our cage and looked right at me. "Well, aren't you a sweetie," she said, poking her finger through the bars of our cage.

I sniffed the air carefully, then I walked right up to her to check her out. I touched her smooth finger with my moist noise. Then my brother came over to say hello too.

The woman turned to Rick and said, "I'd like to visit with both of them."

"Sure thing, Mary," Rick said.

Rick hailed Nancy, the cat room volunteer. Nancy took us into the cat playroom, which was filled with brightly colored toys any kitten would love to investigate. We played with everything! Mary rolled the yellow balls, and we chased them. She teased us with a string on a stick. I loved it.

She picked us up and loved on us too. Even when I was a tiny kitten, I could tell when someone didn't like me. If they took me into the playroom, I felt like scratching their eyes out.

Mary was so nice; I could tell she was a cat person. I decided she could keep her eyes. I hoped that she'd pick both of us and we would get to own her. We'd been together our whole lives—three months already—and it would have been hard for my brother and me to be separated from each other.

It worked! We charmed her into choosing both of us. Mary was impressed with how soft and friendly we were, and she decided adopting just one wasn't an option. She filled out the paperwork for both of us, even though she'd missed the summertime two-for-one kitten deal.

She and Nancy slid us into scary-looking cardboard carriers, my brother in one and me in the other, and loaded us into the back of Mary's Subaru Outback.

I did okay, but my brother threw up in his carrier. After that, he was all right, but what a mess! I wondered if Mary would still want us. Turns out, she did; she didn't return us to the animal shelter. She even stopped at a pet supply store on the way to our new home and bought lots of toys and supplies for us. I knew then for sure that we'd hit the jackpot.

We were free again—this time, for life!

Mary parked in the driveway and lifted our carriers out of the car. It was great to be outside again. The air in the driveway sure smelled fresher than the cold air at kitty jail. Smelled better than the upchuck in my brother's carrier too!

Just then, another car pulled into the driveway. It was Earl, our new dad, home from work. Mary lifted us in our carriers up high and called out, "Happy anniversary, dear! There's one for each of us!"

Earl broke into a big grin. Two more cats! With Matthew, that made three.

I will tell you the most surprising thing about this: Mary and Earl never wanted to have three cats all at once. They just wanted a buddy for Matthew, the cat they already had.

We didn't meet Matthew face-to-face in the beginning. Mary kept us in the downstairs cat room, isolated from Matt and from Tipper the Wonder Husky. It's a nice room, with good natural light, a soft carpet, and a nice place for us to go potty.

A long time ago, the cat room was Mary's cat clinic reception area. When Matthew was a kitten, it was his room; he still hides out in it when he wants to chill out and have some alone time.

But when we first came home, it was just my brother's and my room for a while. Matt and Tipper could sniff at the closed door and tell that we were inside, but they couldn't come in. That protected them in case we had "shelter crud." Lots of pets from animal shelters come home with an upper respiratory disease, kind of like a bad cold. My brother and I didn't have the slightest hint of the sniffles, but it's better to be safe than sorry.

Mary discovered that we had *Cheyletiella* mites, also called "walking dandruff." Mites are really common in animal shelters, and they're so contagious that pretty much every cat and dog at the shelter has them. The mites don't infest people like they do us cats, but they will jump on for a quick snack of blood, leaving tiny itchy bites on the skin.

Mary discovered bites where she had a little hole in her jeans. The bites were challenging, because you can't scratch your butt in public, especially when you're a teacher at a junior high school, where the kids know everything, see everything, and gossip about it. So before the mites could give her any more bites, Mary gave us a bath with a special shampoo. That got rid of our mites. It protected Matthew and Tipper from catching them from us too.

We had fun in our cat room. It was airy and sunny and lots larger than our old prison of steel. And the toys! With all the stuff Mary gave us, we were in kitty heaven! She and Earl played with us a lot. We showed our approval by purring extra loud when they held us.

A few weeks later, we slowly began to join the rest of the household, supervised by Mary and Earl.

Tipper the Wonder Husky loved cats! That was a load off my mind.

Matthew insisted on being Top Cat. He had fun beating up on us, but we overwhelmed him with our charm, and the three of us became buddies. He still insists on being Top Cat, especially over my brother. We've been grown-up for years, but Matt still chases us and occasionally bops us with his paw. Sometimes, he takes a flying leap and lands on top of me. But most of the time, Matt and I just hang out together doing what cats do best, sleeping.

Sometimes, it takes a while before you know what your name is. Mine took a week to appear.

My brother's name was obvious from the first day: Cowboy Joe, because of the brown fur in his black tabby coat. Brown is one of the University of Wyoming's colors, and Earl was a rabid Wyoming Cowboys fan. Mary knew my brother should be named after their team mascot. Matthew is gold, Wyoming's other color. Earl was triumphant—now he had brown and gold cats to match the Cowboys!

At the end of the first week in my new home, I still didn't have a name. Mary even had a kitten-naming contest in her junior high school science classes. The kids came up with many interesting names, but none of them fit me.

Then one evening, I heard Mary and Earl giggling in the family room. They were watching one of their favorite movies, *Men in Black*. They always giggled when they saw Frank, the pug dog alien. They giggled harder. Mary claimed that "Frank" fit me to a tee, even though he was an alien dog and I was a kitten. They started calling me Frank.

"'Franklin' is more dignified," Mary said, but she still called me Frank.

Then, because I have a lot of fur on the inside of my ears, she decided I should have a middle name: Irving, after her grandfather's brother. Great-uncle Irving taught Mary how to make the perfect martini when she was fifteen. He had hairy ears too.

So I am officially Franklin Irving Carlson the First.

Technically, I am also Franklin Irving Carlson the Last, because I am not able to produce any more Franklins, if you know what I mean. Before Mary adopted us, we had had our first deworming, our first distemper combo shot, and our special treatment so we wouldn't make more kittens. While I am personally happy to have neither the responsibility of parenthood nor the distraction of always wanting to search for a mate, it still puzzles me when Mary giggles and tells us that, like the dog in *The Far Side* cartoon, we were "tutored" at the shelter.

While I am confident that I am Best Cat, it's true that my brother and I weren't the first cats here. Matthew wasn't first either. One snowy night, we curled up with Mary as she told us the stories of the cats who came before us.

Pruney was the first. She had been Mary's cat ever since Mary graduated from college. Pruney came to live at our house after Mary and Earl were married. She lived a long time but died when a runaway dog hurt her. Since then, Mary and Earl have never let their cats outside without a leash, though sometimes Matthew sneaks out when no one's looking.

Their next cat was Simon. Mary was working in the anesthesia department at the CSU Veterinary Teaching Hospital, and she brought home a beautiful buff-colored tabby cat from the hospital. He had copper-colored eyes, and he'd originally come from an animal shelter. The hospital spayed or neutered cats who had been left at the shelter and, after they recovered from their surgeries, returned them to the shelter for adoption.

Mary didn't know Simon hadn't been vaccinated wherever he had lived before, and unfortunately, he came down with feline distemper soon after he arrived home and died quickly.

Now Mary and Earl had to wait at least two weeks before considering bringing another cat into their home, to make sure all traces of the feline distemper virus were gone.

A few weeks passed. Mary was having a bad day at her VTH job, so she went to the back of the hospital, where the cats from the animal shelters were being held before their surgeries. That's the same place where she had found Simon.

She spied a huge, long-haired orange boy in a holding cage, and she fell in love.

Mary thinks orange boys are special, and this one was extra special, because he was from the Cheyenne animal shelter. That meant he was a Wyoming cat, and as far as Earl was concerned, orange was really gold, one of his beloved Wyoming Cowboys' colors.

The staff members who worked in the holding area knew Mary

had lost Pruney and then Simon, and they had been saving this six-month-old kitty for her.

When Mary walked up to him, he reached one of his giant slab paws out to her through his cage. Mary melted; she knew he was the one for her.

She waited until he was neutered and vaccinated, and then she held him at the hospital for another ten days to see if he developed feline distemper. He didn't.

Mary visited him often during his waiting period. They cuddled a lot in her lap. He was incredibly soft. He also had mites, the same kind Cowboy Joe and I had. The mites bit Mary all over her tummy; she was covered with small red itchy bumps. Of course, she couldn't just put her hand under her scrub pants and scratch herself whenever she wanted to. When it got really bad, she'd run down the corridors of the vet hospital to the restroom, pull her scrubs out of the way, and scratch-scratch-scratch. Ahhhh, relief. For a little while, anyway.

The big orange boy passed all his health tests. After antibiotics to wipe out his shelter crud and a medicated bath to get rid of the mites, Mary brought him home, and they named him Fletcher.

Fletcher was a good sport, even better than Cowboy Joe. Mary and Earl could do anything with him, and he wouldn't object. They rolled him up in a blanket like a kitty burrito, and he stayed put, no complaints. They pretended to fish for him with a ridiculous fishing rod toy so he would do wild gymnastics jumps. They even held him up to their husky dog, Keli. Keli loved cats, and she would lick Fletcher all over his body. They had fun all the time.

Then Mary moved away.

She went to Virginia for a whole year to practice working with cats at a feline veterinary clinic so she could open her own clinic when she came back home.

Earl and Fletcher stayed home in Colorado with Keli and the horses, Franny and Marcie. It was hard to be so far away, but Mary and Earl visited each other every month and had many adventures exploring the Eastern Seaboard. After her year of practice was finished, Mary came home to stay and opened her own feline clinic.

Instead of being happy that Mary was home, Fletcher started pooping on the guest room bed. How rude!

Mary thought Fletcher might do well with a buddy. I hadn't been born yet, but there was an ad in the paper for free kittens.

There were three tuxedo kittens. Earl's Aunt Elaine and Mary went to check them out. Two kittens ran under the couch and hid. Mary did her special test on the third kitty to see if he would be a good cat, the same test she did on my brother and me.

She held him in her lap on his back and gently turned him upside-down, with his head hanging over her knees. He relaxed and won himself a forever home.

Earl named him Alexander, and Fletcher had a new best buddy.

Alexander and Fletcher weren't just pets. They were members of Mary's cat clinic staff, where they worked as demo cats. "Demo cat" isn't a political party; it stands for "demonstration." They showed frightened clients how to do procedures on their own cats at home. They even let owners of diabetic cats practice giving shots! The clients injected Alexander and Fletcher with saline solution, not insulin, for practice. Al and Fletch let them practice until they were comfortable giving the shots and were confident enough to give insulin to their own cats.

I must admit, I'm glad that Mary closed her cat clinic before she adopted me. I think if I had to put up with clients sticking needles into me all day, I'd want to stick my teeth into them. Needle-sticking practice is not for me!

Fletcher died in 2000, when he was thirteen years old. Mary says thirteen is a geriatric age for a cat, but I don't think it's that old. I am over thirteen years old myself, and I'm just fine, thank you.

Fletcher might have lived longer, but he had a rare heart disease.

It isn't seen much anymore because researchers discovered that it was caused by a lack of one amino acid. Nowadays, that amino acid is included as a supplement in all pet foods for cats.

When Fletcher got sick, Mary took him to the vet hospital. The people there told her that they saw about one case of this kind of heart disease each year, and Fletcher's case was it for that year. They were trying to be funny to cheer Mary up, but she was not amused. Fletcher was a beloved buddy, her special orange boy, and he was gravely ill. No one could cure him, and that was no joke.

Mary and Earl do not just replace cats. How can you replace someone who was a part of your life for thirteen years? Our dad, Earl, died in 2009. Mary is never going to replace him. Personally, I myself am irreplaceable; I am one of a kind.

So Earl and Mary settled into being a one-cat family.

Then one day in October, not long after the terrorist action of September 11, 2001, a new cleaning lady was starting work at the Carlson home. Mary got one of those feelings she gets sometimes. She didn't want to interrupt the cleaning lady, and something told her to check out the kittens at the Larimer Humane Society.

She didn't want another cat. She didn't intend to get a kitten, and besides, it was nearly the end of kitten season. Still, she wanted to go.

There, in a cage, was a three-month-old orange boy. He had short tabby-patterned fur, partially white paws, and a white chest. Short hair? What a mutant! She took him anyway and brought him home. Despite my fine black fur and excellence as Best Cat, Mary is convinced that all orange boys are smart, brave, and friendly, with extra-loud purrs.

It didn't take long to find the new kitten's name.

That fall, Mary had a special young man in her biology class. Matthew was one of the few junior high kids who would carry on a conversation with a teacher outside of the subject matter and class time. He was a voracious reader and an expert on the subject of the *Titanic*. He was also quite knowledgeable about antiques, one of Mary's passions.

The kitten looked Mary in the eye, and Mary knew right away that his name was Matthew. The name definitely suits him.

When Boy Matthew from Mary's class graduated from high school, Mary gave him a framed photograph of Kitty Matthew. Every time Mary sees him, he always asks, "How is little Matthew doing?" Even though he's over thirty years old now and has had five open-heart operations, he still keeps the photo of Kitty Matthew on his dresser.

When Alexander was fifteen years old, he went to the Rainbow Bridge because his kidneys failed. Matthew was three years old. Mary and Earl were a one-cat family again, and that just wouldn't do.

That's where we came into the picture. We were both adorable, of course. We were soft and friendly. We were so hoping to get out of the steel cage and get a forever home. Mary adopted us both, making us a three-cat family.

My brother and I have grown up to be big and strong. I am a felid of massive size—eighteen pounds—a (not so) lean, mean feline machine. My paw is so big that it covers the palm of Mary's hand.

My brother has the longest, fluffiest tail of any cat ever. Mary says it's definitely longer and fluffier than any she's seen, and she's seen a lot of cat tails. Cowboy Joe waves his tail constantly. I know he's showing off. My tail is straggly compared to his, but I am still Best Cat.

Cowboy Joe and I groom each other. That's called "mutual groom-ing." Joe starts, because I am Best Cat and top cat over him. We use our spiky tongues to clean the places we can't reach for ourselves, like our chins and the insides of our ears. We use our tongues to clean our own fur too. We keep at it until we are spick-and-span. Did you know that our tongue spikes go only one direction? They're like a one-way

comb, so I can't get rid of what I put in my mouth. When I'm groom-
ing, most of what goes in my mouth is hair, and the only place it can
go is down my gullet. Eventually, it comes back up as a hairball. I may
not have a great tail, but I am the King of Hairballs. I love decorating the carpet with them. Mary doesn't appreciate my artistry. Thank
goodness she has a new puppy who loves anything I cough up. The
puppy comes running the moment she hears me *hurk-hurking*, and
voilà! Instant floor cleaning.

In addition to his champion tail, Joe has a soft, long coat. I'm jealous, because he never needs a bath. I have a long coat too, but my
skin is dry, and my oily coat gets matted if I don't have a professional
bathing and grooming every other month.

"Frank, your suit is looking pretty rumpled today," Mary says, even
though I do plenty of grooming, and Cowboy Joe helps. Then she
schedules an appointment with the groomer. She schedules one for
the puppy too, because Ivy, the goldendoodle puppy, needs a snazzy
haircut for her fancy curly hair.

I always know when bath day is coming. I hate bath day. Mary
makes the groomers shave my underside—all four of my kitty arm
and leg pits, plus my entire belly, including my personal area. She calls
it a "potty patch"—how embarrassing! Is it any wonder that I'm upset
and try to hide?

I do my best, but I can't get under any furniture; I am too massive.
On bath day, Mary gets up early and shoves me into the guest bathroom so she can find me when it's time to go. She closes her bedroom
door and goes back to sleep, even though I meow and bang on the
door so loudly the whole house shakes. When it's time, she uses the
reverse gravity method to load me into the carrier: she sets the carrier
on the floor with the open end up, then slides me in back feet first,
straight down and in.

After all the fuss and aggravation, I have to admit that when I come
home, I am definitely stylin'! I strut through the house, rubbing all the

corners, happy and *sooo* proud of myself. I jump into Mary's lap for well-deserved praises and pets and plenty of kisses on my beautiful head.

Of course, Matthew and Cowboy Joe are jealous and hiss at me for two days. They finally get used to me being so good-looking, and they settle down and agree that I am Best Cat.

The job of Best Cat carries a lot of responsibility. I figured that out when I was only six months old. Mary was gone for a whole week. When she finally came home, she couldn't walk by herself; she had to use a shiny thing with extra legs. I waited for her beside her favorite chair. It took her a long time to cross the room. She sat down in her chair, then leaned over and picked me up. She held me tight and cried and cried. I kept myself very still and never moved a muscle until she finished crying. That's what a Best Cat has to do sometimes.

She carried things with her teeth so she could keep her hands on her walker. I kept a close eye on her as she carried a paper cup in her teeth from the kitchen to her chair. As Best Cat, I knew I should help, so I carried cups in my teeth to her chair. Cowboy Joe helped carry some too. Pretty soon, we decided she had enough cups.

I noticed she needed pens and pencils. She always kept some near her chair, but pens and pencils are tricky things; they can vanish when you're not looking. So I began carrying pens and pencils and bringing them to her. I insisted that Cowboy Joe help me, of course.

We would carry the pen or pencil to Mary and meow politely so she'd know we'd brought her these important gifts.

I was proud to be so helpful. After Mary could walk on her own again, Cowboy Joe and I continued to carry pens and pencils to wherever they might be needed. We usually move them during the night so we don't disturb anyone. We've left them in her bed and on the floor just outside the bedroom door, as well as by her chair. Once, the cleaning lady discovered our secret stash—twenty-five pens and pencils stuck under the sofa. Another time, a workman left his little pocketknife, open, on the windowsill. That wasn't where it belonged. I moved it to the bed so Mary would see it when she woke up.

But mostly, I stick with pens and pencils. My skill with them is so amazing that Mary decided I should have my own column on her blog. After all, I have a lifelong connection to writing. Or at least to pens.

And I am Best Cat.

The Wayward Horse Trailer

Warm days in Colorado winters are a rare gift. When one happens on New Year's Eve, it's cause for extra celebration and a gas fill-up and car wash, before the next storm front slams us back into the deep freeze.

December 31 that year was a balmy sixty-five degrees Fahrenheit by midday. I was busy preparing for the annual veterinary conference held in Florida. Earl and I were flying out right after New Year's. This year, I was part of an Academy of Feline Medicine work group developing best feline practice standards; my topic was proper and humane methods for feline euthanasia.

Brilliant sunshine flooded the cloudless sky. I decided to take a break and run Uncle Tom's Javelin over to the gas station. I still thought of it as his, even though I had inherited it and was now the official owner. It was a 1968 beauty, still in excellent condition.

The Javelin's gas tank filler neck was in the back, behind the license plate. I pulled the license plate down, unscrewed the gas cap, and stuck the cap between the license plate and car to hold the plate down. I lifted the nozzle from the pump, squatted behind the car, and inserted the gas pump nozzle into the opening. I squeezed the grip and flipped the little metal tab into the groove to hold it in place. Nozzle secured, I stood up to make sure I was visible to other drivers. Everything locked and loaded, just like always, only this time, as I straightened up, the nozzle flew out of the filler neck, spewing gasoline as it went.

I took a direct hit of gasoline in my left eye. Gasoline drenched my clothes. The nozzle fell to the ground, pumping gasoline onto the pavement.

I ran into the station store, dripping gas. "I have gas in my eye!" I told the attendant. "Call 911! Where's the eyewash?"

The young man working the counter (and by "working" I mean "leaning against the counter looking bored, probably stoned") blinked sleepily and said, "Like, dude, we don't have an eyewash."

What? I almost screamed. The law requires that gas stations have an eyewash station. It's part of the OSHA safety regulations, just like having a first-aid kit.

"Okay," I said, holding my temper. "Where is the restroom?"

He yawned and said, "Over there."

"Point it out, take me over there, or get me a guide dog!" The initial shock was wearing off, and my eye was starting to hurt.

I leaned over the sink and began splashing my eye with cold water. The drain was clogged, and water overflowed the sink, cascading onto the floor.

I returned to the counter and asked if he'd called 911.

"Well, like, no, dude."

"Do you know *how* to call 911?"

He stared blankly at me for a minute, then finally picked up the phone and called. As soon as he set the phone back down, I pointed out that it would be a good idea to turn off the gas pump, which had continued pumping gas the entire time. I could see gas spread across a swath of asphalt, flowing from the station's pavement onto College Avenue. From there, it would drain into the river.

After another long pause, Mr. Rocket Science mumbled, "Oh, yeah . . . man, like, the whole place could blow up."

He pressed the remote switch to turn off the pump, then had the gall to tell me that I had to pay for the gas that had gushed out. By this time, I didn't care; I just wanted my eye tended to. Saving my eye was more important than arguing over who was responsible for spilled gasoline.

Paramedics arrived soon after and flushed my eye thoroughly with saline solution. They recommended that I go home immediately and shower, because gasoline can seep through clothes and burn the skin. As soon as possible after that, I should see my eye doctor.

I reeked of gasoline. I washed my hair three times and could still smell gas. I shoved my clothes in the washing machine, hoping that the stench would rinse out and my clothes wouldn't be ruined.

My ophthalmologist of many years had just moved into a brand-new building devoted entirely to the care and treatment of eyes; I felt awful for stinking it up. He diagnosed a grade II chemical injury to my cornea and sent me home with eye drops. At home, I showered again, this time using Dawn dish detergent instead of regular shampoo. Six times I washed and rinsed my long hair; it still reeked, but short of shaving my head, there wasn't any more I could do.

Now that I knew I wasn't going to lose my eye and that my conference and travel plans would be fine, I started to get angry.

I called the president of the company that owned the gas station. He said that he'd heard there was a 911 call at this station, but nothing more. I filled him in on the details.

I don't know if the *L* word—lawsuit—was on his mind, but he raced over to my house. He refunded the money I'd paid for gas and gave me a stack of coupons to use in the future. Then he drove the Javelin to the station, filled it with gas, detailed the entire car, and returned it, gleaming in the late-day sun, to the house. He even offered to pay my medical bill, but I declined, because I was insured and had a small deductible.

I spent the rest of New Year's Eve curled up, nursing my eye. *Tomorrow has to be better*, I told myself.

New Year's Day dawned as bright and beautiful as the day before, with predictions for temperatures in the seventies. I was relieved and delighted. The first day of the new year was going to be great, I just knew it.

My vet school classmate Anna and I decided to go riding. She loaded her mare, Aria, into her rig, and I loaded Marcie into mine. My rig consisted of my father-in-law's twenty-five-year-old three-quarter-ton GMC pickup truck with a class-three trailer hitch on the bumper pulling a twenty-one-year-old horse trailer, currently carrying a twenty-three-year-old mare.

We drove to a nearby natural area and had a lovely ride in the warm weather, happily enjoying the sunshine and peaceful lake. The horses were glad to be out and about too, stretching their legs after being cooped up in the corral after the recent stretch of bad weather.

After the ride, Anna and I loaded our horses into our respective rigs, and first Anna, then I, pulled onto the steep drive leading out of the natural area.

As I began the slow climb up, I glanced in my rearview mirror and gasped. To my absolute horror, I saw my horse trailer sliding down the hill. I slammed on the brakes and honked my horn so Anna would realize something was wrong. I'd need her help to attend to an upside down, injured, or (God forbid) dead Marcie.

We were lucky; the trailer rolled gently down the hill and came to rest against the triangular Western fence that marked a steep drop-off. If that fence hadn't been there . . . I thought I would die of fright at the thought of what could have happened.

I ran past the gathering crowd of curious onlookers and opened the window to the trailer. My placid pony stared at me as if to say, "Hey, that was cool! Can we do it again?"

I inspected the trailer and discovered that the hitch was still attached to the horse trailer tongue. I'd hooked everything up correctly; metal fatigue had caused the hitch itself to fail. The hitch had broken off from the truck, setting the trailer free.

We transferred Marcie to the spare space in Anna's trailer, and Anna hauled both horses back to the corral. Then Anna returned to the natural area and tried to pull my trailer out. Her truck, a little Ford Ranger, didn't have enough oomph to pull it out of the ditch, so she headed back home again. I stayed behind and waited for the police so they'd know why there was a horse trailer sitting beside the fence that night in an area that didn't allow overnight parking.

While we were chatting, I told the police officer about my adventures at the gas station the day before too. He looked at me with a strange expression on his face.

He gently advised me to go home, get into bed, pull the covers over my head, and stay there.

I thought that was excellent advice, and it's exactly what I did.

The Annie Walk

Tipper danced in excitement as I pulled her husky-print bandana from the closet. She knew the bandana meant adventure!

"Go for ride, Tipper?" I asked, tying the kerchief around her neck.

"Yeah, yeah, yeah, *ah-woooo*!" she howled.

I popped open the back of her dogmobile (also known as the Subaru), and she sailed up and in like an Olympic hurdler vying for the gold.

Earl and I were always on the lookout for fun activities to channel Tipper's boundless energy. She ran the annual Fire Hydrant Five, a fundraiser for the Larimer Humane Society, with us. She competed in the Doggie Olympics, a benefit for the Larimer Animal-People Partnership (LAPP).

Today's adventure was the Annie Walk.

This field trip, a fundraiser for the public library, was one of our favorites. It was named for a Fort Collins icon, Annie the Railroad Dog.

In 1934, Brakeman Christopher DeMuth and several other Colorado and Southern Railroad Company workers rescued a pregnant, emaciated mixed-breed collie at a blacksmith shop in Timnath, Colorado. They named her Annie and nursed her back to health at the

Fort Collins freight depot. For the next fourteen years, Annie was the unofficial mascot and greeter at the Fort Collins passenger and freight depots. People still tell stories of how she cheered folks during the Great Depression and how she said goodbye to boys leaving for World War II and licked the tears from their faces when they returned. Newcomers reported that disembarking locals greeted Annie before turning to their own families.

Annie took her responsibilities as a local celebrity seriously. She waited politely against the depot wall until someone beckoned to her, and only then would she approach them to be petted.

When Annie died in 1948, the railroad crew buried her near the depot. DeMuth created a cement headstone to mark her grave. Its inscription reads,

FROM

C and S

MEN

TO

ANNIE

OUR DOG

1934–1948

Over the years, the Fort Collins depot fell into disrepair, and there was talk of moving or eliminating Annie's grave. The community rallied around Annie's defense, and in 1995, the gravesite and the C&S depot became designated as local historic landmarks.

When Loveland, Colorado, sculptor Dawn Weimer heard Annie's story, she decided to create a tribute to Fort Collins's famous dog. The result is a beautiful sculpture of Annie, installed near the front entrance of the downtown library. Annie's paw is raised, ready to shake the hands of passersby. I shake that paw every time I visit the library.

The library organized the first Annie Walk to coincide with the statue's unveiling. This year's walk began just like the ones before: Lions Club pancake breakfast, picnic style, on the lawn outside the old Carnegie building, originally the library but now home to the Fort Collins History Museum. The library now occupies a newer facility next door.

Tables and tents of vendor booths stretched beyond the picnic tables and past the museum's reassembled log cabins. Around the corner, on the far side of Library Park, volunteers were setting up doggie activities for the day.

Ancient cottonwood trees shaded us from the clear August sky as Earl and I settled down with paper plates heaped with pancakes and syrup. Tipper, as usual, sat staring at us with those hopeful blue eyes, begging for just a bite. We didn't share our breakfast with her; we knew her turn was coming.

We strolled past the crowded, pet-friendly booths. Tipper looked longingly at the biscuits and other treats that the vendors were offering, and this time, we said yes. She eagerly filled up on doggie junk food. Earl and I knew we were probably being a little too indulgent, and we hoped she wouldn't puke during the walk itself.

Tipper loved the crowds, and they loved her. People stopped to pet her and admire her beauty. She adored the attention. Being admired for her beauty was Tipper's one and only vanity. She was so well-behaved despite (or perhaps because of) all the attention that I was proud to be her dog-mother.

Soon, it was time to gather at the starting line for the mile-and-a-half walk from Library Park to Annie's gravesite near the old depot.

The crowd assembled itself into a slightly chaotic mass ready to move forward. I recognized a diminutive older gentleman walking slowly with his Harlequin Great Dane named Duke (I think all Great Danes are named Duke). I'd seen them in the downtown hardware store, which sold dog treats as well as the usual nuts and bolts. They stopped by each morning on their daily constitutional. The man purchased a small bag of dog treats and handed the bag to his dog, who carried the bag in his mouth on their way home. I always smiled at the incongruity of this tiny, frail man walking side by side with his beloved 150-pound dog.

Dressed-up dogs had been part of this event from the beginning. Many people spent plenty of time and money on costumes. Ladies with small-breed dogs, such as Chihuahuas, miniature poodles, and Lhasa apsos (we called them "land sharks" in vet school), dressed their little Fifis in ballet tutus. Tough guys outfitted their fierce beasts in studded leather. There was always at least one dachshund in a hotdog costume. As far as we were concerned, Tipper wore a goofy husky costume twenty-four seven; even her bandana made her "costume" a little over the top.

Mayor Ray Martinez and his golden retriever, Oakley, waited at the front of the pack. Ray held out his hands, and Oakley stood up on his hind legs and placed his paws in Ray's outstretched palms. Ray said, "Bow your head." Oakley ducked his head down, and they said a short prayer before leading the procession out of the park.

The roads through downtown were open to traffic, so the crowd squeezed itself onto the sidewalks. Folks enjoying brunch or coffee at the many outdoor restaurant patios gawked at us as we streamed by. Shoppers caught unaware dodged strollers and families and college students and old folks and young ones and every type and size of dog imaginable.

Earl hung on to Tipper's leash—she was bred to pull, and being well-behaved didn't change that—and we moved with the crowd. Tipper was having a blast, first because she was busy moving, and second, because there were people to look at and other dogs to meet.

The official walk was over once the mass of walkers reached Annie's gravesite. We stopped to pay our respects, still surrounded by throngs of people and dogs, and soon after, the crowd dispersed as people began making their way back to Library Park.

At the park, vendor booths were still going strong, plus there were dog-friendly activities to try out. There was an Annie look-alike contest; Tipper wasn't even close, so we didn't enter that. There was a water-filled kiddie pool too, where Tipper and other dogs could cool off as the summer sun beat down.

Every year, the Canine Learning Center set up a professional agility course on the north side of the library. Tipper had never trained in the difficult obstacles that require speed, attention, and that oxymoron, "husky obedience," but she loved jumping over the obstacles and dashing up and down the ramps. She even jumped through a hanging tire and ran into (and out of) a tunnel. I had to let go of her leash for that, and I grabbed it the moment she emerged on the other side. The teeter-totter was a puzzle for her, but once she got over the odd motion of it, she maneuvered it like a champ. Earl and I wondered if we'd missed an opportunity by not training The Wonder Husky in agility; it sure seemed like she had natural talent.

This particular year, the stakes were higher. Next to the agility course, the American Kennel Club (AKC) had set up a "Canine Good Citizenship" testing area. Canine participants who completed the ten-step course with no mistakes would be awarded an official AKC Canine Good Citizenship certificate.

Tessa, one of my former students, bounded over to me, her basset hound, Carmine, in tow. Carmine was competing for a certificate; was Tipper?

I thought about Tipper's natural athletic agility. I considered the true nature of huskies: their high energy, part-time obedience, selective hearing, and desire to run like hell when off-leash. I'd always held her leash when she ran the agility course; this time, she'd be off-leash. But she'd always had so much fun on the agility course.

This could be a triumph or a disaster.

Orange plastic temporary fencing surrounded the course area, so even if The Wonder Husky decided to make a run for it, she wouldn't get far.

We decided to let Tipper try the test.

Earl and I watched as Tessa handed Carmine off to one of the judges and took her place outside of the fence where she could watch Carmine, but Carmine couldn't see her. The judges, stationed at various areas around the course, put Carmine through the paces of basic canine obedience, which reminded me that Tipper had failed novice obedience class. We were headed for disaster, no doubt.

The last challenge on the course was for the dog to lie down away from all people and stay put, a "down, stay" command. Oh my gosh, I thought; that last one will be the deal breaker. Tipper's attention span was shorter than a hummingbird's heartbeat.

Carmine, who'd done everything perfectly so far, lay down on the command, but he was watching the other dogs and waltzed over to join them instead of staying put.

Ding, ding, ding—Carmine's turn was over. Good try but sorry, no certificate.

Next contestant, please!

Tipper progressed through each station, clearly enjoying meeting all these fascinating new people. I held my breath, wondering at what point exactly she would go from obedient charmer to crazy dog. I broke into a sweat when the judges gave the "down, stay" command.

Tipper lay down. Then she rolled onto her side, put her head down, and fell asleep.

I think she even snored a little.

The judge woke her up to proclaim her a winner.

My husky was officially an AKC Canine Good Citizen! I dropped to my knees and wrapped my arms around her neck in a big hug, grinning like a goofball and exclaiming, "You're the goodest dog, you're the bestest dog!" over and over. Tessa and her mom showered Tipper with praise and lots of petting too.

Earl just laughed at us. The only reason Tipper had passed was because she'd fallen asleep, he guffawed. If we hadn't walked the three-mile round-trip to Annie's grave, if we hadn't strolled by every booth and picnic table, if it hadn't been so hot all morning, she never would have passed. He couldn't stop laughing at me and the dog who'd passed the Canine Good Citizen Test only because she'd fallen asleep.

But I didn't care. She was still a winner. My heart swelled with maternal pride.

The official certificate arrived in the mail several weeks later. I framed it and nailed it to the wall above her dog crate in the family room, then stepped back to admire it.

It was better than an Olympic gold medal.

Been Rode on the Ranch

Far and away, the worst place to buy a horse is at an auction. You don't know anything about the horse except what the seller says, and the seller can say anything he wants. You don't know why a horse ended up at an auction rather than at a private sale.

Some horse trainers buy, train, and sell horses for a living. A few abhorrent auctions even sell horses destined for slaughter. Killers come to pick out horses for the ride to a Texas feedlot and that final destination in Mexico or Canada. I don't think I could stand going to this type of auction and still call myself a human being.

But a good auction can be interesting and fun.

One fine day on the last Sunday in March, there was a horse auction at the Equine Center on the Foothills Campus of CSU. Earl and I thought we would go in the gorgeous weather and look at the beautiful horses. We had no intention of buying a horse. We were still dressed in running attire and had no money with us.

There were many horses, mules, and burros tied to fences. Each animal had a numbered sticker adhered to the base of its tail and was identified in a catalog.

One adorable burro with an attitude walked around freely as though he owned the place. I think he did. He definitely did not want

192192

192192192192192192

to be approached. I tried to pet him, and when he went after me, I said, "Little fella, you sure are a cutie."

I particularly admired an adult mule called Jennifer. She was a pretty sorrel color. Mules are very nice under saddle and are popular to ride. I thought Jennifer might make a nice buddy for Marcie. Then Jennifer opened her mouth and let out the loudest bray in the history of the world. "*Eeeeee haw, eeeeeeh haw eh, eh, eh!*" I could imagine our entire neighborhood calling animal control to complain about the noise reverberating down our residential street.

We continued strolling along, looking at the stock before the auction began. Earl came close to me, put his hands on my shoulders, turned me around, and said, "Mare, look at this one."

I felt as though I'd been struck by lightning, just as Michael Corleone had been struck by the thunderbolt upon seeing the girl who would become his wife in *The Godfather*. Ahead was a gorgeous black-and-white paint, #10 on his sticker, shiny clean and impeccably groomed.

I looked at the catalog. Ten was a black-and-white registered APHA gelding, just coming three years old, with the registered name of Scootsritealong. What a cute name! I loved him instantly. Of course, we immediately called him Scooter.

We checked Scooter out medically, and other than a healed wire cut on his shoulder, he was a fine youngster in good physical shape. We petted him, hugged him, and put our hands all over him. We picked up his legs to see if he objected to us handling his feet. He was as cool as a cucumber. We talked to the owner's wife about him. She was in love with him too, but buying and selling horses was her business. It was she who told us that the beautiful shape of Scoot's head was called a baby doll head. It was an exquisite work of equine art.

I decided to bid on him. I didn't think I'd get him, because he was so beautiful and well-mannered. So I first bid on an older, more experienced paint horse called Buddy, but the bidding got out of control, and I couldn't spend that much. Buddy was trained to work and be ridden by hunters, and he sold for a large sum.

I told Earl that I didn't think I'd get Scooter either. Earl thought I absolutely would get him. He said I had three things in my favor. One, Scoot was young. Two, he was short. Three, he was relatively untrained.

So I bid on him. During the bidding, his owner actually got up on Scooter's rump and jumped up and down with his cowboy boots. The little guy didn't even react.

There was only one other bidder.

I won!

Far from being cool and maintaining a poker face, as at an art or antique auction, I was jumping up and down. Definitely not cool.

But I'd won! And I had to go directly home—fast! We hadn't brought any money because we'd only been going for a look. We had our car, not the truck and trailer. We didn't have a cashier's check or cash, which were the only ways to pay for a horse at this auction. Since Earl knew the auction secretary, she agreed to let us pay by personal check. I left him with her as collateral while I sped two miles home to get my checkbook and return with it, along with our rig. I remember taking time to call my sister and leave an out-of-breath voice message: "We've got a new baby! It's a horse! Gotta go pay for him. Talk to you later."

I raced back and paid for Scoot, and he was ours.

Then we had to get him home.

The auction catalog said that he had "been rode on the ranch." It said nothing about getting into a horse trailer instead of a large stock trailer for a two-mile trip to his new home.

It was a rodeo gone bad. Scooter actually ended up with his front legs in the manger where the head goes, his hind hooves scrabbling as he tried to catch his balance. We drove back to the auction to ask the seller for help. The seller, Brent, came with us.

By then, Scooter had turned completely around in the divided trailer, with his head out the back and his lead rope broken. Brent actually stood outside the trailer on the back fender, holding Scooter's head while we drove home very, very slowly. In our college town, of course, people tried to pass us because we were going too slowly. Somehow, they ignored the odd sight of a man balanced precariously on the fender of a horse trailer, holding a broken lead rope attached to a frantic young paint horse whose head was poking out of the wrong end of the trailer.

We managed to avert disaster, as well as the Fort Collins police department. We placed Scooter in Aria's old pen across the street. He kept circling the small pen. I'm sure he was thinking in his equine brain, *What's going on? Where am I? What are those strange people going to do to me?*

Scooter had some minor cuts and bruises from the wild trip home, so I treated his wounds and gave him some pain medicine and a low dose of steroids for the swelling. He was fine after that and inhaled his suppertime hay. To this day, I have only known one time when Scooter refused to eat, and that cost us over $10,000 in veterinary bills and included abdominal surgery for a large, highly infectious equine strangles abscess.

After a week in the small pen, with the horses neighing to each other across the street, we brought him to the corral at our house. He fit in well with Marcie the Barn Diva and Aria, his new best friends.

Earl's dad, Bill, had come up to Fort Collins on one of his many visits from Texas to work around the house and yard. He and Earl were great builders. They were in the barn, sawing wood, driving nails, and generally having a good time preparing a stall for Scooter. Scooter was standing in the corral, placidly watching all the activity.

Remember how the auction catalog said Scooter had "been rode on the ranch"?

I decided to saddle him and see how he rode. I got him all tacked up. He was stunning. I took many pictures. He remained his quiet, relaxed self, so I buckled on my helmet (after getting bucked off Marcie that one time, I never rode without a helmet again) and mounted up.

I gave him the cue to go—and nothing happened. He just stood there like a rock. It was clear that he didn't know how to go with a rider on board. Earl, Bill, and I laughed hysterically about being "rode on the ranch." What, exactly, was that supposed to mean?

Later in the summer, Steve Bowers, who with his twin, Mike, had trained Franny and Marcie, trained Scooter. He became a wonderful horse without any bad habits or mean behaviors.

The first time I rode him alone was close to home in a natural area with a small lake. People liked to fish there. I got Scoot tacked up and was ready to go, whereupon he spotted a man fishing in the water.

I have never seen a horse raise his head so high in fright. The man had waders on and was fishing in deep water. What Scooter saw in his small equine brain was half a man.

Scoot struggled to get away from this monster man, even though we were nowhere near him. Scooter backed up, jumped in the air, and fell down on his side. I panicked because I thought he had broken a leg, but he was okay except for road rash all over his right side. I got on him to ride a few yards or so, just to let him know he was there for a ride, then took his saddle off and drove him home for wound treatment. Oy. So much for riding alone on a young horse.

Scooter is truly gorgeous in any kind of tack—English, Western, or Australian—and draws audible gasps from onlookers. He's such a ham that if someone tells him how handsome he is, he puts on his "Mr. Smooth" act. Kids love to come over and pet him when we are on the trail. We always tell the parents it's okay. He loves to be the first horse a frightened little child gets to ride. I've had eighteen-month-old toddlers on his back. He's also a sucker for a pretty girl, and he's good for geography lessons because he has a perfect map of South America on his left shoulder.

One young woman I know developed Hodgkin's lymphoma as a sophomore in high school. Thanks to working at a stable and riding the horse of her dreams, she sailed through chemotherapy. Eventually, her parents bought her the horse of her dreams, which she rode and took everywhere, including to college, where she graduated in three years with honors, cancer-free. Her horseback experience had begun years earlier, on Scooter—I still have a picture of her riding him when she was seven years old.

I know that Scoot would protect me if anyone tried to hurt me on the trail. One time on a ride in an open-space area, a dog was running off leash—strictly *verboten* in this area. I turned Scoot toward the dog and said, "Get him!" As the dog moved, so did Scooter. The dog made a hasty retreat. I have no doubt that Scoot would protect me if someone were to jump out of a bush and grab the reins to pull me down.

Scooter does enjoy the little pleasures in life. We train our horses to be unafraid of water. There is a nearby lake where we take the horses to splash. Franny and Marcie were dedicated splashers.

I was riding Scoot and Earl was riding Marcie at the same lake where Scoot saw the monster man. I decided to let Scoot go in the water. He stood there watching Marcie splash until Earl was soaked and giggling. Finally, Scooter started splashing too. Then he decided that the cool water felt so good after a hot ride that he would lie down in the lake. He didn't bother to think about the fact that I was still sitting on his back. I bailed out with a splash and ended up standing in the shallow lake with water filling up my cowboy boots. I was soaking wet and laughing so hard that I had to bend over and put my hands on my knees to catch my breath.

Earl was concerned that Scoot would run off and told me to go get him. I said I couldn't—I was laughing too hard; he'd be fine. Eventually, I walked over to get him. After all, there was food where he was. He wasn't going anywhere.

In June, shortly after school was out for the summer, I was part of a weeklong committee to review new biology textbooks. Sunday, the day before the review began, we went riding at the lake. I decided to let Scooter try splashing again, but I would be more vigilant because of what had happened last time.

Bam! He did it again, and down we went.

When horses get up from being down, especially in water, they paddle their hind limbs. Scoot whacked me right across both shins. Ouch! I think maybe that happened because my boot got caught in the stirrup and I was hanging upside down.

I remember Earl shouting my name in fright. Earl was usually a very laid-back man, particularly around horses, but the sight of his wife hanging upside down was enough to scare the daylights out of him. My foot released just in time for Scooter's horseshoes to whack against my shinbones. With only badly bruised shins and some scrapes on my hands from hitting the shoreline, I got back on, we rode home, and I treated my wounds.

The next day at the meeting, I wasn't feeling too well. Before I'd left home, I had taken my temperature and confirmed that I was running a fever from the inflammation caused by Scoot whacking my shins. My doctor's nurse was always after me about how rarely I came in for a checkup, so I called the office. The doctor was trying to get out of the office to visit France with his wife, so I was given an appointment with the physician's assistant. She told me to elevate my legs and keep ice packs on them. I went home for the remainder of the day.

I returned to the meeting the next day and stretched out with my legs elevated and covered with ice packs. The nurse's husband, a math teacher, was also at a textbook review meeting in the same building, so I showed him my wounds of many colors, along with my bandaged elbow, and asked him to tell his wife what they looked like. He said they came under the heading of "unbelievable."

So much for letting Scoot in the water to splash. We did continue to go into water when we rode, but we no longer stopped to let Scoot splash and risk having him lie down on me.

After Earl died and I moved away from the farmhouse, I boarded Scoot at a stable. Every time I tried to ride him, we got into some kind of wreck, such as a five o'clock near ride that turned into a race to his pen for supper, leaving me behind holding a broken lead rope.

I gave Scooter to the woman who owns the stable. Scooter is the type of horse that is unhappy standing around a corral. He loves being ridden, groomed, trained—anything, really, that involves interaction with people. Scooter has a new life giving riding and jumping lessons to students too intimidated to ride huge off-the-track thoroughbreds. He is what is called an "honest jumper." He jumps in business mode only, with no equine chicanery.

Many paints live a long time. Scootsritealong is past twenty now and is still a delight to all who know him and train on him. It is my greatest pleasure to smooch his muzzle when I go out to visit him.

I love this auction horse with my entire being. When Scoot retires from his teaching career, I'll get him back, as arranged with the woman who owns the stable, to have him as a trail horse. He is my equine friend, and even though he is not mine right now, I still consider him my son, Scootsritealong. Someday, we will be riding together, since he really has been "rode on the ranch."

Lost and Found

Our best beloved pets can save us—and make us crazy—sometimes at the same time.

In October 2003, Earl and I went to Denton, Texas, to be with his family. Earl's dad was dying.

We had suspected something was wrong when Bill and his wife, Bev, had visited us in July, just after my niece's June wedding. He'd been portly all the years I'd known him, but that July, he was much thinner. I remember noticing how his watch hung from his wrist. He hadn't had his usual enthusiasm for working with Earl on the house and yard.

In early August, he was diagnosed with stage IV lung cancer. "Stage IV" means that the cancer has metastasized, or spread, from the lungs to other organs or parts of the body. In Bill's case, the cancer had spread everywhere, even into his bones.

It was a rapid form of cancer with a grave prognosis; his doctor recommended chemotherapy. Bill had one dose, but his health was failing so fast that the family chose to halt the chemo after that first treatment. Chemo wasn't going to work fast enough to save him, and they wanted to avoid his suffering from noxious side effects as he took the journey to his passing. As far as I know, no one in the family told

Bill why his treatment didn't continue, but I believe Bill would have agreed with the decision.

Earl and I planned to alternate months going down to Texas to help out; I'd go one month, Earl the next. But that never happened.

Dr. William D. Carlson—Bill—was an internationally known veterinarian as well as a wonderful father-in-law. He'd developed the field of veterinary radiology in the late 1950s by transposing techniques from human radiology. He wrote the first textbook on that specialty after being a resident in radiology at the human hospital and earning a PhD in radiology from the University of Colorado School of Medicine. CSU's College of Veterinary Medicine then launched their radiology department, complete with professors trained by Wild Bill.

Bill also started a colony of beagles, housed at the Foothills Campus of CSU, to study the long-term effects of radiation on animals. The colony was active for fifty years. I am sure that his research caused his cancer—today's careful precautions against radiation exposure didn't exist back in the 1950s and '60s.

In addition to his work as a professor, researcher, and administrator at CSU, Bill was president of the University of Wyoming for eleven years; was head of St. John's Medical Center (a human, not veterinary, hospital) in Jackson, Wyoming, where he initiated a therapy dog program for the nursing home associated with the hospital; and, as his final job before retirement, served with the United States Department of Agriculture (USDA) in Washington, DC, as the administrator of federal dollars given to land grant colleges. If you were a land grant college (such as CSU) seeking federal research money, you had to go through Bill. His work with the USDA took him on many travels—wherever there was USDA research. He told me of trips as far flung as Micronesia and as close to home as Louisiana. Louisiana was one of his favorites; he visited humid Avery Island, which is owned by the McIlhenny family, the manufacturers of Tabasco sauce. The sauce, Bill said, sat in barrels on that island for three years to age to gastronomic perfection.

Not bad for a vet whose first boss after graduation told him he'd never amount to much in veterinary medicine.

Bill was the kind of father I wished I'd had. He actively enjoyed his kids and was willing to turn the smallest outing into a great adventure.

He and Bev still lived in Arlington, Virginia, when I graduated from vet school. I knew I needed intense cat clinic experience if I wanted to open my own feline-exclusive clinic, so I joined a feline-exclusive practice in nearby Falls Church, Virginia. Bev was a real estate agent, and thanks to her, I was able to buy a studio apartment sight unseen across the street from where she and Bill lived. It was a great little apartment in a nice building; I counted the surgeon general, many members of Congress, and Larry King among my neighbors.

I rode the elevator with Larry every now and then, and we'd always talk about horses. That began when Larry asked me what the letters AAEP, emblazoned on my jacket, stood for. "American Association of Equine Practitioners—horse doctors," I said, slightly awestruck that this big-name guy had even noticed me. I was a huge fan. I always listened to his radio show and had even called into the show a couple of times. I never thought I'd talk with him face-to-face, never imagined that he'd be so cordial, especially considering how we met: I'd dropped my bags of groceries at the door to the building, spilling stuff all over the place. He'd helped me pick everything up while I babbled stupid question number one—"Aren't you Larry King?"—and stupid question number two—"Do you live here too?"

Bill, Bev, and I visited back and forth frequently; I even took my laundry over to their house and ran my things through their washer and dryer when they weren't home. The laundry room in the basement of my building was creepy, and the one time I did use it, the security guard was there, drinking whisky straight out of the bottle. After that, I sneaked my laundry out the front door of my building in a gym bag and across the street to Bev and Bill's.

Tippling security guards aside, the neighborhood was pretty safe.

Even so, if my visits lasted until after dark, Bill always insisted on escorting me from their home through my parking lot to the front door of my building.

Earl had stayed back in Colorado the year I worked in Falls Church. Once a month, I had a three-day weekend, and one of us would travel to the other. We'd get together on vacation days too—my contract with the clinic allowed for three weeks of paid time off. When Earl came to Virginia, we'd go on excursions to places like Gettysburg and Tangier Island.

The rest of the time, it was Bill, Bev, and me exploring and seeing the sights, from local adventures—hiking to Roosevelt Island, attending free military concerts and the DC Fourth of July fireworks, going to the theatre—to cruising Skyline Drive in the Blue Ridge Mountains and traveling to Charlottesville to visit Bill and Bev's daughter, Susan, and her family. Susan was working on her PhD in health education at the University of Virginia, complementing her RN degree, in order to become a college professor.

The Falls Church clinic owner asked me to continue working with them, but I was ready to move back to Colorado when my yearlong contract was up. Eventually, Bev tired of the climate in Northern Virginia and announced to Bill that she'd bought a house in Denton, Texas. Her decision wasn't as strange as it sounds; Susan had accepted a position at Texas Woman's University in Denton.

Bill retired and they moved, despite the fact that Bill detested the hot, humid climate of their new town. The plus side of their move was that Bill especially spent a lot of each summer with us in Colorado, enjoying our cooler temperatures and much (much!) lower humidity. Every summer, he and Earl had all sorts of projects in the works, and they even finished most of them. Bill's energy and enthusiasm for life seemed endless.

In September, not long after Bill's diagnosis, Earl and I went to Denton for a short visit to help out. Bill kept wondering what was happening to him and why it was happening. He said repeatedly that he didn't understand how he could have gotten sick.

I understood his confusion—how could someone who had always been so robust and full of energy now be so weak? It was a painful reminder to me that being a patient is profoundly different from having technical medical knowledge and that it is very hard to rationalize, let alone understand, your own illness when it's a terminal condition.

On a Wednesday morning in October, just a few weeks after we'd returned home, Earl had an emergency call from Susan saying to get down to Denton ASAP; Bill was fading fast. Tickets would be waiting for us at the airline counter that evening.

Earl called me in tears—I was in my classroom—and I couldn't understand what he was saying, because he was crying so hard. He finally got through to me: we had to go *now*.

I started to cry, and so did some of my students. I'd warned them early on about my father-in-law's illness and that I might have to leave suddenly, even though at the time I hadn't believed it would be so soon.

I made a panicked call to my friend Nancy. There wasn't time for us to get Tipper to her regular kennel, where she stayed when she couldn't travel with us. Nancy and her husband, David, had dog-sat Keli for us for years and were well-versed in the challenges of husky care. They knew Tipper, and Tipper knew them. Could she—?

Nancy said yes, they would be happy to dog-sit. I heaved a sigh of relief; one less thing to worry about. I knew they would take good care of Tipper.

We got into Denton Wednesday night after dinner.

Bill's hospital bed had been set up in his and Bev's bedroom. He was awake when we arrived, but it was clear that he was rapidly failing.

Hospice oversaw Bill's end-of-life care, but Susan was a registered nurse and handled his pain medication, opening the small red vials of morphine and dripping the contents under his tongue. Sometime Wednesday night, Earl fed his father a dribble of vanilla ice cream, which was the last food he ate.

After that, all we could do was wait.

Earl and I stayed by Bill's side almost nonstop. We managed to duck out for groceries to restock the kitchen, but I refused to leave Bill alone while family members were off doing other necessary things. Susan slept on the floor next to the hospital bed. I took naps on Bev's bed, ignoring Bill's death rattle. This prodrome of death can be disturbing, but it didn't bother me. The sound comes from fluids that accumulate in the throat and upper chest as we lose our ability to swallow, which can begin to happen two or three days before we die. When we're close to death, it's difficult, if not impossible, to swallow at all, even a tiny bit of water.

The next day, Thursday, Bill slipped into a coma.

I woke up early Friday morning and padded into the bedroom to look at Bill, expecting to find him dead. Susan woke up from the floor and said he was all right. I returned to the guest room and went back to sleep.

Friday evening, Susan, her husband, their two daughters, plus my little great-niece and great-nephew and Bev, Earl, and I were gathered in the bedroom watching TV. Bill's condition hadn't changed; he was still comatose, and we knew death was coming.

We were watching a show about the progress of Elizabeth Smart, the kidnapped Utah teen who had been rescued by police officers after nine months of brutal captivity.

The minute the show was over at ten o'clock, Bill drew his last true breath.

Whether animal or human, after the last breath, there are several "agonal respirations," which are loud, deep postmortem breaths. Bill had three of them.

I looked at Earl; he was weeping silently. I hugged him, then went to Bill's bedside to talk to him and kiss him goodbye. Everyone else had left the room immediately.

In my faith, a body isn't left alone. After the last breath, the brain is still alive for about five minutes; that's why I talked to Bill after he died.

The hospice nurse was out in the field, so we had to wait for her to return and officially pronounce Bill dead, a little over an hour later. My niece, who was pregnant, had already gone back to her home in the country, so Earl and my brother-in-law drove out to pick her up and bring her back to the house. I waited up for them; they returned about two thirty in the morning.

The funeral directors arrived. They transferred Bill's body to the gurney, wrapped it with a special cover, and maneuvered it down the steep stairs. All I could think was, "God help you, don't drop the body!" We followed along behind, out to the waiting van.

Over the next few days, to take some of the workload off my mother-in-law and to distract myself from my own grief, I arranged Bill's obituaries for four newspapers and reminded our hometown paper that they had done an article on the family the previous year, when Bill celebrated his fiftieth vet school graduation anniversary and Earl his twenty-fifth. Since Bill was a giant in the world of veterinary medicine, the paper wrote a kind article about him. A colleague whom he had trained wrote a warm memorial piece for the *Journal of the American College of Veterinary Radiology*. Three years later, this veterinarian would also die of a radiation-related cancer.

I held my emotions together until Sunday, when Nancy called.

"I need your voice mail code," she said, sounding half-panicked. "Tipper's escaped, but there's a message. Maybe someone found her, and I need the code."

Nancy and David live near one of the most dangerous intersections in town.

Tipper had slipped through their fence at the one place they hadn't known was loose.

It was typical husky escape behavior. And huskies are known for running far and fast without stopping, let alone looking both ways before crossing the street. Numbly, I recited the access code, then hung up the phone.

I was sure the worst had happened to my beloved girl. I began to cry and couldn't stop.

I was still crying when Nancy called back: Tipper was safe!

The message was from a nice lady who had taken her son to the two-dollar movie theatre located across the intersection from Nancy and David's place. Tipper, her tail wagging furiously, had come up to them in the parking lot to say "howdy" and (I knew) to be admired for her beauty. She'd let the lady look at her signature ID tag, a hot-pink dog bone. This kind stranger had taken Tipper home, where her little boy and Tipper had had a fine time playing together until Nancy had arrived to take my adventurous girl home.

I didn't know whether to laugh or cry. I was completely wrung out from the emotional vortex of the last two days: grief from losing Bill, the trauma of Tipper's escape, the joy of her safe return. I lay like a wet noodle on the guest room bed, beyond exhausted.

My lucky dog had managed to cross eight-plus lanes of heavily traveled road safely. I'd never know how many new friends she made in the parking lot before the lady and her son realized that she needed rescuing. I giggled to myself, imagining her trotting up to the box office, buying a tub of popcorn and a Coke, and settling into the theatre to watch a double feature. I thought of her beautiful face with those crystal-blue eyes. I was so grateful that she'd been found and that I would hold her in my arms in a few days.

Another day to get through and then, on Tuesday, Bill's funeral. Bill's sister, Elaine, and her husband flew in from Colorado. Their son, Dan, an ER doctor who had just finished a twenty-four-hour shift, flew in too, then immediately out again after the service to face another shift. I was touched by, and am still grateful for, Dan's generosity and kindness, spending those precious hours to honor Bill.

The church was packed. Bill had been such a humble man, I don't think anyone in the congregation really knew all he had accomplished in his life or how famous he was in the veterinary community. There was no doubt, however, that the people here knew, loved, and respected him. Later, I learned the generous donations received by the church went to two exquisite wall hangings in the sanctuary in memory of Bill.

A luncheon followed Bill's memorial service. I know it's a cliché to say that everything is bigger in Texas, but this meal was huge, even by Texas standards: roast turkey and all the trimmings, plus at least twenty different side dishes weighing down the sagging buffet tables.

I hadn't eaten much since arriving in Denton—I tend to not eat when I'm stressed out, and I usually can't eat in a crowd of strangers. But these parishioners, people who had loved the man I was so proud to have had as my father-in-law, felt more like old friends. As I tucked into the feast, filling my belly with roast turkey Texas-style, I thought about how funerals are really for the living. Meals like this one weren't just hospitality; they were for caring, for sharing stories and memories, for nourishing our hearts as well as our bodies.

After the luncheon, Earl and I headed to the airport and home—no time to spare, because not only did we have to prepare for the open house we were hosting on Friday in Bill's memory, we also had to arrange to bury Gram's ashes.

Gram—Jewell Bradshaw—was Bev's mother and Earl's grandmother. She'd lived on the other side of Bill and Bev's duplex. Bev's brother Ralph—Earl's favorite uncle and his kidney donor—had lived with Gram. In early October, Gram had suffered a massive stroke and been brought home to hospice care.

On October 12, Earl and I had been at our home, getting ready to go out on a trail ride, when the phone had rung: Gram had died. She was ninety-four years old.

I loved Gram so much and miss her to this day. She and I liked to shop together, and she'd always suggest that I buy masses of clothes— she was definitely a power shopper! We loved discussing the stock market. Back when she and Ralph lived in Utah, they'd drive over to Nevada to play the slot machines. When Earl and I visited, we'd go to the casinos in Wendover, Nevada, and Gram always won more than I did. She was sharp as a tack her whole life. Her only symptom of old age was a bit of deafness that sometimes got in the way of conversation.

Gram's original plan had been that when she died, her body would be brought to Fort Collins and laid to rest beside Gramp, who had died twenty-five years earlier. Instead, with the need to stay focused on Bill's care and impending death, her body had been cremated, and her ashes had been set aside to be brought home with the family later.

Later was now.

On Wednesday, October 29, Fort Collins weather was sweltering, extremely unusual for late October. I arranged for Gram's grave to be opened, her stone engraved, and Gramp's stone cleaned in preparation for Gram's burial on Thursday. I picked up Tipper and, in spite of her misdeeds, hugged and kissed her, thankful to have her back safe and sound. Earl and I worked to get our house in shipshape condition for the crowd of people we expected to visit on Friday—Halloween, of all days.

Exhausted from the heat, the travel, and the emotional upheaval, heartsick from the loss of both Gram and Bill, I wandered outside. Marcie was standing in the corral. My beautiful palomino paint mare turned to look at me, seeming to understand what I could not. She stood patient and still as I wrapped my arms around her neck and let the pent-up tears flow, soaking her hair.

Thursday, the weather did an about-face: the temperature plum- meted from Wednesday's high of eighty degrees Fahrenheit to near freezing. We called family coming in and told them to prepare for serious cold. Then, shivering despite bundling ourselves against the weather, we buried Gram's ashes.

Friday was even colder, but the house was ready, and Earl and I were as ready as we could be. And as we'd hoped, about five hundred friends and colleagues filled the house, keeping each other warm with their memories of Bill.

A Lesson in Newtonian Physics

It didn't hurt at first.

I lay there, feeling a little disoriented, peering up at Hannah. I could tell she was wondering what the heck I was doing on the ground.

I wasn't supposed to be riding Hannah. It was Earl's turn, but he had a sore on his leg, and when he rode, his boot rubbed the painful spot.

I was supposed to be riding Marcie. She was up there in years by now, but no horse had ever been a more dedicated and focused jumper. When I steered her toward a jump, she took my cue and sailed over like the finest champion, her forelimbs tucked up in tight flexion above the rails.

Earl and I were here with both horses so Hannah, "The Baby," could take her jumping lesson from Sue, the trainer. Hannah had turned four years old that year, and, as with our other horses, we'd begun a year of jumping lessons to teach her agility and discipline and to teach us how to ride our young horse. Earl and I alternated lessons; one week, he'd ride Hannah, and the next, I'd ride her.

When Earl and Hannah worked with Sue, I would ride Marcie with English tack, watch the lesson, and practice some moves and jumps with Marcie.

I'd volunteered to swap with Earl. We'd traded mounts but not English saddles.

Sue talked Hannah and me through various basic leg commands. Hannah hadn't yet picked up her right lead when I asked her to canter. It was difficult urging her to take the correct lead.

The natural inclination for the rider is to lean forward in the saddle to help the horse along. That's what I was doing as I worked with Hannah on taking the correct lead, and it's the opposite of what you really should do. Sue noticed and advised me to sit back in the saddle.

I did as Sue asked at the same moment Hannah changed to a fast trot. As I sat back, Hannah brought her hips up in the gait, our butts crashed together, Hannah swerved unexpectedly to the left, and I was launched like a rocket.

So, technically, at that precise moment, I wasn't actually riding Hannah.

I soared into the summer sky, evidence of Newton's first law of motion: "An object will remain at rest or in uniform motion in a straight line unless acted upon by an external force." The external force of my hitting Hannah's tushy had triggered my upward trajectory. I continued in that direction while her sharp turn took her elsewhere, riderless.

I'd learned about Newton and his laws during my first semester as an undergraduate physical education major, in one of our required courses, Basic Body Movement and Rhythms. We PE majors called it Basic Bod. My father, who was a medical doctor, sneered at the course content, but it was a wonderful class. Newton's laws helped me understand how my field hockey cleats worked. A variation on Newton's first law, conservation of angular momentum, addressed the angles of rebound and spin, which forever improved my pool game.

Most people think of Sir Isaac Newton as the guy who discovered gravity when an apple fell on his head. His law of gravity, commonly stated as "What goes up must come down," seemed especially appropriate just now, considering my upward trajectory and the opposing force of gravity.

"Hang time" is the length of time that something stays in the air, whether the "something" is a leaping cat, a football arcing its way down the field, or a horseback rider ejected from her horse. Hang time often seems much longer than it really is. It's one of those cool illusions of nature.

"Suspensory motion" is the sweet spot as you round the top of the trajectory, right before gravity overtakes you and you begin your descent. It includes that fraction of a moment when the force of your upward trajectory exactly matches the downward force of gravity, and for the briefest moment, you're motionless and weightless.

I contemplated hang time; surely, I was almost to the top. What would suspensory motion feel like? Everything was happening in slow motion—another of those weird illusions we humans are prone to, this one due to the adrenaline surge—so perhaps there would be plenty of time to notice being weightless before time resumed its normal pace.

I couldn't see Hannah, but I knew she was somewhere below me. She wasn't weightless. Or soaring, for that matter.

Neither was I, I noticed; gravity was winning, and I was falling.

I hit the dirt fully extended on my right side, squarely on my right hip. I couldn't have nailed it better if I'd painted a bull's eye on my hip and aimed for dead center. I didn't exactly bounce, but the force of the rebound rolled me onto my belly.

Cats are much better experts at dissipating the landing force than people. The two new kittens we'd adopted a couple of months earlier, brothers Frank and Cowboy Joe, were already masters at marvelous gymnastics moves that I'd never accomplished back in my heyday. They had excellent hang times too.

I tried to get up. I got as far as my hands and knees and then discovered that my right leg wouldn't move forward.

"Earl, call 911!" I yelled.

He squatted down beside me and said, "No, it's okay—I'll take you to the hospital."

I groaned and shifted over to half-sit on my left side. "No! I need 911!"

No cell reception at the arena, thanks to the surrounding mountains, so Sue rushed back to her house and called the paramedics from the landline. There was a fire station close to Sue's place; they sent a truck immediately and dispatched an ambulance from Poudre Fire Authority Station 2, which was only about a mile from our house but ten miles from Sue's place.

While we waited, Sue's son drove their Mule—a type of farm vehicle that looks like a cross between a golf cart and a small but mighty pickup truck—to the arena. I grabbed the edge of the open bed at the back of the Mule and hoisted myself up.

Oh, yes, I'd definitely broken a bone. I could feel the edges grinding together when I put a little weight on my injured leg. Trying to step on my leg felt like wobbling on top of a pond, only with a lot more pain.

By the time the fire truck arrived, I'd made it onto the Mule's padded bench seat, and Sue's son had driven us to just outside the arena, where it would be easier for the firefighters to reach us. I drew on my years of yoga practice, using breathing techniques to stay calm. I had only one minor episode of nausea and dizziness.

Before the firefighter had a chance to do anything, I barked out, "Whatever you do, do not cut my boot off!" It had taken me all my life to find a pair of English knee boots that fit. I'd used my late sister Natalie's boots for thirty years, but at long last, I finally had a pair of my own. My beautiful brand-new, black, shiny boots were English field riding boots, the kind with shoelaces over the ankle and part of the instep. Injury or no injury, I wasn't going to lose those boots.

The firefighter smiled and promised no boot cutting. He was patient and worked with me to remove the boot intact and without pain.

The ambulance arrived; time to transfer me onto the gurney. "Give yourself a hug," one of the EMTs said.

"What?"

He demonstrated, wrapping his arms around his own shoulders. "That way, you won't try to move yourself onto the gurney. That's our job," he said, smiling.

The lack of control I had frightened me more than my injury, but I wrapped my arms tightly around myself, and they loaded me gently into the ambulance.

"How about lights and sirens? And high speed?" I asked. If I had to ride in an ambulance, at least it could be first class.

The answer was, "Sorry, no."

Bummer. I was hurt badly, but evidently, I was stable enough that I didn't warrant that much excitement.

I studied my injured leg. It was rotated, the foot turned totally to the outside, the classic position of a fractured hip.

I noticed a few visual disturbances too. Sometimes, the clock in the ambulance had black spots on it, or only half of the clock was visible. I knew this was a sign of mild shock, but when I asked the EMT about it, he didn't say anything. I suspect he didn't want to scare me.

I gave myself another hug as the EMTs transferred me to the emergency room bed. The ER staff took over my care, inserting an IV line and administering much-needed pain medication before sending me off to radiology. The ER doctor never touched me; he could tell just by looking exactly what my injury was. He did, however, bill me for the exam.

X-rays were the worst part of emergency treatment. The room temperature was frigid, especially for a trauma patient. I swear the radiology technician was a heartless witch. She insisted that Earl leave, and then she left me alone on the X-ray table with no safety railing. I couldn't correct my balance because of my injury, and I had just been pumped full of strong narcotics. I worried that I'd fall a second time.

Moving my leg into the position the tech wanted caused such horrific pain that the tech had to call in other aides to hold my leg. I was shaking and crying by then. I didn't know my husband was just outside the door; they never asked me if I wanted him beside me in between attempts at X-rays, and they never asked him if he wanted to join me. I thought he was waiting for me back in the ER bay.

On the way back to ER from radiology, I overheard one of the techs say, "Surgery."

I already knew I would be heading for surgery because the ER doctor had ordered a chest X-ray, which is a mandatory precursor to surgery.

I said, "*Stop!*"

The gurney stopped. I explained that I was aware of confidentiality rules, but since I couldn't see their faces, could they please tell me what was broken.

"The femoral neck," one of them said.

The femoral neck is the thinnest part of the largest bone in the body. It attaches the long shaft of the femur to the head of the femur so the bone can fit into the pelvis, creating the hip joint.

Since I wasn't critical—this wasn't a life or death situation—I was transferred to a room on the orthopedic floor, where I spent the rest of the day waiting for the orthopedic trauma surgeon. I'd launched from Hannah at eleven in the morning. I had a long, uncomfortable, scary wait, offset in part by powerful pharmaceuticals, before it was time to transfer me to the pre-op area at six o'clock.

By late afternoon, my body was reminding me that I hadn't used the bathroom since before we left home for the riding lesson. Between that and a day's worth of IV fluids, my bladder started talking to me. I couldn't get out of bed, of course. The nurse tried to help me use a bedpan. No way—moving was agony.

By the time I was moved to pre-op, my bladder was screaming at me. I was gritting my teeth to prevent an explosion of urine.

In pre-op, the nurse noticed that my hands still had some blood on them from the IV insertion. She began to wash my hands with a warm, moist towel.

That did it! My bladder could not wait any longer.

I informed the nurse that I had to be focused to talk to the surgeon when he arrived, and I couldn't do that with a basketball-sized bladder. I understood that bladders are usually catheterized under anesthesia, but I didn't care how much it hurt; she had to do it immediately.

She didn't argue or question my reasoning. She gently inserted the catheter—painlessly too, I might add—and nearly a liter of urine gushed into the collection bag. I have never felt such utter, joyous relief.

That evening, I underwent surgery to put my hip back together. Three screws—$500 a pop, each one 85 millimeters (3.5 inches) long and sturdy enough to be used on farm equipment—were installed across the fracture line.

I could have been featured in a John Deere calendar.

Physical therapy began the next morning. The first exercise was to get out of bed with the therapists' help and hold on to a walker. I couldn't move my leg; the therapists had to move it for me. The pain was excruciating.

Before I could be discharged from the hospital, I had to learn to walk using the "touch-down weight-bearing" method, which would be how I'd get around for the next eight weeks. I advanced with my injured leg barely touching the floor, no weight on it. Then I moved the walker and then moved my uninjured leg. My arms trembled from the exertion, and I shook with pain.

Simply standing and hanging on to the walker was the first task. Next, I had to learn how to use the walker to actually move myself and, after that, learn how to use crutches.

Did I mention the excruciating pain?

I quickly reached the point where any time any hospital staff person came into my room, I startled in fear of impending pain. "Mary, no one's touched you yet," they'd say, trying to reassure me, but that didn't help.

My morphine drip compounded the pain issues.

Research shows that when patients are able to control the delivery of their pain medication, they use less medication. I controlled my morphine delivery by pushing a button on a special pump attached to the IV apparatus. Push the button, and the PCA (Patient-Controlled Analgesia) pump delivers the correct dose of morphine directly into the vein. Then the machine locks you out for ten minutes. If you need more painkiller, you can push the button again after the ten minutes are up.

Morphine is an effective pain medication, but it made me itch all over, talk like a crazy woman, and hallucinate. (It's now on my medication "do not use" list.)

I had no clue that I was hallucinating. I just thought I was in a different room every day for my six-day hospital stay. One day, my room had a kitchenette. The next day, I wondered where the kitchenette had gone. Over the weekend, I was sure my room was on the first floor. I was actually "the hip in 3029," on the third floor of the hospital, during my entire stay. And my room definitely did not include a kitchenette.

When I closed my eyes to try to sleep, I saw visions of my childhood home on Indian Tree Drive in Highland Park as façades for new condominium buildings. I watched animals morph into other animals. I have to admit that was pretty cool, and it was in Technicolor too!

Not all of the hallucinations were enjoyable. In one especially disturbing vision, I saw Marcie walk across the corner of my visual field. Marcie was twenty-nine that summer, and I always worried about her health, even though she was doing well. I was terrified that she would die while I was hospitalized because she'd appeared in my waking dream. I cried and cried, convinced Marcie was about to die, while my wonderful night nurse, Sara, comforted me. After I'd cried myself out and Sara left, I was finally able to sleep for the first time in three days.

The hallucinations became quite complicated when I had the TV on. Certain channels made things worse or more intense. When I listened to the Spanish channel, the hallucinations were more relaxing. When I turned the TV off, the hallucinations gravitated toward mild subject matter—not exactly relaxing but not especially disturbing.

A couple of teacher friends visited Saturday morning, and I told them about the weird visions I was having. They're the ones who told me that my visions were hallucinations, laughing so hard that they nearly fell off their chairs. I had no idea. In my college days (clearly different from theirs!), I'd been a field hockey team member, too busy being a pioneer for Title IX to want to do drugs. It took a twenty-first century hip fracture and hospital stay, complete with tubes sticking out of my body and screws holding the broken parts together, for me to have that experience.

Friday, the day after my surgery, I called the school district's director of human resources in a panic to tell him that I wouldn't be able to start school in the fall. He arranged everything, including notifying the benefits department to start my long-term sick leave so I wouldn't lose any pay. He asked permission to tell others about my accident. I was a little hesitant, but he pointed out that I was a former board of education director and a longtime teacher, and people would want to know. I agreed and gave him the go-ahead.

Gary, the acting superintendent of schools, stopped by that afternoon. He was so kind. During his visit, I took my scheduled dose of oral narcotic painkillers. "Uh-oh, now you've seen a teacher taking opioid drugs," I commented.

Later, a giant flower arrangement was delivered to my room, courtesy of the superintendent and the board of education. I was a survivor—I mean alumna—of the school board, and I felt like an honored member of the club when I saw that bouquet.

The weekend in the hospital was dreadful. I developed a fever from the inflammation in my fractured leg and felt even worse. I would have appreciated an opinion from the doctor, but my temperature was a few tenths of a degree shy of the point where anyone would call him. The only bad nurses I've ever had—one who was hearing-impaired and was shadowing another who had a speech impediment—assisted me with my first in-hospital shower. They seated me precariously high in the air on a special stool and did nothing to help me feel secure. Instead, I felt like I was in danger of falling any second. I was so embarrassed by my fear that I wrapped a bath towel over my head and face when they wheeled me back to my room. I felt mostly clean, but then I noticed dirt and hay still packed into my belly button, leftovers from hitting the deck in the arena.

Fortunately, Jean, my dear friend and fellow vet school classmate, came up from Denver to visit me on Saturday. She did some relaxation exercises with me, then taped acupuncture seeds to important meridian points to help me with the pain and to relax.

My nurse that afternoon was fascinated with Jean's acupuncture work. She had a little headache, so Jean applied seeds to the nurse's hands, which alleviated her headache.

The best—or funniest—part of Jean's visit was when I used the orthopedic triangle pull-up bar while giving the classic middle digit salute. We both giggled, and she took my photo. I keep that photo in my date book to remind myself that things do get better with time.

Things improved when the morphine pump was removed, and I was allowed to switch to an oral narcotic. I was finally able to sleep. I became a rock star at physical therapy. I started eating, although it was uncomfortable because the outer edge of my tongue had a gigantic ulcer on it, probably from biting it while coming out of anesthesia. I also had a sore throat from the too-large endotracheal tube that had been inserted to help me breathe during surgery. I coughed up some bloody stuff that was really gross, directly from my injured trachea.

Friends left tons of chocolate for me to enjoy, but chocolate never tastes good to me when I'm sick, and I was having a hard time eating anything because of my sore throat and mouth. The chocolate piled up until there was so much that we converted an entire table into an official "chocolate table." It didn't take long before nurses I'd never seen began wandering in to ask, "Is this the room with all the chocolate?" and pluck a goodie or two from the colossal stash.

Ortho docs are really busy, and while I saw my trauma surgeon daily, there never seemed to be enough time to ask him about my prognosis. I was feeling better now that I wasn't hallucinating, but I was still worried. I finally had the nurse put a sticky note in my chart: "Patient requests that Dr. Lundy please sit down and talk to her about her injury."

It worked.

Doug Lundy, a fine doctor, sat down with me to assuage my fears. We developed an excellent doctor-patient relationship, one that would last for two years, until he moved with his family back to his home state of Georgia. Doug made me laugh with stories from his med school days, including one about dropping an old guy on the floor that cracked me up. Laughter is great medicine, and laughing during adversity has always been important to me—enough so that I had the nurse add a note about it on the white board near my hospital bed. Next to "Mary—R. hip—a 'rock star' at PT," she wrote, "Humor works well."

I was scheduled to be released on Tuesday.

Monday, a woman who worked in some office (I never found out which office, specifically) barged into my room and announced that my insurance program paid for only four nights in the hospital for this type of injury, and if I "insisted" on staying an extra night, I would have to pay for the room and all associated services myself.

"I haven't even learned to use crutches yet!" I sputtered. "My doctor isn't releasing me until tomorrow."

She shoved a paper at me, demanding that I sign it. The paper said I would be responsible for the extra day and its costs.

I refused to sign.

She insisted.

My irritation blossomed into rage. I told her that I wouldn't sign anything and to get the hell out of my hospital room.

She left, paper unsigned, and I called the school district's benefits office. The wonderful experts there straightened out the mess, and I was allowed to stay one more day.

What should have been a quick goodbye after physical therapy on Tuesday turned into an all-day process. I remember very little of it. I know that whenever food came, someone pushed it away for unknown reasons. I had no clothes at the hospital, so Earl and his mom, Beverley, who had arrived from Texas while I was in the hospital, went home and brought back something for me to wear. I did have the presence of mind to take the remaining chocolate—a single bag of Hershey's Kisses, which were a gift from my principal, Mike—home with me.

It was late afternoon when I arrived home. I made my slow way from the car to the house, supporting myself with my youth-sized walker. Earl followed behind, carrying my new crutches.

The first thing I saw when I made it through the door was new kitten Frank. I sat down, picked him up, and began to cry.

Summer, for me, was over before it began.

I was looking at eight weeks of sitting in a recliner, stumping around with a walker, and hobbling on crutches. No horseback riding. No outside jaunts with Tipper. No tending my beloved rose garden.

The first full day at home, I stayed in bed, exhausted but not alone. Principal Mike had included the news about my injury in our school's latest email blast, and visitors began trooping in to wish me well.

On day two, I began outpatient physical therapy. Earl drove me to the Orthopaedic Center of the Rockies and watched me stump my way with my walker to the evaluation room.

Dr. Lundy had hand-picked my physical therapist. Todd's personality was a perfect match for me. My mindset was that I was not in rehabilitation; I was in training, just as I would be for a sports competition. I needed to focus on training for future performance instead of rehabbing a past injury, and Todd understood that immediately.

During my first appointment, Todd asked me to raise my fractured leg. My brain kept telling my leg to rise, but my leg didn't move. I could move my foot back and forth and slide my leg side to side a little, but no matter how hard I tried, my leg stayed on the tabletop.

Gradually, over many weeks and PT sessions, I was finally able to lift my leg.

Home itself provided plenty of challenges. Going to the bathroom was problematic. First, I had to maneuver myself and the crutches through the narrow space between Earl's side of the bed and a dresser to get to the bathroom. I had to be especially mindful of not falling with my new crutches. I crashed into the dresser more than once.

Once in the bathroom, there was the problem of actually sitting on the toilet. I'd discovered in the hospital how painful lowering myself onto the seat was, and that seat had been higher than a standard toilet seat, as well as having grab bars for extra support. Why hadn't anyone told me about potty risers before I got home? With one of those in place, I didn't have to bend so far, and sitting down was less painful.

Taking a shower involved sitting on a transfer table in the bathtub and using a handheld showerhead, which our plumber had installed specifically for my recuperation. I could get myself onto the table, but at the beginning, I couldn't move my leg to get it into the tub. Earl had to lift my leg up and over the side of the tub for me.

I yelled at him the first time we practiced this in the hospital's therapy room. I sat beside a mock-up of an automobile (the movement to get into a car is essentially the same as getting into a bathtub, except the wall of the tub is higher). Earl wasn't paying attention, and instead of gently lifting and moving my leg, he hoisted it up and dumped it over the side of the automobile. I would have laughed if it hadn't hurt so much.

By the end of my first week home, I could lift my leg well enough by myself to shower on my own. It seems like such a small thing, but I felt tremendous freedom when I finally reached that milestone, showering alone except for Cowboy Joe, our other new kitten, who sat between the shower curtain and liner and watched me—my very own Peeping Tom.

Because space was tight upstairs, we kept my walker at the bottom of the stairs. I navigated the stairs and second floor with crutches.

I mastered the stairs faster than I expected. Going up, the good leg leads; going down, the bad leg (with the crutch) leads, or, in crutch-walking parlance, "The good leg goes to heaven; the bad leg goes to hell."

Six steps marched up from the first floor to a small landing. Another twelve steps finished the climb to the second floor. To get to the second floor, I parked the walker, tucked one crutch under my left arm, and held the other crutch by a finger in the same hand. I gripped the banister with my right hand. Next, I hopped on my good leg onto the first step. Then I brought my bad leg and the crutches up on the step. Hop to second step, bring bad leg and crutch alongside, hop to third step, repeat until I reached the landing.

The banister from the landing up was on the left side, so when I reached the landing, I switched the crutches to my right arm, gripped the banister with my left hand, and resumed the good-leg hop-up until I reached the top and could switch to using a crutch under each arm.

Coming downstairs was the same thing in reverse: crutches on the outside, spare hand gripping the banister; put crutch on first step, bad leg bent so that the foot barely touched the step; then, supporting my weight between crutch and banister, move good leg to the step.

The first day home, I got the hang of it right away, zipping up and down the stairs with no problem. I wasn't ready for crutches full time, so when I made it to the bottom of the stairs, I leaned them against the corner and switched back to the walker.

At night, I went upstairs and stayed there. During the day, I camped out downstairs. I created a nest of sorts next to my reclining chair, where I stashed the TV remote, pens, paper, and meds.

I put my mealtime vitamins in a paper cup and carried the cup in my teeth as I stumped my way back to my chair, carefully observed by Cowboy Joe and Frank. Soon, both of them began carrying paper cups around the house in their mouths! Eventually, they switched from paper cups to pens and pencils; it wasn't unusual to wake up and discover half a dozen pencils in bed.

My friends, vet colleagues, and school family were wonderful, bringing meals, sending cards and flowers, visiting, and calling. One friend, a retired flight surgeon who had an artificial knee, took Tipper the Wonder Husky for a long walk each week, a lovely treat for Tipper and one less thing for me to worry about.

My mother-in-law, Beverley, had been widowed eight months to the day when I had my accident. She needed to work on settling Bill's estate in Colorado and Wyoming. Despite her social schedule and heavy workload with estate issues, she helped out too, shuttling me around when Earl wasn't available. And she helped me with the compression stockings I was supposed to wear, until I decided they weren't worth the effort and threw them out.

Those stockings! TED hose—thromboembolism-deterrent hose—are supposed to help prevent deep vein thrombosis, which are blood clots in a deep vein, usually in the leg. They can form when you don't move around much. It's a life-threatening complication, because a clot can break loose, travel through your bloodstream, and get stuck in your lungs, blocking air flow. That can be fatal.

So there's a good reason to wear them, but this was the middle of summer. The outside daytime temperatures hit the nineties most days and cracked the hundred-degree mark more than once. We didn't have air conditioning, and the upstairs bedroom was an oven until sunset brought cooler air and a gentle breeze through the open windows behind our bed. Downstairs was marginally better. It was a struggle to get the stockings on, and once on, they were truly vile in the heat. I figured I was taking an anticoagulant anyway, and my weekly test to check my blood-clotting ability would help flag any concerns.

A few days after coming home from the hospital, I made my clumsy way to the barn, not an easy feat with a walker on our flagstone path. Hannah was relaxing in the barn, looking out the window.

I shuffled over with my walker, stood close to her on my good leg, and burst into tears. "It's not your fault," I sobbed, hugging her head and stroking and kissing her soft muzzle. I think she understood.

Over the next several weeks, I gradually shifted from mostly walker to only crutches. In the process, I figured out how to sweep the barn on crutches. I placed one crutch against the gate to the hay room and supported myself with the other crutch and the push broom, sweeping the stalls without putting weight on my injured leg. It took strength and balance, skills I'd first developed long ago in gymnastics. Scooter skulked around the barn and, when he thought I wasn't looking, would nab the spare crutch and chew the top of it or toss it in the air. The work and watching Scooter's silly antics were a wonderful psychological boost for my banged-up self. I left the manure shoveling to Earl. Shoveling took two hands, and besides, my banged-up self didn't need that big a boost.

I had taken long-term sick leave from my work as a junior high school teacher because I knew that I needed to be as physically and emotionally fit as possible to interact with this age group. I would return to teaching biology part time in November; until then, a substitute teacher would cover my classes. Beginning in November, the sub and I would each work half time.

Despite feeling miserable—bone pain is horrible—and taking one of the strongest narcotics available to manage the pain, I spent all of July writing a full semester of day-by-day lesson plans for the substitute teacher to use. After I finished each unit, Bev would drive me to school, and I'd stash the huge binder on my office desk. I placed the orders for papers to be printed for the kids, and I reserved the dates the classes would need the library too, which helped me feel calmer.

I discovered later that since I was on long-term leave, I wasn't required to do any plans, but even if I'd known that up front, I would have done them anyway. I knew it would be a great help for my substitute, who wouldn't be hired until a week before school started. It also gave me something constructive to do and was one of the few things I could control . . . not to mention the irony of "Just say 'No' to drugs" and creating lesson plans while under the influence of high-octane painkillers.

The highlight of my long and miserable summer was seeing my beloved Chicago Cubs play the Colorado Rockies at Coors Field in Denver. Long before my fall from Hannah, I'd purchased seventh-row seats in the "pay attention" foul zone of right field. I didn't care that it had been barely six weeks since my great crash. No force in the universe was going to stop me from going to the game!

Our group included my cousin Michael and his wife, Debbie, visiting from Chicago; my golf buddy, Diane; Earl; and me. We got to the ballpark with plenty of time to spare. The ballpark attendant wheeled me to our seating section.

And only as far as the section. I had to clamber down thirty rows on my own to reach my specific seat.

But we had a plan. Diane would go first, to catch me if I fell forward. Earl would follow behind me, holding on to my spotting belt, a souvenir from my hospital stay. Michael and Debbie were backup and would run for help if needed.

"Bad leg goes to hell," I muttered and lowered my crutches to the first step. I swung my bad leg into position, shifted my body weight from my good leg to the crutches, and landed my good leg onto the step. One row down, twenty-nine to go.

Diane shouted something that sounded like encouragement. I swung down to the next step. It wasn't as hard as I'd feared. I didn't even notice Earl holding on to my spotting belt.

Oh. That's because he wasn't holding on to my spotting belt—he was now in front of me, ahead of Diane, intent on finding our seats. I had no idea where Michael and Debbie were, and I wasn't going to risk a fall by turning around to look. I ignored the faint whispers of "gravity is a constant" and kept moving: crutches, bad leg, good leg, crutches, bad leg, good leg. I reached our row, proud of myself for making it on my own and resisting the temptation to smack Earl with a crutch for spacing out on what he was supposed to do.

The ballpark was a sea of red and blue. It was Cubs fans, after all, transplants from Chicago like me, who had brought Major League Baseball to Colorado. Coors Field even looks a lot like Wrigley Field, including an ivy-covered wall.

The game was exciting, and like everyone else, I jumped up from my seat many times—up and down on my good leg, using Earl's or Diane's shoulders for balance.

One fan a few rows above us took a foul ball to the head, left to get stitched up, and returned to the cheers of the crowd a few innings later, proudly displaying his new row of black sutures. A few rows in front of us, people started yelling and pointing. As the crowd shifted, we could see two guys fighting. Security collared them and threw them out as the crowd cheered its approval.

Two and a half hours later, I made my way up the thirty rows (*good leg goes to heaven*), exhausted but thoroughly happy. I knew all that up and down during the game wasn't my best idea, so I took my pain meds while waiting for the wheelchair assistant. I slept all the way home. Even with pain meds and plenty of rest after the game and back home, it took me five days to fully recover.

The Cubs won, five to one.

Sometimes, the pain is worth it.

Two weeks after the Cubs game, I was finally allowed to walk without crutches. "Wean yourself off crutches and use a cane" was the advice. I carried the cane with me, but I discovered I could walk without it. Walking was not, however, pain-free. My hip had collapsed, and the neck of the femur had disappeared. I now had about an inch of the screws sticking into my hip muscles, so I walked with a limp. I continued with physical therapy twice a week. I tried running with Tipper, but it was uncomfortable, so we settled for walking.

I also contacted an equine clinician at the Veterinary Teaching Hospital who had suffered a fractured hip the year before and asked her what to expect during recovery. She recommended that I buy a packet of ten Pilates lessons with Don Spence of Big Toe Studio. Don, a certified Pilates instructor with extensive experience in rehabilitation and sports fitness, offered both group and private classes using the full complement of Pilates equipment. When I met with him for an evaluation, I told him point-blank that I wasn't interested in "rehabilitation"; I was in training. That appealed to him. I've been practicing Pilates with him ever since; he's still one of my best cheerleaders.

About the same time I was transitioning off crutches, we took Hannah to Steve, our horse trainer, for remedial ground lessons. He determined that at the time of the accident, Hannah had had a sore hip herself. It had healed by September, and she'd done well with her lessons.

I was itching to ride again. A week or so after I was officially off crutches, I was sitting on top of a chuck wagon, watching Hannah's lesson. I asked Steve to bring Hannah over to me.

Steve held the lead rope while I tentatively mounted Hannah. Then he walked us around a little.

Rudimentary as it was, I was back on a horse again. On Hannah again.

In October, the month before I returned to teaching, I was able to ride and move around enough that I could drive our rig alone to take Marcie to Lory State Park to ride.

Free at last, except for the step stool I now needed to get on her. The fracture had done a number on my right leg's range of motion, though when I mounted Marcie, the limited range of motion seemed to come from my left leg—my "good" leg. That's the leg you mount with; it was tough reaching up to the stirrup for a long time after the accident.

To psych myself up for returning to work in November, I took a trip to celebrate my freedom. My cousin Barbara was getting married in late October, near Chicago. Earl was invited too, but the Colorado State–Wyoming football game was the same weekend as Barbara's wedding. Some people attend church services; some go to the "Border War" game. Earl was definitely in the latter category. There was no way he was going to help his crippled wife negotiate suburban Chicago during that all-important game. He remained home to cheer on his beloved Wyoming Cowboys with friends at the stadium on the west side of town.

And so I trekked solo to Barbara's wedding. I hadn't been alone all summer, and I was tired of being a patient. It was time for some fun.

I imagined I was a queen with my personal staff wheeling me through the airports. The Orthopaedic and Spine Center of the Rockies had given me a wallet card that said I had orthopedic hardware in my body, but the security agents said that bad guys carried those cards too. I had to "assume the position" just like everybody else: from queen to criminal and back to queen again.

In Chicago, I rented a car and used my shiny new handicapped hangtag to get convenient parking places. One of my greatest pleasures in life is to stay in nice hotels by myself, and this time, my handicapped status snagged an extra-special hotel room for me.

Although I wasn't walking very well, I managed to shop till I dropped in between all the wedding activities. At Northwestern University in Evanston, where I'd earned my master's degree, I cleaned the gift shop out of alumni items, including T-shirts, sweatshirts, a nice jacket, and key chains.

I drove up Lake Michigan to my hometown of Highland Park and visited some of my former neighbors. Doc Canmann, who had been my pediatrician as well as our neighbor, was ninety-three that fall. We reminisced about those days when all the neighborhood kids played in his yard while his sweet wife watched out for us.

I cruised along the scenic North Shore with great enjoyment. It is a lovely area, cursed only by dreadful weather. In October, the beauty was breathtaking. I played tourist, snapping pictures of Lake Michigan. I swung by our former home on Indian Tree Drive, which had been enlarged and remodeled over the years. On impulse, I knocked on the door, in case anyone inside wondered why I was photographing the house. The nanny let me tour the house; three little girls lived there with their doctor parents, just as the three girls of my family had.

The real estate market had taken a turn for the worse when we'd sold the house after Mom died. Now the market had recovered, and with the over-the-top remodeling (it even had a butler's pantry!), it was now close to a million-dollar property. I think that would have surprised my mom.

Barbara's wedding was a fancy affair at her brother Michael's suburban country club. Cocktail party-attired guests swirled everywhere.

No cocktail attire and fancy shoes for me; I don't even own a cocktail dress. I wore a regular dress—nice but not fancy—with sturdy Merrell Jungle Mocs, which helped me walk without disaster. They mostly matched the dress. I had a large backpack instead of a purse so my hands would be free if I needed to use my cane. Michael quietly put my backpack out of sight in a closet, but I didn't care that I had the dumpy old lady look; I was just happy to be able to stump along with my cane.

After the visits, the shopping, and the wedding, I returned home in a wonderful mood, ready to return to teaching.

To keep my spirits up at home, there were the boys—our cat, Matthew, and the kittens, Frank and Cowboy Joe—and Tipper the Wonder Husky to play with. There were horses—Marcie, Scooter, and Hannah—to take care of, talk to, and ride after school.

Knowing that Marcie was there for me, whether I called it rehabilitation or training, was a huge comfort. Marcie was a stable, reliable mount for rehab riding. My rehab team included excellent professionals, from trauma surgeon and physical therapist to Pilates trainer and massage therapist, but Marcie, my lovely old mare, gave me equine therapy, which was the best rehabilitation modality of all.

I visited school the day before my official return to work and told some staff members hanging out in the lounge that I was going riding that afternoon. They looked at me in surprise. Was I really going to ride horses again?

I was equally surprised by their question. I asked them, "Have you ever had a car accident?"

Heads nodded.

"Do you still drive?"

"Of course," someone said.

"It's the same," I said. "What happened was a freak accident. My surgeon said one millimeter's difference in the way I hit the ground would have avoided disaster." I shrugged. "I've had more car mishaps than equine incidents."

I returned to school on Friday, November 5. We were supposed to begin the unit on genetics. Instead, I spent the day debriefing the kids about my summer and fall semester and showed them the X-rays of my fracture with the huge screws holding things together. They listened with rapt attention.

Despite my dedication to recovery, I was still scared of going through the school hallways packed with students rushing to classes.

I didn't want to be junior high roadkill, so I waited in out-of-the-way pockets until passing period was over before moving from place to place. Other than that, I got around all right, but I was definitely looking forward to welcoming a student teacher during spring semester.

On the last day of school before winter break, I was scheduled to check into the hospital again so Dr. Lundy, my trauma surgeon, could change the screws to a shorter size. I skipped breakfast, headed to school at my regular time, and taught as usual all morning. Earl picked me up at noon, and we headed to Poudre Valley Hospital.

The second surgery was a cakewalk compared to the first one: eleven minutes total surgery time, twenty-three hours total hospital time, a little fentanyl for pain (much easier on the system than morphine). Recovery at home was easier too; I didn't need any pain medication at all, and I was up and walking almost immediately.

That might have been the end of this particular story, were it not for my adventures with my new student teacher, Leah, and her horse, Dancer, less than two months later, in February.

Dancer was Leah's "dream horse," whom she'd gotten for free. Dancer was being treated for a leg injury, and Leah asked me to take a look at her. I packed my vet bag and took it with me to school on Friday.

Leah was an enthusiastic horse owner, but the horse hadn't had much training. I took one look at Dancer as Leah led her into the barn and thought that it was great that Leah could jump three-foot fences with this mare, but if Dancer didn't get in some solid ground training and learn manners, she had the capacity to seriously injure or kill someone.

Being aware of the danger, when I changed Dancer's leg bandage and put on a Furacin sweat (a type of bandage to keep heat on the injured leg), I knelt on the concrete floor of the barn with the knee of my injured leg on the concrete. I kept my left foot flat on the floor, my left knee up, ready to launch myself with my good leg away from

Dancer, should she blow up. Most of my body weight was on my bad leg.

Dancer behaved herself, but by the time we finished, I could feel how big a mistake I'd made by positioning myself bad-leg-down on the concrete. I was in agony.

The next day, Saturday, Earl and I went for a short ride. Earl was on Marcie; I was on Scooter. Thirty minutes in, I was in so much pain that we had to stop. Earl untacked the horses and loaded them up, and we drove home in silence.

By Sunday morning, I could barely walk. I called the Orthopaedic Center, and Dr. Lundy happened to be on call. He was getting his kids ready for church. I was near tears from the pain and was panicking. In a gentle voice, he asked me what was wrong. I told him about the pain and that I could barely walk. He said to skip breakfast and go to the hospital for X-rays.

No breakfast? Did that mean he thought I'd have surgery that day?

Well, that ship had sailed—I'd already had my oatmeal and apple juice.

The X-rays were unspectacular, but my leg steadily declined. I dug out my crutches and started using them again. Soon, it hurt when I got out of a chair, and the pain continued for the first few steps after getting up. Not too bad after that, which is not a good sign.

The symptoms were classic for avascular necrosis, or death of the bone from lack of blood supply. My hip was dead.

I called Dr. Lundy's office and made an appointment. Strongly suspecting what we'd find, I also called the office of Dr. Kirk Kindsfater, the total hip replacement surgeon, and scheduled an office appointment with him for hip replacement surgery for the Tuesday of spring break. I knew how busy Dr. Kindsfater's schedule was, and if I had to have another surgery, I wanted it to be when school wasn't in session.

Dr. Lundy's voice was soft when he broke the news to me. "Mary, this is the first time I'm thinking this won't work out for you." He showed me the new set of radiographs, and I knew I would be keeping my appointment for the total hip replacement.

Even though I'd expected this and understood what I had to do, I began to cry. I'd followed all the rules, spent my required eight weeks on crutches, done all the therapy, behaved myself during my long-term sick leave from school, and had the screws swapped out. And yet my fracture repair had failed.

Although kneeling on the concrete floor to work with Dancer had triggered this latest crisis, I suspect it wasn't the actual cause. I think it was probably game over when I hit the ground after coming off Hannah. The impact had smashed and trashed my blood supply to the injury site, causing more damage than just the severe bruising that turned my leg and backside black for weeks afterward.

I was originally scheduled for surgery late Tuesday afternoon, but thanks to a cancellation, they moved me up to seven in the morning, which meant a five thirty check-in time at the hospital. There was a short delay because I had specified that an MD anesthesiologist perform the spinal anesthesia and monitor me during surgery. The staff hadn't planned for that and had to wake up the doctor, who rushed over.

The spinal anesthesia was cool. I had to sit over the side of the bed so that the doctor could access my back. I had to grasp a nurse's arm for balance. First, the doctor injected a local anesthetic so the spinal wouldn't hurt. Then she began the spinal itself.

It was a fascinating experience. First, my feet became paralyzed. The paralysis moved upward until it reached my waist. I couldn't help but think about Socrates drinking hemlock and being forced to walk around; he would have experienced the same sensations.

In the OR, I was catheterized, then rolled onto my left side, with my right hip up. My arms were tied to splints, one of top of the other, so I could be given continuous sedation.

It took Dr. Kindsfater fifty-five minutes to replace my dead hip with a new stainless-steel model.

I don't remember a thing about the actual surgery. I learned later that during the surgery, Dr. Kindsfater discovered my hip had a non-union fracture—that is, the break had never healed. He could actually toggle the pieces of my femur back and forth. I wonder what Newton would have said about that.

Dr. Kindsfater retrieved the screws that had done their best to hold my hip together. I added them to my original set; they had cost $500 apiece, bringing the grand total value of my six-screw set to $3,000. Alas, he refused to let me have my bone as a souvenir.

When I awoke in the post-anesthetic care unit (PACU), my legs were spread-eagled, with a pillow between my feet. That's how I had to sleep for the next six weeks.

I was wheeled to my room, where Earl met me. I kept asking him, "When are they going to put me into a bed?"

"You are in a bed," Earl said.

"No, I'm on the transfer gurney," I insisted. "Call the nurses to put me into a bed."

"Look around."

My "gurney" was where beds were placed in the room; I was indeed in a bed, not on a transfer gurney. The OR staff had placed me in the bed, positioned with a pillow between my feet, so I wouldn't have to be transferred while awake.

I still felt disoriented, but I finally accepted the fact that, yes, this was a bed, and I was in it.

A spinal takes effect from the feet up; it wears off from the abdomen down. Nurses came in regularly to draw a line with their fingers on my abdomen, asking me, "Can you feel this?"

The answer for most of the day was "nope," but as the day wore on, I could say "yes" to higher points on my abdomen. By the next morning, I was back to normal, my abdomen covered with ink timelines.

This time, there was no physical therapy. Nurses, doctors, and everyone else hammered the message into my brain that I was to stay off the leg and sleep on my back with a pillow between my feet. There would be no PT at home either; rehab for total hip replacement would involve taking it easy for six weeks and using crutches to move from one spot to the next. After that, it would involve walking and other ordinary day to day activities.

I was supposed to stay home for six weeks.

Hip replacement surgery wasn't nearly as painful as fracture surgery. By three weeks post-op, I no longer needed any pain meds. I was also bored.

I found I could drive pretty soon after surgery. After the accident, I hadn't been allowed to drive for five weeks, but I didn't have any restrictions this time around, beyond the "no weight bearing" and "pillow between feet while sleeping" commands. I was also under strict orders to not flex my new hip past ninety degrees, to guard against dislocating it.

Dr. Lundy renewed my handicapped parking hangtag, upgrading it from a temporary tag to a permanent one. Because of the way I had to position my hip, I couldn't reach down to adjust the seat of my Subaru, so I used my little Mercedes as my rehab car. It was lower to the ground but had electric seat adjustments.

Being able to get myself where I needed to go and feeling the need for something more interesting than sitting at home, I decided to return to school. Leah, my student teacher, was still teaching by herself, supervised by others; I only had to be there to oversee her activities. I spent most of my time in the office, planning lessons for the end of the school year.

Leah's time with me was ramping down just before the practical exam for the fetal pig unit. Exam setup was my last day on crutches, and I had a doctor's appointment after school, so I fudged a little and walked carefully around the classroom without crutches. I did keep them close by, and I used them to get from station to station, but that didn't prevent Nikki, one of my students, from scolding me. "Now,

Doctor C., you have to use your crutches!" I wasn't surprised to learn that Nikki grew up to be a nurse.

After missing almost half the school year, I suppose I shouldn't have been surprised that I was missing from the yearbook too. But on the last day of school—a half-day, when the kids spend pretty much all the class time outside signing their yearbooks—I was battling the beginnings of what would turn out to be a killer three-day migraine. I thumbed through the yearbook and discovered that I hadn't been included. Sure, I'd missed photo day, but they could have run the one from the previous year, couldn't they? They didn't even mention my name as "not pictured." I felt invisible, as if I'd never existed at the school. The headache made the omission feel even worse, so when the kids were released to wait for the buses, I told an office staff member I was leaving and crawled home to take my migraine medication and go to sleep.

The migraine didn't let up. I missed the staff lunch, missed the surprise announcement that our principal was retiring, missed every-thing. Thursday was more of the same agony. On Friday, feeling a little better, I emerged long enough to attend an end-of-year party at a teacher's house, but I paid for it the next day. I was back in bed again, writhing in pain: an awful end to a miserable year.

When the migraine finally released me, I noticed that summer was truly here. It had been almost a year since my accident. I wasn't allowed to ride yet, but I'd been walking, feeding the horses, and giving Marcie her acupuncture treatments.

The earliest I was allowed to ride was June 15, two weeks after Marcie's birthday. I hated waiting! I needed to be on my horse. A few days before the fifteenth, we put the saddle and hackamore on Marcie, and I climbed up.

It was tough getting up on Marcie. The stretch felt weird, although my hip didn't hurt.

But I was up! I was sitting on my beloved Marcie. It was my first time on horseback since that painful day on Scooter, the day after I'd helped Leah with Dancer. And I didn't ride; I just sat.

I raised my hands in triumph, and Earl took my photo to send to Dr. Kindsfater. (I'm not riding! I'm just sitting!)

It was a perfect day, with perfect weather: sunny, warm, clear, everything green and beautiful. And I was sitting on my horse.

With a small regretful sigh, I slid down after a few minutes. It wasn't enough, but it would have to do.

Looking back on that year of orthopedic misery and the year that followed, I realize Marcie launched me too—not high into the air the way Hannah did but back into a lifetime of horseback riding.

Snow Day!

Several months after my hip replacement, a monster blizzard descended on Fort Collins.

Snow day!

No school, no work, no necessary errands to run; nothing but staying snug at home.

Tipper was more of a house dog than Keli had been. Keli preferred to be outside, even in extreme cold; we had to insist that she sleep inside when the temperature dropped too low. Tipper preferred inside, and during the Great Blizzard of 2006, she wanted to be in the house. That was fine, but before settling down for the night, she needed to go outside to do her usual business. That meant getting her from the house to her pen and back again.

Three feet of snow covered the ground, with a higher pile of it along the walk where Earl had shoveled a path to the dog pen. A nice walled walkway; no need for a leash. I could just walk with her to the pen and back.

We stepped outside.

Tipper vanished into the snow.

Had I learned nothing in all those years of Keli's adventures or from Tipper's escape from Nancy's yard?

I couldn't follow her; I could barely walk, let alone run high-stepping through the drifts.

I didn't see her anywhere. I finally climbed into the pickup truck and drove slowly around the block, hoping she'd surface. I looped the neighborhood just once; the roads were in terrible shape and unsafe. No one else was out, which was a small comfort; it was unlikely she'd get hit by a car.

Mortified by my carelessness and stupidity, I called Animal Control and told them that my dog was on the loose. They reassured me that because of the blizzard, they weren't ticketing anyone. I was halfway through giving them Tipper's description when I glanced out the kitchen window and saw a dog speeding by the house.

It was Tipper! Holy crap!

I dropped the phone and opened the back door to yell for her, but I didn't have to: she was sitting right there, like the obedient dog I'm sure she thought she was, waiting for the door to open. She was covered in snow and panting like a champion sled dog who'd just won the Iditarod.

What to do?

The only thing to do was compliment her profusely for being a good dog. As far as she was concerned, she *was* a good doggie; she had come home and was sitting on the stoop, and I'd opened the door within the three seconds her memory could track the action—returning to the back door—with my praise. Her running off in the first place was well beyond the three-second limit; she'd long since forgotten that action. Scolding her now wouldn't help prevent a future escape.

I welcomed her home and promised myself that I'd never again forget that huskies are born and bred to race through the snow.

A Life Well-Lived

It is never easy to make the ultimate decision about animal family members. Being a veterinarian doesn't change that.

On Monday, Marcie's last day, Earl and I stood with her in her stall at the vet hospital. That long day of medical exams and tests had confirmed what we'd already suspected: it was time.

Earl preferred not to watch the euthanasia, so he stood outside the padded anesthesia induction stall. I couldn't *not* watch; I realized that this was something I had to do myself, for my best girl.

The equine staff of the CSU hospital inserted the catheter into Marcie's jugular vein. They administered the anesthetic, and Marcie sank down into slumber.

A tech handed me the first of two syringes filled with the euthanasia solution. I inserted the syringe into the catheter and quickly depressed the plunger into the thick liquid, then swapped out the empty syringe for the second one and administered the last of the solution.

I knelt beside Marcie, speaking softly to her and stroking her head and neck, and watched our beautiful friend drift peacefully out of this life and into the next.

The next morning, halfway through my bowl of Rice Krispies, I said to Earl, "Let's go watch the necropsy."

I don't know that being a veterinarian makes it easier to watch the necropsy of an animal you've treasured. I do know that, to me, the physical body left behind wasn't Marcie. Even so, I was a little worried that my breakfast cereal wouldn't sit well during the procedure. I hadn't originally planned on observing Marcie's necropsy, but now, this morning, I was determined to attend.

Earl and I sat in the viewing area. Marcie's body lay on its side on the concrete floor of the necropsy room. It took me a moment to get used to seeing my dead horse on the floor, but my Rice Krispies stayed put.

The vet students made a long incision beginning under the chin and continuing down Marcie's chest. They began pulling out the "pluck," which includes the tongue, trachea, lungs, and associated structures. They'd gotten as far as the tongue when the lab supervisor said, "Stop!" and immediately called for Marcie's medical team from the day before.

When Marcie's team arrived, the lab supervisor explained that they'd found something significant.

There was a fist-sized tumor on the far back of Marcie's tongue. It had grown large enough, and was positioned in just the right spot, to begin blocking her airway. The blocked airway explained her abnormal breathing during our Saturday ride.

The tumor was a squamous cell carcinoma. Those are fairly common, but it was in an extremely rare location. No one, student or longtime vet, had ever seen this before. Even if we'd known for sure that the tumor was causing Marcie's problems, we wouldn't have been able to save her. The tumor's location couldn't have been reached surgically, and Marcie's advanced age—she was thirty, which is quite old for a horse—would have made the surgery itself extremely risky.

We had our diagnosis and left the necropsy comforted by the knowledge that we had done the right thing for our sweet Marcie.

I had attended equine rounds during every one of Marcie's frequent hospitalizations for colic, so it seemed only right that I attend pathology rounds the Friday after she died. In many ways, it was no different from what I had always done for her, even though this time it was the last rounds presentation about her. I made my way to the observation area outside the necropsy room. A line of trays inside the room held the organs of the various animals that would be the topics of this morning's rounds. Marcie's pluck was on the first tray, the cancerous mass on her tongue clearly visible.

Before pathology rounds began, the students on Marcie's case gave me a hoof print with Marcie's name embedded in it and a gorgeous braid they'd made from her tail skirt (the long hairs of her tail) with a pale green ribbon woven in. Before Earl and I had taken Marcie to the hospital, I'd brushed her thoroughly, put a rubber band around a thick hank of her white mane, and clipped it close to the skin. I have kept and cared for these precious mementos ever since.

My mom always said that kids should not have pets or grandparents because they just lead to grief and tears, but there is a lot to be said for the human-animal bond. I am a believer that things happen for a reason. I believe that Marcie lived so happily in her last year to help me relearn riding three times after the misery of my orthopedic trauma, which had begun the year before. After the broken hip, after surgery to replace the screws, and after surgery to replace the hip, Marcie was there, helping me recover and ride again. I was heartbroken that she was gone, and I was grateful she'd been with me for this tough journey.

Earl and I weren't the only ones who grieved Marcie's passing. Scooter whinnied all that night and into the next day, looking for her after we returned with an empty trailer. Hannah seemed puzzled that there was no one to trade stalls with to search for after-dinner morsels. Our dogs and cats knew too.

There is a quote from Stephen King's book *Pet Sematary* that still brings me comfort: ". . . time passes, and time welds one state of human feeling into another, until they become something like a rainbow. Strong grief becomes a softer, more mellow grief; mellow grief becomes mourning; mourning at last becomes remembrance . . ."

The story "Rainbow Bridge" gives me hope for the future, with no fear of death when it comes.

The Rainbow Bridge

There is a bridge connecting Heaven and Earth.

It is called the Rainbow Bridge because of its many colors. Just this side of the Rainbow Bridge is a land of meadows, hills, and valleys, all of it covered with lush green grass.

When a beloved pet dies, the pet goes to this lovely land. There is always food and water and warm spring weather. There, the old and frail animals are young again. Those who are maimed are made whole once more. They play all day with each other, content and comfortable.

There is only one thing missing. They are not with the special person who loved them on Earth. So each day they run and play until the day comes when one suddenly stops playing and looks up! The eyes are staring! You have been seen, and that one suddenly runs from the group!

You take him or her in your arms and embrace. Your face is kissed again and again and again, and you look once more into the eyes of your trusting pet.

Then, together, you cross the Rainbow Bridge, never again to be separated.

Author Unknown

I know that she will be there at the Rainbow Bridge, ready to carry me over riding joyfully on her back.

Marcie had what we all hope for: a life well-lived.

Ten Days

I didn't want to talk about it, let alone write about it. He got sick, and he died. It happened at the same time Tipper got sick and died. What more is there to say? How can I possibly explain the anguish that comes from such profound loss? Why would I want to remind myself of that pain? Why would I want to burden anyone else with it?

It started with what looked like a scrape on his face, near his right temple. Earl, like many of us who had spent so much time outdoors in the days when no one thought about sunscreen, had had several basal cell skin cancers removed over the years. This didn't look like one of those. When I asked, Earl shrugged it off and said it was nothing.

The scrape didn't heal. By December, it had expanded to a large, round lesion covering most of his temple.

I spent Christmas week in Chicago, visiting my cousins. Earl stayed home to concentrate on finishing the paper he would be presenting at the North American Veterinary Conference (NAVC) in January. Two days before we left for the conference, his dermatologist used the Mohs technique to remove the rapidly growing squamous cell carcinoma from his face.

Layer after layer of cancer cells were removed, leaving a clean and cancer-free border—and an incision from Earl's temple down his face to about the level of his ear. And sutures—his face was a forest of black suture threads. Not the most handsome face to put before an audience, but at least the worst was over, we thought.

We flew into Orlando, Florida, and met up with Earl's mom, who had invited us to stay with her at her vacation condo. On Saturday, January 17, 2009, we both attended Earl's presentation, "An Analysis of Greyhound Injuries: a 14-Year Study." Bev returned home, and Earl and I treated ourselves to a night in a plush hotel, a nice dinner, a visit to one of the free Disney venues, and the just-released movie *Marley and Me*. It was a peaceful, relaxing trip, a brief vacation we both needed.

Our flight home was on January 19, the day before President Obama's inauguration. Once home, all Earl wanted to do was sleep—unusual, but perhaps not surprising, considering how hard he'd been pushing himself and that he'd just had extensive facial surgery.

Inauguration Day was the same. I went by myself to retrieve our horses from where we'd boarded them during our travels, then picked up Tipper from the kennel. I was a little concerned that Earl didn't want to watch the inauguration; we both shared an intense interest in politics, and Obama's inauguration would be one for the history books.

Follow-up tests revealed that the cancer had metastasized into Earl's facial lymph nodes.

One of the questions we ask when cancer appears is, "What caused it?" Often, there isn't a clear-cut answer. In Earl's case, the cancer, and everything that came after, had its beginnings in his kidney transplant.

When he was born, Earl's kidneys were swollen due to a blockage that prevented urine from draining properly, a condition called bilateral hydronephrosis. Surgery corrected the problem, and although his kidneys were damaged, they did their job well enough through his childhood. They began failing in his teens, and he started dialysis when he was seventeen. He had a kidney transplant in 1970, when he was eighteen and the procedure was still relatively new. His Uncle Ralph was his donor.

He'd done well with his transplant for thirty-nine years—he was one of the longest surviving transplant recipients at that time—but the antirejection drugs suppress the immune system, and that increases the risk of certain cancers, including skin cancers.

The next step would be radiation treatments. First, a form-fitting mask would be created. The mask would keep Earl's head positioned properly so the machine would target the specific areas in his face to be irradiated. If all went as hoped, the treatment would eradicate the cancer. It would also damage his salivary glands and temporarily destroy his ability to taste anything. With no sense of taste, most people won't eat enough, so standard procedure is to install a feeding tube, also called a stomach or gastrostomy tube, through which supplemental nutrients are administered.

Earl also had an incisional hernia—a hernia that had formed long ago at the site of his transplant incision. It had worsened and now needed repair. On March 11—our wedding anniversary—Earl had successful surgery to repair the hernia. At the end of March, his doctors gave the go-ahead for the radiation treatment preparations.

But before anyone could jump into surgeries for stomach tubes, I pointed out that Earl, who was fifty-seven, had never had a colonoscopy; perhaps we should start there.

The GI specialist who performed the colonoscopy identified a large mass. He was certain the mass was colon cancer.

In early April, fairly soon after the colonoscopy, Earl's surgeon removed the suspicious mass, along with half of Earl's colon.

I had dozed off in the waiting room. I woke when the nurse liaison knelt down in front of me and rested his hand on my forearm. He looked me straight in the eyes and said, "It is not cancer." Relief flooded through me: finally, some good news.

The mass was a benign tumor that had formed from platelets

clumping, which had its origins in a patent foramen ovale that had been discovered a little over a year earlier. The foramen ovale is a "hole in the heart" that usually closes and seals shut soon after birth. In about 25 percent of people, it doesn't close ("patent" means "open"). For most of them, the hole doesn't cause problems, even though blood leaks from the right atrium to the left. They'll never know they have it unless it's discovered while testing for something else. In Earl's case, his thumb turned so blue it was purple, and I nagged him to get it checked out. That was in December 2007. I remember the timing so well because on Friday, December 28, as we were leaving to pick up the test results, I got the call telling me that my closest friend, Jean, had just died after her six-month battle with gastroesophageal cancer. I'd spent almost all my time with her during the months she was sick. I'd only returned home for dental work on Thursday and Earl's doctor's appointment on Friday.

After the colon surgery, Earl's liver began to fail. His kidney was fine, but a biopsy showed cirrhosis of the liver, most likely caused by years of taking the antirejection drugs necessary to keep the kidney safe and him alive. The cirrhosis had created a body full of fluid, and his abdomen swelled with it, a condition called ascites.

Fluid began building up in Earl's chest. He was having trouble breathing. His entire stomach had crossed the diaphragm and was now in his chest cavity. We were heading for another surgery. My mother-in-law, Bev, came to Fort Collins for a short visit to help out.

In mid-April, the doctors inserted the stomach tube. Earl had trouble with the anesthesia and landed in the intensive care unit. When the surgeon came into the recovery room, his mask still in place, I asked him if Earl was critical. After a long pause, he said, "Yes."

Bev turned away and said, "Damn it."

Earl was in and out of the hospital all of April. I finished settling Jean's estate in April too—she'd named me as her personal representative—and finally let myself cry to Earl about losing my dear friend.

Throughout everything, Tipper and I had kept up with our usual routines of daily walks, pets, and playing. Then, in mid-April, I noticed that she seemed to be having trouble eating. A few days later, while Earl was resting, I was petting her and noticed that the lymph nodes in her neck were hard and swollen. Our dear friend and go-to vet, Dr. John Mulnix, thought it was because her teeth were acting up again, so she underwent dental surgery.

Despite the tooth extractions, Tipper started to slow down.

The problem wasn't her teeth.

At the end of April, a needle biopsy revealed that the swelling was lymphoma, a common type of cancer in older animals. Tipper was twelve years old, which is fairly old for a large dog, and lymphoma treatment doesn't have a great outcome in dogs. Earl and I would rather Tipper have four months of feeling pretty good without medicine than eight months—the best we could hope for—during which she would feel miserable from the treatment. Better her final days were happy and comfortable, we decided.

In early May, my mother-in-law came back to Fort Collins to keep an eye on Earl as he recovered from his latest round of hospitalizations, so that I could drive to Lubbock, Texas, to visit the campus of the Texas Tech University School of Law, where I'd applied before any of this began and had been accepted for admission to begin in July. When I returned home, Earl seemed okay, or at least no worse than when I'd left. But fluid continued to build up in his abdomen, and he felt terrible.

At the same time, lymphoma was taking a toll on The Wonder Husky. One day in mid-May, Tipper and I went on our regular walk around the neighborhood. About a fourth of the way in, she stopped in the middle of the street and wouldn't move ahead. She just stood there until I turned us around, and we made our sad way home. That was her last walk for exercise.

Tipper always slept inside, often pressed against the back door. By late May, she couldn't get up when I came through in the wee hours of the morning, after spending the day at the hospital with Earl and then cleaning the barn. Cleaning the barn at two in the morning may sound odd, but I derived a lot of comfort from it. When I'd finished in the barn, almost tired enough to sleep, I'd have to push the door hard enough to slide Tipper across the floor so I could enter. Once I helped her up to all fours, she could still walk, though sometimes I had to run a towel under her like a body sling to help her along.

She was no longer a happy dog. She had that look in her eyes that animals get when they're close to death. I knew it was time.

Earl was in the hospital again, and I couldn't stand the thought of that "last ride" for Tipper, so John—Dr. Mulnix—agreed to come to the house early on the morning of June 2 to euthanize Tipper.

The night before, I slept on Tom's old couch in the family room, Tipper by my side, a DVD movie playing so I could fall asleep.

It had been raining and hailing on and off all spring, turning our corral into a small lake. The next morning, it was pouring rain again. I heard Tipper's tags rattle; she was standing ramrod straight at the back door in her "I have to go out" position. I let her walk along the sidewalk at her own pace. It was really quite beautiful at six o'clock. Everything smelled so good—the blooming peonies in our flower garden, the spruce and pine trees in our yard, the wet grass.

We stopped by the barn so she could see the horses for the last time. Then I took her in the house and fed her a peanut butter and jelly sandwich laced with pain meds and tranquilizers, which she snarfed down. She had reached the point where I was feeding her anything so she would eat at all; regular dog food was not on her end-stage cancer menu.

John arrived promptly at seven in the morning and gave her an anesthetic before administering the euthanasia solution. The instant he gave her the stinging shot, I gave her a Hershey bar to distract her. Chocolate is extremely toxic for dogs, but chocolate was not going to be her cause of death this day.

I told her to go to bed, and she obediently went into her crate. I stroked her beautiful head as she fell asleep for the last time.

After Tipper was peacefully released, I asked John if he would have someone come take her crate away so I could put the house back in order before Earl came home the next time from the hospital. We threw the crate into the backyard so that one of John's staff members could pick it up when they had time.

We wrapped Tipper's body in a large black bag and carried her to John's car, a Porsche, which I thought was perfect, as she had been a good dog and deserved the best. I confirmed that we wanted Tipper cremated and her ashes saved. I already knew that I'd keep them beside Keli's, in a discreet place in the living room where visitors wouldn't notice them.

Earl had been taken by ambulance and admitted to the hospital the day before Tipper's euthanasia. It was his fifth admission that spring. When I arrived at his room, I hung Tipper's collar from his IV pole. He was conscious but so ill that he didn't notice her hot-pink dog tag.

He came home again on June 4. We woke up early that next morning, June 5. I remember thinking that it was my late mother's birthday. Earl said he wanted to feed the horses. I asked him if he wanted me to come with him. He said no.

I honored his request, but I peeked through the bedroom window curtains and watched him make his way to the barn. I didn't want him to think I was spying on him, but he was so weak, I worried that he'd fall. He didn't; he went slowly about his tasks and made his way back to the house unattended.

Later that day, I was at the eye center ordering new computer glasses. Earl called, literally breathless, saying he couldn't breathe.

His mother was there at the house with him but never called 911. *What could she be thinking?*

I called 911 immediately from the eye center and bolted out the door. I ignored every speed limit and got home just as the ambulance arrived.

At the hospital, Earl's doctors inserted two painful tubes in his chest and began pulling fluid out of his pleural and mediastinal cavities. They discovered that the fluid from both sites was infected, one with bacteria and the other with a fungus. The bacterial infection might be treatable, but the fungal infection had a 99 percent mortality rate.

Earl never came home again. A week later, he sank into a coma and died, surrounded by his family, just before one in the afternoon on June 12.

It's funny what you remember. On June 9, I'd called my sister-in-law, who is a nurse, to come to Fort Collins to help my mother-in-law, who was coming apart at the seams. My sister-in-law brought my niece Olivia. They stayed in our little guest room while Earl was in the hospital. On June 10, my sister-in-law informed me that she would stay with Earl at night. It felt like she was ordering me out of Earl's hospital room. Overwhelmed, I said okay. At seven thirty in the morning on June 12, Olivia woke me abruptly, saying, "We have to go, we have to go!" Her mom had just called her to say something bad had happened.

I knew the horses still needed to be fed, so I called the surgical floor where Earl was and asked the nurses for a status report. They said, "Yes, we think it's a coma." I needed to come, but there was no reason to rush.

I fed the horses and drove to the hospital. Olivia's sister, Amanda, had flown in. I asked her for oatmeal; I couldn't remember when I'd last eaten, and I knew I needed something in my stomach. She found some in the hospital floor pantry, which is stocked with simple foods for patients and visitors.

I called Terry, our insurance agent and one of Earl's closest friends, and asked him to contact the funeral home to tell them we would need them today. Terry came by immediately, in tears. The room was crowded with Earl's relatives, who had taken all the available seating. I was relegated to the windowsill, far from the bed.

Friends and other doctors visited, not knowing how sick Earl was; they just happened to stop by on that morning. As the morning wore on, I quietly pointed out Earl's blue fingernails to my sister-in-law, who just nodded. Later, Earl's arm was blue; his circulatory system was shutting down.

We asked Earl's doctor how long he thought it would be. He said it could be as long as three days.

It was three hours.

Immediately after Earl died, Amanda screamed, and then she and the rest of Earl's relatives left. I remembered how the family had deserted Bill, my father-in-law, right after he died; Amanda had screamed then too. I don't know how long I stayed beside Earl; I only know that eventually, several hours after the resident doctor had pronounced Earl dead, the chaplain came in the room and gently said, "You know, there are things the nurses need to do. . . ." I knew he was right. I nodded and found my way to the car and home.

Ten days: that's what I kept thinking. Ten days between putting Tipper to sleep and my husband dying. I thought I would be crushed by the weight of the pain.

I think I was crushed, for a long time. But I was determined to remember the deep friendship Earl and I had had, fostered first through the horses, a friendship and love that deepened and sustained us in our twenty-seven years of marriage. I was determined to remember all the fun we'd had with Tipper the Wonder Husky, to remember her love of snow and all things naughty, to remember our laughter at her silly dog tricks and sneaky antics.

And I realize now that, even though I will always grieve for them, sharing their stories, even the hard stories, honors and celebrates the gift of sharing our lives with each other.

27

The Cobalt-Blue Bag

Ashes. What do you do with ashes?

My father-in-law's ashes were in a pine box urn. His wish had been to be scattered at the family cabin by the Cache la Poudre River, but my mother-in-law had kept the box next to her bed. I shuddered. No way was I sleeping with my dead husband's ashes.

Keli's ashes were in a lacquered heart-shaped box on a shelf in the living room. Tipper's ashes were in another box, beside Keli's, identical except for the amount of accumulated dust. A smaller heart-shaped box on the same shelf held the ashes of Kitty Alexander, the twenty-pound tuxedo cat.

The boxes were sealed, but I'd opened one to peek inside: just ashes in a plastic bag. Looking at them didn't feel creepy or scary. Even though I'd loved those pets and still missed them, looking at their ashes and the decorated boxes didn't trigger new waves of grief.

But putting Earl's ashes on the shelf . . . well, that didn't seem right. I was sure Earl didn't want to be on the shelf either. Besides, I'd be moving to Texas when winter came, to attend Texas Tech University's School of Law. My acceptance letter had come after Earl's health began failing, and the dean had allowed me to defer my entry for a year. So no more ashes on the living room shelf. Plus, I doubted that Earl would want to be in Texas any more than he'd want to be stuck on a shelf. He'd always been a Wyoming man, through and through.

The only thing I knew for certain was that he hadn't wanted a church service. He'd been emphatic about that, not that it had stopped his family from having one anyway.

My mother-in-law, Bev, was staying at Earl's and my house—technically, her house, since we'd been renting it from her and Earl's dad from the beginning, despite my wanting to buy it when we married—while I prepared for the open house I was having for Earl. She'd wanted the open house the previous Tuesday, but I'd pointed out that since that was the same day that Earl's obituary would appear in the papers, no one would know yet that he'd died. She'd already been there for two months and had managed to steamroll a church service through. I'd just shrugged; everybody grieves in different ways, and if the service was what she needed, I figured it wouldn't bother Earl all that much. It did, however, bother me. Right after the service, the rest of Earl's family packed up and left. Bev announced that she'd stay until after the open house, because it was important that people see her.

The day after Earl's death, the funeral director met me at the house to discuss arrangements. Bev wouldn't come downstairs and made it clear by her action that she didn't want to have any input into these final decisions. So I met with the funeral director alone and said, "Cremation, save the ashes, no urn, I'll take care of the rest." Then I gave her a copy of the obituary I'd written the night before, when Bev and the rest of Earl's relatives had gone out to dinner without me to plan the unwanted church service.

And now it was four days later, and the funeral home had called and left a voice mail saying that they had "things for me to pick up." The "things" were Earl's ashes and the death certificates.

I pulled the car into the drive and turned off the engine. I stared at the cobalt-blue, faux-velvet bag on the seat beside me. The box containing Earl's ashes was inside the bag.

I sighed and pulled the bundle into my lap. I knew how upset my mother-in-law was. I knew that she'd been dealing with depression and insomnia for a long time, as well as so many deaths so close together. Earl was my husband, and he was her son. I could at least do her the small kindness of not displaying the ashes in a way that might cause her more pain. I had to admit that I didn't want to risk her disapproval either—I could imagine her berating me for not buying an urn to keep by my bedside.

I would scatter the ashes but only after Bev left, which wouldn't be for at least another week. For now, I had to stash the ashes somewhere, some spot where Bev wouldn't find them. That ruled out the house. I stared through the windshield, wishing I didn't have to deal with in-laws who clearly thought I was an interloper.

The house was never going to be mine anyway. She'd made that clear: after she died, her entire estate was going to Earl's sister. If I wanted to stay, she'd have her lawyer draw up a lease for me.

But I was moving to Lubbock for law school; I didn't care about the house. Without Earl, the house didn't feel like home anymore anyway.

I blinked away tears that were trying to form. I would not let my mother-in-law's issues derail me.

I missed Earl so much. I remembered watching him the last morning he was home, as he walked slowly to the barn to feed the horses.

What about the barn?

Earl had spent so much time in the barn with our horses, especially Scooter and Hannah, the last two horses we ever owned. Horses had brought us together at the beginning and were part of every important event of our shared lives. They'd brought us joy all the years we were married.

The barn.

I closed the car door softly behind me and carried the blue bag and its contents to the wide opening. I stepped through and stood for a long moment, inhaling the rich smells of hay, dirt, and horse. Late afternoon sun filtered through the doorway. I took a deep breath and made my way to the hay room.

Stacks of hay bales lined the room. I gently laid the blue bundle on the center of a bale and stepped back to examine the result. I nodded to myself: this would do. It was safe and secure and protected from the weather. Bev never came into the barn, so she'd never find it. If she asked, I would simply shrug and say that the ashes were safe.

Tux, a feral black-and-white cat who'd adopted our neighborhood as his mousing grounds, strolled in to offer a second opinion. He leapt onto the bale and curled up next to the blue bag. When I came out the next morning to feed the horses, I discovered Tux snuggled up asleep in the same spot. Tux slept next to the bag every night after that.

We made it through the open house, though instead of "being seen," Bev spent the entire time in her bed in the guest room with the door closed. She finally emerged when the only visitors left were three of Earl's high school friends. Earl had been best man for one of them, John Duke. John had flown in from Utah just for the day and flew back that night. Now that was love and loyalty.

None of Earl's other relatives returned for the open house, and none of them ever contacted me again. Bev went home a few days later. For the next year, she would occasionally call me to complain about the state in which I'd left the house when I moved out, and then even those calls stopped.

After she'd left and I was alone in the house, I gave in to angry grief—not at Earl but at his family. Had they only put up with me for his sake? On our very first date back in 1977, I'd said to him, "You know I'm Jewish, don't you?"

He'd said yes and that it didn't matter—and to him, it didn't.

But his family . . . had their acceptance of me been just a show all those years? Was the awful behavior and their disregard for me that began when Earl died long-hidden anti-Semitism? Earl and I had had such a wonderful married life, and I had loved his family, especially his dad, our nieces, and his grandparents. Now, when I needed a family, they had abandoned me without warning, without reason.

I'd spent those long hours by Earl's bed after he died. Toward the end of the afternoon, we put Earl's few things into my car. Earl's sister announced, "We're going out to dinner. Are you okay getting home alone?"

Of course I wasn't okay. I was too numb to protest but not so numb that I wasn't suspicious of how dismissive she'd been. Later, I realized that none of them cared that Earl didn't want a church service, or maybe they didn't believe me or didn't believe that it mattered to me.

I called two friends and asked them to meet me at home. I spent the rest of the evening writing an obituary to send to four newspapers and, with my friends' help, cleaning up the rubble my sister-in-law and her daughter had left in the guest room.

Earl's relatives spent their evening planning a very strange church service to be held Monday afternoon. I was outnumbered and over-powered; there was nothing I could do to stop them.

I had called Sid, a longtime friend of Earl's who lived in Laramie, and invited her to the service. Early in our relationship, Earl had been worried that Sid and I might be jealous of each other—he'd taken Sid to the high school prom—but we never were. We became good friends instead.

Sid didn't come. Later, she told me that my mother-in-law had left a message on her answering machine telling her not to come to the service. My mother-in-law never mentioned it, of course, and neither Sid nor I ever figured out a reason Bev would do such a thing.

As my rage the night after Bev left wore itself out, I thought about what it was like to go through death and what we do with the remains—the ceremonial rituals, the actual disposition of the body, and honoring someone's wishes.

Dealing with death, whether it's a beloved human or cherished animal, is always daunting. In my veterinary practice, before I put a pet to sleep,

I always gave the owner several options. The language I used had to be courteous and comforting, a little cautious too. I never used the word "disposal"; that sounded too much like taking out the trash. A client couldn't dispose of a beloved cat's body any more than I could dispose of Earl's body. Instead, I said, "disposition": the *disposition* of the body.

Concerning the pet, there were three options.

The first option was to take the pet's body home and bury it. There is a city ordinance that bans this, but as a police officer once told me, no one goes around town checking for pet burials. I buried two cats, several songbirds, and Keli's raccoon in our orchard across the street from the house.

My old cat Pruney was the first to go into the ground of the orchard, in 1987, four months after I graduated from vet school.

She'd been diagnosed with chronic renal failure when she was fifteen, but she lived for another two years. Back then, there were only two methods of treatment. One was a special canned kidney failure diet. It didn't come in dry form like it does today.

Pruney hated the canned food and immediately went on a feline hunger strike. She lost more weight until I decided that chronic renal failure was better than starvation and returned her to her usual diet of Meow Mix, water, and milk.

The other treatment was subcutaneous (under the skin) administration of fluids to help flush out toxins that build up in the blood when the kidneys start to fail. Pruney never reached that stage of renal failure.

I just left her alone, rechecking her blood work on a regular basis, and Pruney went about her normal life in fine enough condition. That's the way it is with animals sometimes; they feel well even though their test results are awful. When my clients puzzled over this seeming contradiction, I always told them it was because animals don't read their lab work.

And in the end, Pruney didn't die of renal failure.

When Pruney was seventeen, the vet student and his wife who were renting our renovated chicken house got (wait for it . . .) a husky puppy. Unfortunately, they never trained the puppy. It hopped its fence and ran away frequently, usually into our yard.

One Friday afternoon, I returned home from work at the hospital and, as usual, called for Pruney using my special whistle display that told her to come into the house.

There was no response.

Oh well, I thought, *she'll be back later. Perhaps she climbed a tree or was munching on a mouse she'd caught in the barn.*

I changed my clothes to go running with Keli, as I did most days after work, but we didn't get far.

I opened the back door, and there, under the bush right by the door and the family room window, was Pruney.

She was alive but motionless in the dirt.

I called Earl's old clinic, which our friend Dr. John Mulnix had bought, and told them we were coming right over.

As we examined her, we found tiny maggots around her anus. That meant she must have been lying there all day under the bush and that there must have been a wound with dead tissue for them to eat; that's what maggots do.

When John and I carefully turned Pruney over, there was blood on the table. It matched the area where her neck had been before we rolled her over.

She was paralyzed from the head down and in a coma. The wound was from the vet student's husky; it had attacked Pruney, for no reason anyone would ever be able to identify beyond the husky's innate ability to hunt. I called Dr. Ingram, who had been my neurology professor at CSU, and asked him about options. Her radiographs were unconvincing about whether or not there was a fracture. On a seventeen-year-old cat, treatment was a poor option. The bottom line was there was nothing to be done but end her life.

We prepared to put Pruney to sleep.

She already had an IV line with fluids running. John let me sit in his office chair in the back so I could spend some time with Pruney on my lap. She wasn't in any pain, but I was a wreck. I sobbed and talked to the greatest cat of my whole life. I couldn't see through my tears and went through almost an entire box of Kleenex.

After a long time, I told John I was ready. He brought in the syringe filled with 1 cc of euthanasia solution. I asked, and he agreed to let me inject it into the IV line. Pruney slept away in my lap.

I left the clinic soaked with tears, carrying Pruney's body in her carrier.

Earl was at work, so I called my best friend, Nancy, to come over and be with me. She was eight months pregnant, so I did the grave digging. We wrapped Pruney in a towel, lowered her into the hole, and covered her with dirt. I made a cairn of flagstones on top of the refilled hole to prevent wildlife from disturbing the grave.

The second and third options for disposition of an animal body are variations on the same thing: cremation and not saving the ashes or cremation with the ashes returned to the owner. Keli and Tipper were too big for me to bury, and Kitty Al died in the winter, when the ground was too frozen to dig. So all three had been cremated, and we'd had their ashes returned to us.

So now I had the cremains of three pets and my husband.

Slowly, a plan began to form. Earl and Wyoming, always Wyoming. Those wide-open spaces, the sense that the Wild West was still there and always would be. Laramie, with the University of Wyoming and its football team, the Cowboys, Earl cheering them on every chance he got.

Earl's ashes belonged in Wyoming.

Wyoming also has wind, a lot of it, all the time.

If I was going to scatter Earl's ashes without literally scattering them to the wind, I needed to practice.

I also wanted my pets' ashes out of this house, which was no longer my home. And I didn't want to take the pet ashes with me when I moved.

I lifted the heart-shaped boxes from the shelf and lined them up in a row on the kitchen table. I could solve all those problems at the same time.

The next morning, I stood beside the dog pen Tipper and Keli had so loved. I remembered the currency in the dog feces, the horrible screech of the juvenile raccoons, the splash Keli made in the fishpond, the way the dogs frolicked with Marcie across the fence shared by the dog pen and the corral. This was the right place for them now.

I opened Keli's box and pulled out the plastic bag. I poured her ashes in a slow stream onto the ground of the dog pen. There was no wind; the ashes went straight down. I opened Tipper's box and repeated the procedure for her ashes. Still no wind. I tried to scatter a few ashes, but tossing them didn't work, so I went back to pouring. I sprinkled some into Tipper and Keli's husky holes, those spots they'd dug out for the comfort and luxury of sleeping in the snow. There were enough ashes to make a thin layer over everything.

When I was done, I put the boxes and bags in the trash and retrieved the smaller box. Alexander would not appreciate being mixed in with husky ashes, so I carried his box to the orchard. I poured a few of his ashes on Pruney's grave and the rest on Fletcher's. Pruney had been a solitary cat; Fletcher and Alexander had been buddies, so it felt right that most of Alexander's cremains would rest with Fletcher.

Mission accomplished: I felt reasonably confident that I could scatter Earl's ashes without making a mess of things.

There was still the question of exactly where in Wyoming. I tried to think like Earl. I have never met anyone as passionate about the University of Wyoming as my husband; he was even more devoted to that fine school than his father, and his father had been president of the university. Earl was a fanatic! His enthusiasm for UW and the Cowboys was obvious every day—most of his clothing was from UW.

I decided to take a chance. I called UW's sports information director, who'd been good friends with Earl. Would it be possible for me to scatter Earl's ashes on or near the football field at War Memorial Stadium? I expected him to say no; no one was allowed on that field, especially, I thought, if she wanted to scatter ashes.

Much to my amazement, Kevin said yes, he would arrange it.

Then I called two of Earl's friends, a UW professor named Dave and Sid, Earl's friend from high school. Both were enthusiastic about joining Kevin and me at the stadium.

I felt better than I had in weeks. I knew Earl would have been proud of me for coming up with such a unique plan for his ashes, and I was delighted that I'd connected with these dear friends of his.

The night before driving up to Laramie, I went to the barn to retrieve the cobalt-blue bag that held the box containing Earl's ashes. As usual, Tux was sleeping alongside. I nodded at him and said, "You'll have to be on your own again." I picked up the bundle, brushed the hay off it, and carried it back into the house.

That night, the blue bundle rested on the antique oak chair in the family room. I sat on the sofa beside it, surrounded by our three cats, watching TV.

Earl and I had had a mixed marriage—not Jewish and Christian but Mercedes and BMW. I bought my Mercedes Benz SLK 320 in 2004, six weeks before I fractured my hip. It was an award-winning show car in its early days, turned into my rehab car, and then became a parade car to chauffeur dignitaries. It was still my favorite car for the Fort Collins to Laramie drive. My man deserved the best, including zipping along that gorgeous stretch of 287 in a compact luxury roadster.

Of course, I'd have to slow down to pokey-old-lady speed once we crossed the state line into Wyoming. Wyoming State Patrol loved to nab speeders who had Colorado license plates, and one of their favorite hiding places was behind the "Welcome to Wyoming, Forever West" sign at the border.

Earl had talked his way out of more than one Wyoming patrol encounter. Once when we were homeward bound after a vacation road trip to South Dakota, he was cruising well above the speed limit. Wyoming's finest pulled him over.

Because Earl was wearing his Wyoming cap, he and the officer began a long conversation about UW. It felt like old home week out on the prairie south of Gillette. The officer remembered Earl's dad as UW president and, eventually, let Earl go without a ticket. After that, I always kept a Wyoming cap in my car—and added caps for every state I knew I'd be driving through on any trip. Safety ritual, good luck charm, or silly superstition to avoid a speeding ticket—I didn't care. It had worked for Earl, and maybe it would work for me too.

This morning, just to be extra safe, I was wearing my favorite UW attire, a brown-and-gold T-shirt with "Cowboy Nation" emblazoned across the chest.

We made it to Laramie without incident. I picked up Sid at her house, and after stopping at a local florist to buy lilies (yellow with brown spots, because UW's colors are brown and gold), we rendezvoused with Kevin and Dave at the north parking lot of the stadium.

I opened the blue bag and slid the box partway out. The return on cremains is about one pound of ashes for every ten pounds of original weight. Earl normally weighed about 150 pounds, but by the time he died, I doubt he weighed more than 120. That meant I had about twelve pounds of ashes to disperse.

I started scattering ashes at the north entrance outside of War Memorial Stadium. I thought that's all I'd be allowed to do.

But Kevin invited me onto the field.

"Oh . . . really?" I stammered, fighting off tears.

Kevin smiled, and we followed him through the gate. "You know, I wish Earl had called me more often for tickets," he said. Earl asked only occasionally, he explained, but he would have given him anything he wanted.

That's my Earl, I thought, *not wanting to take advantage of someone's generosity.* I was a little sad that he hadn't asked more often but grateful for Kevin's kind story about Earl.

Now that I was on the field, I placed some of the lilies on a statue called "Cowboy Tough." I realized how sheltered our spot near the entrance had been. The wind was blowing hard; there was nothing to get in its way. If I poured the ashes the same way I'd practiced, I'd end up coating our friends. I held the plastic bag close to the ground in the end zone and shook it carefully. Most landed on the ground, but I still managed to get some on Dave's pant legs.

Kevin suggested that I use the whole field. I didn't have to stay in one small spot, which would be better visually too. The field was a mixture of grass and synthetic grass, with crumbled rubber as the turf base. It was never vacuumed, groomed, or mowed much, which meant the cremains would pretty much stay where I put them. Spreading them out over the whole field would make them less noticeable.

I decided that twelve pounds wasn't much to scatter on the entire field, so I kept to the end zones and the fifty-yard line.

I finished the north end zone and walked to the image of the dark brown bucking bronco at the fifty-yard line. I bent low and scattered—or more accurately poured—a little heavier than I should have. Whoops! The white ashes made a striking—and extremely visible—contrast with the dark brown. I finally got the hang of it, scattering low and wide.

Finally, the south end zone. Sid held up a bone spicule and asked if she could have it. I said no, but she was welcome to take the blue bag and box and to use anything left in them for her flowerbed.

I straightened up, holding the bag with a few remaining ashes that I'd saved to put around Bill's memorial bench, a way of honoring Earl and his father's strong relationship with each other.

I gazed across the expanse of the football field, trying to memorize everything—and realized I'd left my camera in the car. "Would you mind if I ran back to the car?" I asked these three dear friends who had already spent so much of their day with me. "I'll try to be quick."

They graciously insisted that I retrieve my camera, and I took off at a run.

Technically, I wasn't supposed to run; the surgeon who'd replaced my hip had forbidden it. After my hip fracture and replacement, I'd fantasized about running the length of an athletic field on a warm, sunny day under a deep blue sky. And here I was, doing just that. I felt like Scarlett O'Hara finally realizing what her nightmare of running through the fog really meant in *Gone with the Wind*.

I took photos of the entire field and Bill's bench. Sid, Kevin, Dave, and I took pictures of each other. After I'd scattered the last of the ashes around the bench, Sid and I sat on it with the leftover lilies and posed for more photos.

Earl was now forever part of the University of Wyoming. Surrounded by the love and companionship of these good friends, comforted by their patience and gentleness, I felt the first step toward closure.

The four of us finally made our way back to our cars.

There was still the house to empty, horses to send to Arizona where my sister would care for them while I was in school, and the move to Texas itself—but all of that would come later. Today, I had taken care of my husband with joy and a peace of mind I hadn't felt in a very long time.

Suddenly, I was hungry. I hadn't eaten much since Earl had died, but now I was ready for a solid meal. Sid and I drove the Benz to the Village Inn for lunch. Afterward, I dropped her off at her house, hugged her goodbye, and watched as she carried the box and cobalt-blue bag through her front door.

I tugged my UW cap firmly into place and headed for 287.

Epilogue

As I sit at my desk writing these words, there's a leash wrapped around my foot. The other end is attached to the cutest puppy born in the twenty-first century.

She's a goldendoodle, a cross between a golden retriever and a poodle. Her curly coat is parti-colored, a mix of white, tan, sable, and gray. Her eyes are olive green, framed by four-inch-long eyelashes.

I named her Ivy in honor of my beloved Chicago Cubs. The outfield walls of Wrigley Field are covered in ivy, and in 2016, when my pup was seven weeks old, the Cubs won the World Series. Those two events—the World Series game and Ivy's arrival—plus the Denver Bronco's Super Bowl win earlier that year, were bursts of sunshine in what had been a long stretch of darkness.

Since Earl's death, I'd struggled with depression. Grief was part of it, of course, combined with the multitude of transitions that follow such life-changing events. Therapy, grief-recovery retreats, and good friends all helped, but it wasn't until the previous summer, over six years after scattering Earl's ashes on the UW football field, that I had finally started to enjoy life again. A year after that, I was ready for a puppy.

It had been twenty years since I'd had a puppy. I'd been dogless since Tipper died, and I decided it was finally time. My first thought was for a Siberian husky; I love the breed and had fond memories of the years with Tipper and Keli.

But I was older now, with orthopedic issues. Realistically, I couldn't provide for a husky's needs. I began looking for alternatives, with the idea that my future puppy would also serve as a therapy dog to help others.

My search led me to Ivy, and I brought her home just a week after the Cubs' winning game.

Ivy's a "Velcro" dog: she sticks to me everywhere I go. That's a new experience for me.

Huskies are loving dogs; they're also happily independent and incredibly stubborn. Put a husky in its pen, and it will say, "See ya, whatever." Not Ivy; she goes outside to do her business, then comes inside to be with her human. She can be ornery, but she's not stubborn. We've been through puppy kindergarten and puppy obedience training already, and unlike Tipper or Keli, Ivy actually comes with boundless enthusiasm when I call her. She finished her Canine Good Citizen class and passed the AKC test too.

She's the only dog I've ever allowed on the furniture; she doesn't shed, another big difference between goldendoodles and huskies. I sit in my recliner, Ivy snuggled in my lap, and brush her soft, curly coat.

Occasionally, someone will criticize me for getting a "designer dog" or a "specialty puppy" instead of a rescue dog. I've rescued plenty of critters in my time, including the cats who still live with me, so I don't have any guilt on that score. Besides, the heart wants what the heart wants; Ivy wanted me, and I wanted her.

Ivy's growing fast, and when she's a little older, we'll begin her therapy dog training. In the meantime, we're happy to revel in the ridiculousness of puppyhood. All the time-consuming, love-filled moments with her have sealed the deal for me: everything is going to be okay.

Ivy romps through the house, closely watched by her feline brothers, the cats. I follow her antics and realize I'm giggling once more.

Acknowledgments

I would like to thank all the animals and people who helped this book become a reality.

Thanks to Judy Fort Brenneman, writing coach and editor extraordinaire, who has been patient, kind, and enthusiastic about my work. Thanks, too, to Mary Jo Morgan for helping me with social media, blog posting, and sorting out my website and to Rebekah Robson-May for saving my sanity where technology was concerned. Your encouragement and clear instructions prevented the need for a straightjacket.

I truly believe that what we do as writers is a gift. My mother, Carol Lederer Elson, was a talented writer herself who worked in radio before her marriage. Her gift to me was a love of words and of reading, and a prodigious vocabulary. She left us too soon, at age fifty-six, when I was twenty-six. She was my advisor, life coach, and best friend, and I loved her dearly. May her memory be a blessing.

Thanks to my husband of twenty-seven years, Earl Carlson, for your love, your bravery in all things, and your mantra, "Get it done and move on." I know you and Mom are here in spirit and are proud of me.

Thanks to Anna Fails, DVM, PhD, for jogging my memory about freshman year adventures, especially the watch alarm story.

Thanks to the Purple Cup Cafe in Fort Collins, Colorado, for tasty treats and a quiet corner to work in.

I thank my Edgewood School seventh grade teachers, Mrs. Lee Erickson and Mr. Larry Uramkin. Mrs. Erickson, my homeroom teacher, taught vocabulary reading, or VR. Mr. Uramkin taught typing, where I got my first D ever—remember those old-fashioned manual typewriters? My hands were too small to type on them! I type much better now than when I was eleven.

Thanks to all the teachers I had at Highland Park High School in Highland Park, Illinois too. They gave me a fine public education by making me rise to the highest levels in reading, writing, and Latin.

And, of course, thanks to the cats, horses, and dogs, past and present, who have filled my life with stories and love.

About the Author

Mary Carlson, DVM, MA, CVA, has been a physical education and science teacher, a community volunteer and school board member, a lecturer in anatomy at the Colorado State University College of Veterinary Medicine and Biomedical Sciences, a guest researcher studying *Yersinia pestis* (plague) at the Centers for Disease Control and Prevention, and a veterinarian specializing in cats through her feline-exclusive practice. She is internationally certified in veterinary acupuncture. Mary is a rabid Chicago Cubs fan, avid horsewoman, enthusiastic dog owner, and, according to her cats, excellent support staff. She is active on Facebook and channels her love of and experience in veterinary medicine through her blog (https://marycarlsondvm.com/). She lives in Fort Collins, Colorado and Tucson, Arizona. Her work has appeared in both professional and lay publications. *Drinking from the Trough* is her first book.

SELECTED TITLES FROM SHE WRITES PRESS

She Writes Press is an independent publishing company founded to serve women writers everywhere. Visit us at www.shewritespress.com.

Seasons Among the Vines: Life Lessons from the California Wine Country and Paris by Paula Moulton. $16.95, 978-1-938314-16-2

New advice on wine making, tasting, and food pairing—along with a spirited account of the author's experiences in Le Cordon Bleu's pilot wine program—make this second edition even better than the first.

In the Game: The Highs and Lows of a Trailblazing Trial Lawyer by Peggy Garrity. $16.95, 978-1-63152-105-8

Admitted to the California State Bar in 1975—when less than 3 percent of lawyers were women—Peggy Garrity refuses to choose between family and profession, and succeeds at both beyond anything she could have imagined.

Filling Her Shoes: Memoir of an Inherited Family by Betsy Graziani Fasbinder. $16.95, 978-1-63152-198-0

A "sweet-bitter" story of how, with tenderness as their guide, a family formed in the wake of loss and learned that joy and grief can be entwined cohabitants in our lives.

This is Mexico: Tales of Culture and Other Complications by Carol M. Merchasin. $16.95, 978-1-63152-962-7

Merchasin chronicles her attempts to understand Mexico, her adopted country, through improbable situations and small moments that keep the reader moving between laughter and tears.

Not a Perfect Fit: Stories from Jane's World by Jane A. Schmidt. $16.95, 978-1631522062

Jane Schmidt documents her challenges living off grid, moving from the city to the country, living with a variety of animals as her only companions, dating, family trips, outdoor adventures, and midlife in essays full of honesty and humor.

Operatic Divas and Naked Irishmen: An Innkeeper's Tale by Nancy R. Hinchliff. $16.95, 978-1-63152-194-2

At sixty four, divorced, retired, and with no prior business experience and little start-up money, Nancy Hinchliff impulsively moves to a new city where she knows only one person, buys a 125-year-old historic mansion, and turns it into a bed and breakfast.